Essentials of Software Project Management

Essentials of Software Project Management

Richard Bechtold, Ph.D.

MANAGEMENTCONCEPTS
8230 Leesburg Pike, Suite 800
Vienna, VA 22182
(703) 790-9595 • FAX (703) 790-1371
www.managementconcepts.com

About the Author

Richard Bechtold, Ph.D., is founder and president of Abridge Technology in Ashburn, Virginia. He has 19 years of experience developing and managing complex software systems, architectures, and environments. He is also an adjunct faculty member at George Mason University in Fairfax, Virginia.

Management Concepts, Inc.
8230 Leesburg Pike, Suite 800
Vienna, Virginia 22182
Phone: (703) 790-9595
Fax: (703) 790-1371
Web: www.managementconcepts.com

Printed in the United States of America

Essentials of Software Project Management
ISBN 1-56726-085-3

Acknowledgments

I would like to acknowledge the contributions of the spring 1999 Software Project Management class at George Mason University, Fairfax, Virginia. The students' review and comments provided valuable insights throughout the development of this book. I owe special thanks to Azin Farshadfar, who so ably developed most of the graphics in the book.

Preface

"Far too many software projects are still managed as unending death marches or, conversely, frenzied firefights."

Nearly two decades ago, I was a volunteer firefighter and paramedic for the state of Maryland, and a career firefighter for the city of Washington, D.C. Sensing the timing was right, I moved to California in search of paid paramedic work. Two weeks after I arrived, California passed its massive tax revolt initiative and even California firefighters and paramedics were finding themselves without work. So much for my keen sense of timing.

Several jobs later and another cross-country move found me working in the mailroom of an Atlanta computer company. Third shift, minimum wage, but they were willing to provide on-the-job training. The mailroom was right next to the computer room, one thing led to another, and so I began a new career in computers.

Regrettably (or fortunately?), I keep finding that my training and experience at fire and rescue were very useful in my work as a software engineer and later in a variety of software project management and research positions. Although there is no obvious connection between the two fields, on close examination, they do have one thing in common: Both are characterized periodically by a sustained state of near-crisis where everyone works as rapidly and effectively as possible while trying to keep panic in check.

While it is true that not all software projects operate in a state of crisis, it is certainly true that most do (more on this later). Accordingly, this book approaches software project management from two directions: (1) how to plan and manage a software project; and (2) how to regain control of a project that has been overwhelmed by events.

Particularly in the software industry, this two-front philosophy is invaluable. Half of this philosophy is consistent with what you find in all the other management books: Plan for success, then execute the plan. The other half, however, asserts that you should just go ahead and expect things to go wrong—and be capable of dealing with software project emergencies in a preplanned and professional manner.

Statistics indicate about a 90 percent likelihood that the software project you are on is failing. A failing project is any project that exhibits one or more of the following characteristics: (1) over budget, (2) over schedule, or (3) inadequate quality. If you are currently the manager of your project, then executive management likely expects you to restore the project to success—soon. If you are currently a technical member on the project, you may suddenly find yourself promoted to manager; management changes sometimes happen fast on failing software projects.

Hence, most commonly the question is not simply "Are you prepared to manage a successful project?" An equally critical question is "Are you prepared to rescue a failing project?"

This book is designed to ensure that you can answer "yes" to both questions. The intent is to prepare you to manage a project successfully regardless of the state or history of the project. Additionally, this material does not presume that you have had the luxury of being placed in charge of the project at project inception. Instead, it generally presumes that you were more or less dumped into the middle of a project already in progress—and already in trouble.

Perhaps this hasn't happened to you. Perhaps it won't. But the advantage of preparing for the worst is that everything less than that seems comparatively easier.

Most of us find the software industry to be absolutely fascinating. We truly enjoy the rapid advances in technology, the incredible audacity of some of the projects, and the ongoing need to learn. And learn. And learn still more. Indeed, the constant learning may be what is most attractive to many of us. In this industry, there is no notion of knowing 100 percent of what you need to know, or even 50 percent. There are just too many subdisciplines, too many technologies, too many tools, too many alternatives. But when you look at what has happened with software-based technologies over the last 30 years, it's obvious that we can legitimately claim an astonishing level of success.

Nevertheless, with a 90 percent software project failure rate, clearly we are capable of doing much better. If we succeed, then software projects will not only be fascinating, but they will also simply be more survivable. Far too many software projects are still managed as unending death marches or, conversely, frenzied firefights. This book is intended to help you ensure that your project isn't one of them.

HOW TO USE THIS BOOK

Arguably, you should read this book backwards. That is, if you are in the middle of a project crisis, the chapters on project recovery are of more immediate interest to you than the chapters on project planning and control fundamentals. However, this book is organized with the fundamentals first because the last six chapters depend extensively on your understanding of the principles and techniques discussed in the first five chapters. Hence, in most cases, it makes the most sense for you to read this book more or less in the order the material is presented.

Depending on your familiarity with the concepts, you will certainly find that some sections require only a light skim, while other sections require deeper study, analysis, and thought. This will depend entirely on your background, education, experience, and skills. Undoubtedly, at least some of the material will be familiar to you. However, the book does not assume any prior management experience or training; everything you need to know to help ensure project success is discussed. Figure 1 offers some options for navigating your way through the book.

If you are a highly experienced or executive manager, you will likely find the greatest value to be the material in the last six chapters. Nevertheless, a quick review of the first five chapters will familiarize you with the terms and context used in the final six chapters.

Finally, if your project is moving along quite peacefully, you may be inclined to read only the first five chapters and skip the chapters on recovering failing projects. I don't recommend this approach. Each of the chapters on project control begins with discussion of the symptoms that offer early warning that something is going wrong. Knowing these techniques before you need them is far preferable to trying to learn them in the middle of a crisis.

However, learning them in the middle of a crisis is certainly better than not knowing them at all!

Richard Bechtold, Ph.D.
July 1999

Figure 1
How to Use This Book

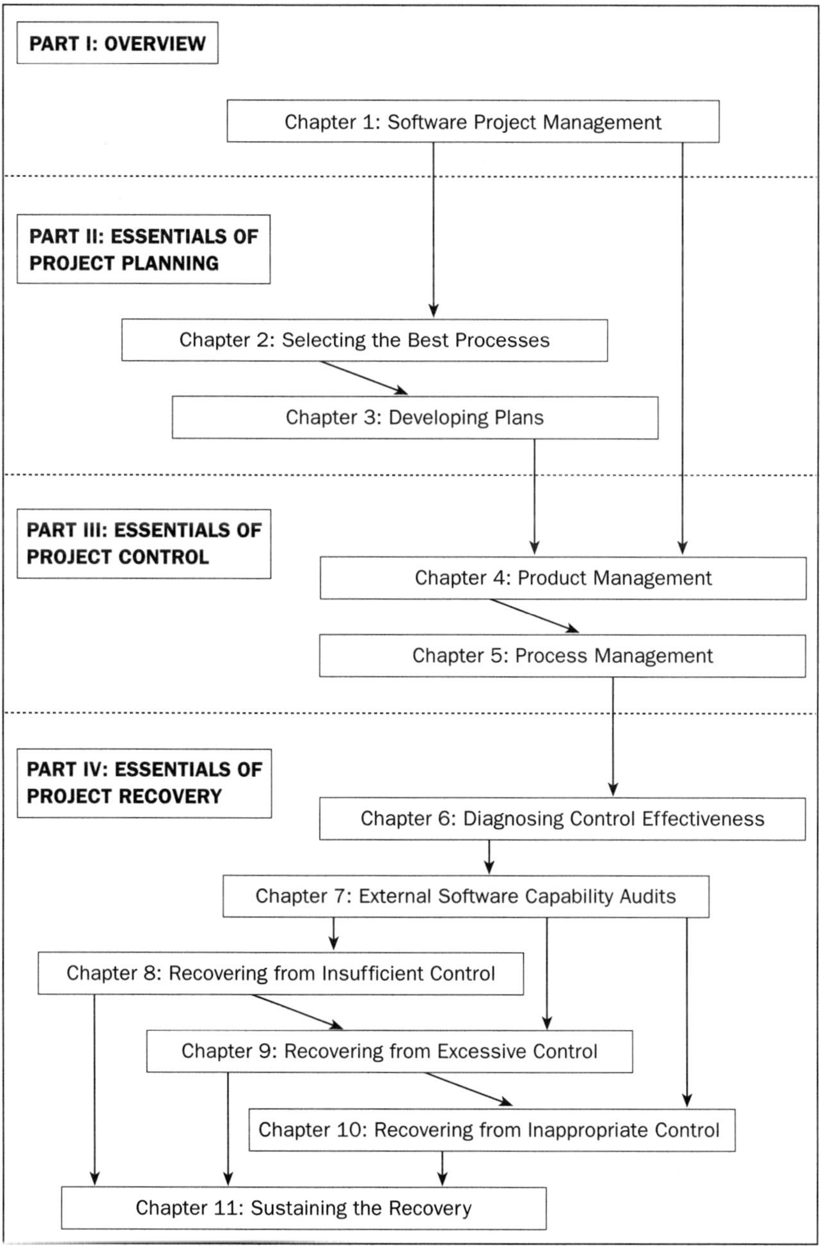

PART I

Overview

1 Project Management in the Software Development Environment

"Software is not natural. It does not age, rust, decay, break, melt, evaporate, vibrate, or float. The laws of nature do not apply to software."

The purpose of project management is, in part, to deliver quality products on time and within budget. An organization's motivation for putting you into project management is to achieve maximum resource leverage. If you are successful, then your well-managed team of technical people can accomplish more, and will encounter fewer problems, than the same group working in an uncoordinated manner.

WHY DO PROJECT MANAGEMENT?

When building complex software-intensive systems, well-managed teams typically accomplish more work in less time than do unmanaged or poorly managed teams. Although management often appears to be a relatively simple process, managing technology personnel involved in the design, development, deployment, and maintenance of a software-intensive system is extremely challenging.

At the simplest or most abstract level, to manage a software project successfully, you must understand:

- the goals of the project,
- the obstacles that may prevent or hinder your project from achieving those goals, and

- the resources and techniques available to you for overcoming those obstacles.

Project Goals

One of the challenges facing the first-line project manager is to recognize that even on very small projects within small companies, people are trying to achieve layers of goals, and those goals are sometimes incompatible and occasionally in direct conflict with each other. Therefore, another motivation for performing project management is to clarify, negotiate, and communicate project goals within the organization in a manner that best enables the overall organization to be successful.

A clear understanding of a project's goals is the only objective and reliable means for developing a plan and for measuring progress toward those goals. In the development of any software-intensive system, there are usually many levels of goals. At the lowest level, you have a first-line manager planning and directing the work of technical personnel in the design and development of the software system. That manager's primary goal is to implement a high-quality software system within the planned budget and time constraints.

At the next higher level, you have a second-line manager who is planning, monitoring, and directing development activities across multiple projects. The projects are often related because the products being developed are usually considered to be of a similar product line. Hence, the goal of this second-line manager may be to identify and implement steps that maximize the reuse and efficient sharing of resources across projects, and thereby increase the likelihood of success not only of an individual project but the entire product line.

A third-line manager might oversee a set of product lines that all relate to a particular industry. This manager may have the dual goals of trying to ensure that (1) each product line properly supports the others, and (2) in combination, the product lines all deliver cost-competitive value within their target industry.

In view of the legitimate existence of multiple, sometimes conflicting goals, the communication and negotiation of shared success values and criteria with other managers are important and sometimes critical factors affecting the success of your project.

Project Obstacles

Project management also involves overcoming obstacles that hinder or prevent the attainment of project goals. The first step in overcoming obstacles is accurately identifying the obstacles. Classic software project management obstacles include:

- unstable goals,
- inadequate funding,
- poor planning,
- insufficient resources, and
- resource conflicts.

With the exception of inadequate funding, the project manager can directly influence each of these obstacles. You can strive to stabilize the goals (at least temporarily), put more effort into planning, arrange the resources into a team structure that maximizes the skills and expertise available, and ensure that the project progresses with a minimum of interference or conflict with other groups.

Project Resources

What really distinguishes the great project manager from the mediocre project manager is the ability to motivate, coordinate, and lead the project personnel. In short, success doesn't depend on the latest hot technology, but on teamwork and attention to human factors.

Success depends largely on your ability to understand your team, their personal needs and capabilities, and their fears and concerns. You must also understand how to shape them into a team, and how to provide them with what they need to be successful. Finally, you must lead your team, both with direction and by setting examples, until—as a team—you secure project success.

DIFFERENT APPROACHES TO PROJECT MANAGEMENT

There are numerous different approaches to project management. With highly organized and experienced teams, self-management may be an option. With a newly formed team of novice software engineers, extensive and detailed management guidance may be necessary. Some teams need only to understand the goals, and then they need flexibility. Other teams need to understand not only the goals, but also the specific steps necessary to reach those goals. Sometimes a team can be managed primarily by consensus; at other times, management by decree may be required.

Consequently, it can seem that there is a bewildering number of approaches to software project management. Indeed, it may often seem like no two managers approach project management in the same way.

To simplify the problem of understanding alternative approaches to management, you should examine software project management approaches from the perspective of:

- discipline, and
- direction.

Specifically, any project manager can approach management responsibilities with varying degrees of:

- flexible management discipline versus more strict discipline, and
- sparse management direction or guidance versus detailed direction.

To help introduce this concept, six approaches to software project management are discussed in the following sections. It is important to realize that each of these approaches is appropriate in certain circumstances, and inappropriate in other circumstances. Details about how to adjust your approach to project management as a function of project strengths will be discussed in Chapter 2.

Combining the extremes of management discipline and direction yields the following four general categories of approaches to management:

- flexible discipline and sparse direction,
- flexible discipline and detailed direction,
- strict discipline and sparse direction, and
- strict discipline and detailed direction.

Nearly any approach to software project management can be placed into one of these four categories. However, it is more accurate to plot the location of any given software management approach along an axis of relative amount of discipline and an axis of relative amount of direction. In Figure 2, six common approaches to project management are plotted relative to the amount of discipline typically associated with them, and the amount of direction provided to project personnel.

Figure 2
Approaches to Project Management

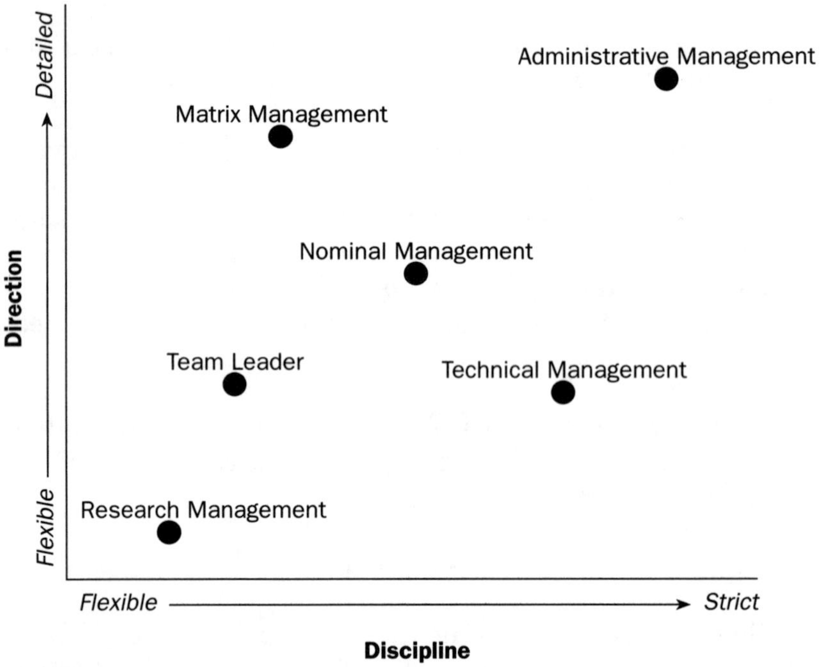

This diagram serves only as an example and is not absolute. For example, one company might employ "matrix management" using a highly flexible approach. Another company might implement a relatively strict style of matrix management. Hence, after reading the following descriptions, reconsider the management approaches your company employs and rebuild the diagram in a manner that accurately reflects your company and immediate environment. List any other approaches your organization uses to perform project management and plot their locations on the figure.

In all cases, the reason for understanding different approaches to software project management is to ensure that the management approach used matches the needs of the project personnel.

Matrix Management

As a matrix manager, you often have flexibility regarding management discipline, but you may need to provide a fair degree of detailed management control and oversight. In principle, matrix management organizations are set up to share management responsibilities equally among two or more managers. In practice, this almost never works. In the interest of efficiency, someone has to be a tie-breaker when two managers cannot come to an agreement.

This management approach requires a flexible management attitude because most of the decisions you make have an impact on the decisions of one or more other managers. Similarly, their decisions often affect yours. This environment requires considerable communication, negotiation, and compromise.

Administrative Management

With an administrative manager, management processes tend to be quite detailed and the overall environment is relatively inflexible. This is often a useful management approach to take if you have moderately good management skills and are put in charge of a group of people in a situation where you understand very little about the type of work they are doing.

You may be well qualified to monitor the group's progress, ensure that all necessary activities are occurring, facilitate intra- and intergroup communications, track hours and schedule, collect, monitor, and report metrics, and carry out a variety of other management activities. However, in this scenario, you don't have the qualifications to make significant technical decisions about the project. Most of those decisions, when they cannot be made within the group, are usually passed up to higher levels of management.

Technical Management

If you take a technical management approach to the project, you often need to be somewhat strict with regard to management direction because many of your decisions are tightly bound to technical constraints and objectives. However, since there are often multiple technically capable personnel on the project, you will likely find that the amount of direction you need to provide is comparatively sparse. Indeed, pure management activities may require only, for example, 25 percent of your time, thereby leaving most of your time free for design, development, and other technical or engineering activities. If you have a comparatively less experienced team, you will make most of the technical decisions and usually look to other technical managers for any decision support you need.

Research Management

As a research manager, you are managing a team of experts who are pushing for research breakthroughs. You can successfully manage such a team even if their domain experience far exceeds your own. This approach is characterized by a highly flexible management style coupled with a relatively sparse amount of management direction.

Research management allows the experts on the team to make most of the decisions. Additionally, the team usually contributes extensively to any planning or scheduling activities. When, on occasion, the team cannot come to consensus, you will typically raise the issue to the managers above you and wait for their decision.

Nominal Management

A nominal management approach is characterized by a generally balanced approach between flexible and strict, and between sparse and detailed management direction. In the absence of other factors, this is typically the best approach to take initially. Then, as the management needs of the project team (and the overall organization) become more apparent, you can modify your approach accordingly.

Team Leader

As a team leader, your approach to management generally favors a flexible style and relative sparse management direction. The team itself often makes most of the low-level management decisions. You often take the position of decision facilitator. Periodically, as lead, your decisions will need to override the opinion of one or more team members. However, you would typically strive to keep this situation relatively rare.

One variant of this type of approach to management is sometimes referred to as a self-managed team. In a true self-managed team, the team members all participate jointly in the decision-making process. However, this can become a very time-consuming process. Hence, someone is usually assigned the role of facilitator and given responsibility to ensure that the group dynamics are efficient and effective, and that a lack of consensus does not unnecessarily delay the team's progress.

These management types are clearly a simplification of the great diversity of management alternatives. Numerous companies have "technical managers" and "research managers" whose responsibilities are nothing like what is discussed here. However, regardless of the labels used, the amount of flexibility in the management discipline and the overall amount of management direction required are key defining characteristics of the management dynamics. For a project to succeed, the project team and all levels of management must agree on these fundamental dynamics.

THE CHALLENGING ENVIRONMENT OF SOFTWARE DEVELOPMENT

Part of the motivation for the numerous approaches to software project management is the extreme diversity of software projects. Much of this diversity is directly attributable to the highly challenging environment in which project teams develop software. Characteristics that make this environment so challenging include:

1. Software is unnatural.

2. There are no natural limits to software complexity.

3. Key solution decision-makers have negligible background in the solution domain.

4. Key problem decision-makers have negligible background in the problem domain.

5. Technical or tool specialists understand very little outside their specialty.

6. Staffing authorities overrely on specialists (especially with regard to development tools).

7. Theoretically, there is virtually nothing "impossible" to implement in software.

8. Customer needs change faster than software development tools.

9. Software development tools change faster than software development methods.

10. Software development methods change faster than management disciplines.

To understand how to manage a software project successfully, it is necessary to appreciate the magnitude of the software challenge and the major characteristics of that challenge.

Software Is Unnatural

The fact that software is unnatural leads to huge problems. One of the most significant is the fact that successful engineering principles from other disciplines—such as electrical engineering, mechanical engineering, and architectural engineering—often work poorly, if at all, when applied to software development. The primary reason for this failure is that other engineering disciplines can rely extensively on highly reliable laws of nature. But software is not natural. It does not age, rust, decay, break, melt, evaporate, vibrate, or float. The laws of nature do not apply to software.

No Limits to Complexity

Even worse, there are no natural limits to software complexity. A construction company that builds single-story houses would never consider attempting to build a 20-story office complex. However, software organizations will routinely attempt to develop software products that are 20 times, if not 100 times, more complex than anything they have built before.

An airline manufacturer would not consider building a jet that is 20 times larger than its largest existing jet. However, that same manufacturer may quite willingly attempt an avionics upgrade where the software is 20 times more complex than existing software. In software, there's often an attitude that nothing is too complicated—if we can get it to work.

Lack of Domain Expertise

Characteristics 3 and 4 from the list of challenges cover lack of expertise in both the problem domain and the solution domain. Expertise in the problem domain consists of direct experience with and understanding of the problem that the software system is intended to solve. If the software is going to be an accounting system, then problem domain expertise includes understanding general ledgers, accounts payable, accounts receivable, payroll, purchase order management, sales order management, inventory management, and other areas related to accounting.

Expertise in the solution domain consists of experience and understanding in the tools and techniques that will be used to solve the problem. Continuing with the accounting system example, solution domain expertise may include experience at distributed computing, development using JavaScript and PERL, and the integration of COTS spreadsheets and mass market databases.

The problem is not necessarily that the project lacks sufficient expertise; the problem is more likely that key decision-makers lack the expertise. This is, in principle, an easily correctable problem. Decision-makers simply need to defer certain decisions to those who have the expertise to make the most informed decision. This deference often does not occur because many decision-makers think they are quite qualified to continue making decisions. However, unless the decision-makers are making a concerted effort to keep up with the extremely rapid pace of change occurring in high technology, their relevant expertise typically degrades over time.

Overspecialization

Developers often tend to become accidentally overspecialized. This occurs because the developer has a particular skill—for example, in a recently released development tool—that the company wants to leverage. The company keeps putting that developer on projects that require the use of that specific tool. As time goes by, new tools appear but most organizations do not have the time or the inclination to cross-train. Eventually, the developer is extremely adept in that one aging tool, and has had almost no exposure to or experience in anything else.

As personnel become increasingly specialized, it becomes more difficult for companies and managers to move these people between projects, or to use them at all on smaller projects. Multidisciplined and multitalented personnel are easier to leverage, but are quite difficult to find.

Overreliance on Specialization

Ironically, the software industry tends to hire people with specific tool or other specialized experience. What they generally end up with is exactly that: a person specialized in one area who has very little understanding of anything else. One reason for this overreliance is that it is easier for human resource departments and for project managers to determine if someone has two years of experience with a specific tool than it is to determine if he or she is a "senior software engineer." It's much easier to make the hiring decision. The problem is that even on large teams, if everyone is a specialist, it is likely that some fundamental computer science and software engineering capabilities will not be available from anyone on the team.

Nothing Seems Impossible

In software development, it generally is not a question of "can" it be done. If it seems like it could be done, it almost certainly can be done. The real questions are: Is there enough time, and is there enough money?

But when you look at some of the spectacular failures associated with extremely complex systems, such as the modernization of large federal government agencies, automation of airports or mass transit systems, and immense telecommunications projects, then it appears that, practically speaking, some projects really are impossible. They are not impossible in principle, but the magnitude, complexity, duration, plan, design, and attempts at implementation all combine to render the project's goals effectively unachievable.

Fast Pace of Change

Finally, to understand the challenges facing a project manager in the development of software-intensive systems, it is crucial to understand the impact of change on the software development environment. Arguably, no other industries are subjected to the rapidity of change that is common in software engineering. Regrettably, the rate of change is essentially uncontrollable. As a software project manager, you have to learn to plan for change, constantly monitor the impacts of change, and manage those impacts as you manage the overall project.

As shown in Figure 3, change occurs at different rates within the various elements of the software engineering environment.

Figure 3
Fast Pace of Change

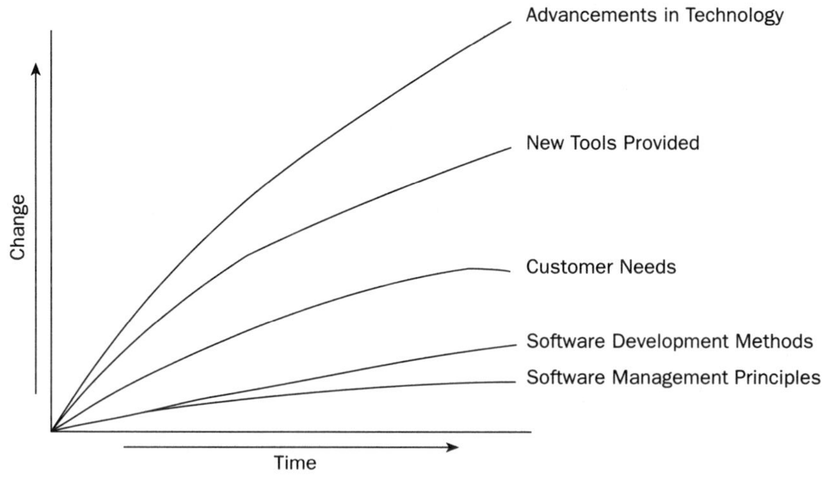

The fantastic opportunity afforded by developing, marketing, and delivering software—either as a stand-alone product or as part of a software-intensive system—has led to an extremely dynamic and competitive market. Software can allow people or companies to do work, or make better-informed decisions, that considerably exceed what their competition is capable of if that competition is using even moderately dated software and technology.

The rate of advancements in technology is so fast that the typical customer only partially understands what its company will likely need a year from now and, frankly, has virtually no idea what it will need five years from now. The market, the competition, and the opportunities all change far too rapidly.

To aggravate this problem, software tool providers are simply not able to keep up with the rate of change in the needs of their software development customers (who are aggressively trying to keep up with the needs of their software purchasing customers). However, the software tool providers certainly try their best; consequently, there is a steady flow of new tools and supporting technologies into the software development environment.

These new tools and technologies almost always afford a new and improved way to perform software engineering processes and methods. Indeed, sometimes the new tools are outright incompatible with the old way of working. Software developers modify their work habits to take best advantage of the new tools. Periodically, a small team may even take the time to document the new process or to establish a robust supporting methodology. But typically, they cannot do this nearly fast enough to keep up with the constant stream of new tools and technologies available for use on their projects.

In the middle of this maelstrom of change is you, the software project manager. To help you perform your responsibilities, you may have had some training in project management business principles—principles that date back to the beginning of the industrial revolution. Of course, many of these principles are somewhat timeless and are as useful now as they were when initially developed. But they were never designed to work in a software development environment. It is little wonder that approximately 90 percent of all software projects fail. And out of every 100 project starts, there are 94 restarts. Moreover, of the 175,000 information technology development projects that occur annually in the United States, 31 percent are canceled outright before completion.

To attempt to address these problems, principles of software project management are also changing. But the rate of change in management principles historically has been slower than the rate of change in engineering principles. This may be due, in part, to the sometimes entrenched belief that a really good manager can manage any group doing anything. While this certainly is true in some industries, the failure rate of software projects provides ample evidence that this belief is fatal for software development managers. It is not enough for you to know how to manage a project—you must understand the essentials of managing a *software development* project.

WHAT IS PROJECT MANAGEMENT?

As we will discuss later, project management (software or otherwise) includes a considerable number of responsibilities. You need to:

- find and hire the right people,
- ensure that they have the tools they need,
- keep up with the latest technology,
- develop and maintain comprehensive plans,
- negotiate compromises with other managers,
- make presentations to executive management,
- spend some time with each of the project personnel during the summer picnic, and
- handle numerous other responsibilities.

But at its essence, project management consists of three simple things: planning, tracking, and controlling.

Planning

Planning is fortune-telling. That is, as you develop a project plan, you are attempting to predict the future. In many industries, this is relatively easy—their future is quite predictable. In the software industry, this is exceedingly difficult and becomes exponentially more difficult as the duration of the project increases.

Because it is so difficult to develop an accurate project plan, many software project managers simply operate with no plan at all. They tell project personnel to work as fast as possible for as long as possible, and the manager spends virtually all his or her time responding to an endless succession of problems. This type of management style is often referred to as "firefighting," but that is grossly misleading. It is far more accurate to refer to it as "arson."

For the relatively few managers who do develop project plans, these plans are commonly abandoned shortly after project initiation. The reason for the abandonment is often that relatively little content of the plan had true value. The planner knows that numerous wild assumptions were made and has no faith in the accuracy of the plan. As the project unfolds, the divergence of real events from planned events quickly becomes obvious. But still the project manager may see little value in updating the plan now. Why bother? There are still too many unknowns. So the manager decides to wait until things become more certain. And continues to wait. Most often, the plan is never updated because things never become certain until the project is nearly over, and why update the plan then when you've gone so long without one?

Difficulties notwithstanding, it is imperative to have a comprehensive plan that is as accurate as you can make it. The key is to remember that any plan can be usable as an initial draft. When you make assumptions while building the plan, document those assumptions. If you need to make some guesses, document those guesses. If you perceive uncertainty and risk, document those also. Put together the best plan you can and remember: *Your software project plan is a living document.*

Be prepared to update your plan on a regular basis. As details become apparent, add them to the plan. As actual resources are added to the project, update your estimated resources accordingly. When some of the assumptions turn out to be incorrect, analyze the impact, adjust the plan, and document any revised assumptions.

On some projects, the development and maintenance of project plans could easily require 50 percent—or more—of your time. While this may initially seem excessive, keep in mind the critical importance of a good plan. The plan is a reflection of your best attempt to anticipate what is going to happen so that you can have the necessary resources available when you need them. Without a plan, you have no strategy and no means for reliably tracking closure toward your project goals. Without a plan, the project is just a daily succession of accidents and reactions to accidents.

Tracking

Once the plan is in place, use it continuously to track the project. Tracking involves collecting status data and updating the various parts of the plan to reflect the latest developments. Collecting this data can range from a formal system of metrics to informal weekly meetings with project personnel.

Most project managers track at least hours worked, dollars spent, and size of product completed relative to total estimated size. In addition to these basic items, you may need to track defect density, milestones achieved, staff turnover, and any other items that help you achieve additional insight into the efficiency, effectiveness, and overall health of your project.

Tracking depends on the achievement of discrete and objectively verifiable events. For example, when a programmer is working on a software module, do not bother asking that programmer what the "percent completion" is on the module. As a general rule, the vast majority of programmers think they are around 90 percent done. This number is meaningless. Instead, ask for status data such as "design complete," "module ready for inspection," and "module ready for integration testing." These are discrete events that you can verify and monitor easily. If these types of transitions do not seem to allow you to track progress closely enough, then you can take the original module, divide it into multiple submodules, and track the progress of each separate submodule.

The key to tracking is to have data available that is sensitive enough to developing events that you get the earliest warnings possible, and yet not so sensitive that it results in wild fluctuations and repeated false alarms.

Controlling

Controlling the project is where everything converges to determine success or failure. You can have a perfect plan, and you can perform impeccable tracking, but it is all useless unless those efforts contribute directly to successful project control.

Project control includes all efforts and activities that are intended to establish, develop, direct, manage, motivate, and coordinate the human resources on your project. It also includes your activities in acquiring and deploying nonhuman resources such as computers, software tools, documentation, training videos, and anything else that is necessary to the success of your project.

A key ratio for evaluating the effectiveness of your project control efforts is the ratio of actions you take in anticipation of events to actions you take in reaction to events. Generally, if the original planning was done properly, you are tracking the project closely, and you are updating your plans regularly, then you will be able to anticipate most events and prepare to take the necessary actions when the events come to pass.

Control is a key element of software project management. You are leading the project, not chasing it. The more reactive you become, the farther "behind" the project you get, and the dynamic changes from you controlling the project to the project controlling you.

THE ROLE OF THE PROJECT MANAGER IN TODAY'S SOFTWARE-INTENSIVE ENVIRONMENTS

The activities of planning, tracking, and controlling are certainly activities that are common across all types of project management. But what is it that makes management different for the person managing a software-intensive project?

In addition to the problematic environment of software development and the huge impact that change has on software development projects, another recognizable characteristic of software projects is that they are commonly staffed with uncommonly intelligent people. Successful software development is clearly not easy. If it were, project failure rates would not be so abysmally high. The challenge of software tends to attract very intelligent people. Successful software teams typically include smart people who are talented, educated, and experienced. Any given individual on the team may not have all three traits, but the team overall certainly will.

This leads to a paradox in the role of the software project manager. You carefully build a team of smart, talented, educated, and experienced people and now you are going to start telling them how to do their jobs. This can lead to a very confusing relationship between you and the project personnel.

Again, this is why the principle of alternative approaches to management is important. Most of the time, your role is not to control each person on the project, but to lead the team through each successive project lifecycle phase, and navigate around the obstacles. As the project proceeds, the management approach that fits the project best will usually change. Indeed, if you have a stable project team, it is likely that, over time, you can become more flexible in your management discipline and provide relatively less direction. This is simply because, over time, the project team becomes progressively more experienced.

With an experienced team, once an operational plan is in use, most of your efforts at project control will focus on removing obstacles. You should be asking yourself and your team regularly what obstacles or problems the team is encountering or anticipating, and how can you remove those hindrances. Your goal is to do everything possible to allow your team to make the greatest progress possible.

Do this right and you maximize the likelihood that your project will be a success. This is because all team members on the project will be making their maximum contribution. They will be able to make their maximum contribution precisely because you are out there anticipating, preventing, or removing obstacles, problems, and anything else that could impede their progress.

WHERE TO START?

There is another paradox regarding project management. To develop a plan properly, you need answers to numerous questions about the characteristics of the project, associated technologies, and the people with whom you will be interacting. However, the answers to nearly all those questions will change as a function of what you decide to put into the plan. So where do you start? Delay planning until you have more answers, or commence planning with considerable uncertainty?

Where you start as a project manager is typically by doing everything in parallel. You start the planning process even though you know there are major influences whose impacts you cannot yet estimate. You start searching for answers while you plan, and revise the plan as those answers become apparent. Typically, you may even start work (presuming that work is not already well underway). All these activities occur in parallel; in principle, none of them is complete until the project is over. That is, throughout the life of the project, you continue refining the plan, looking for answers, and leading the team as the various members perform their work.

However, if you are on a project that looks like it is out of control, or does not have a plan that is both usable and current, then the answer to "Where to Start?" is easy: Before you do anything else, you have to start developing a usable plan.

PART II

Essentials of Project Planning

2 Selecting the Best Processes

"The purpose of a lifecycle is to organize. . .activities in a meaningful, efficient, and effective way, and to help ensure that all important activities are performed. If you begin to suspect that a particular lifecycle approach is making your life more complicated, you are probably right."

When you commence planning for a software project, a variety of things should already have been done by other people, and a variety of items should have been provided to you. Typically, most of these things haven't happened, and the items don't exist. If any of these items do exist, they are often outdated or of questionable usefulness. Depending on what does or does not exist, the work you have to do to plan the project can vary significantly.

One scenario is that system-level requirements are well-defined, a subset of those requirements has been allocated to software, and someone has provided you with a comprehensive requirements specification. Another scenario, especially if the project is entirely software development, is that you have been provided with a statement of work, or with some type of detailed functional product description. A more likely scenario is that you've been given only informal verbal explanations and suggestions about the ultimate objective of the project, and you are expected to start planning anyway.

Regardless of the scenario you find yourself in, your first step is to start identifying and selecting the best processes to use on your project. This begins with deciding on the best software lifecycle to follow, and then determining the most appropriate general software engineering processes.

Before you can determine the best lifecycle and processes to use on your project, you need to develop a conceptual model of your project by defining the project's key strengths.

IDENTIFYING YOUR PROJECT'S KEY STRENGTHS

Numerous strengths can be analyzed to help you classify your project and select the most applicable lifecycle. Listed below are twelve areas of possible project strength; conversely, you may consider one or more of these areas to be intrinsically weak.

Because there are such extreme differences between software projects, you will likely find that this list is not all-inclusive. Add to this list any other areas of strength (or weakness) that you think, if left out of the decision process, might cause you to select an inappropriate lifecycle. However, in the interests of remaining focused on the "most important" areas, strive to keep the length of the list to no more than fifteen.

Key project strengths that can contribute directly to the success of the project include:

1. Appropriate processes
2. Capitalization
3. Customer focus
4. Historically based, relevant, predictive data
5. Modern support environment and tools
6. Project brevity

7. Requirements stability
8. Strategic teaming
9. Team cohesiveness
10. Team expertise
11. Training support
12. Your expertise as a manager

For each of the areas on this list, carefully consider your project and develop a relative strength rating based on the sufficiency, availability, or value of the item. Rate the strength of each area using one of the following ratings:

- very low,
- low,
- medium,
- high, or
- very high.

The more areas where you rate the strength as "high" or "very high," the greater the overall strength and the lower the overall risk of your project.

Guidelines for how to rate your project in these areas are presented below.

Appropriate Processes

Do you consider the processes currently in use on the project to be one of the project's major strengths? Is the requirements management process keeping up with changing requirements? Is configuration management occurring regularly? Are the developers all using a relatively consistent and well-understood development methodology? If you can answer "yes" to these and similar questions, then rate this area as "high" or "very high." Otherwise, use one of the weaker ratings.

Capitalization

Is the project backed by sufficient capitalization? Are funds sufficient for proper computers and support software? Is money available to train project personnel? Is the travel budget adequate for providing on-site customer support? Are sufficient funds available to give the developers appropriate annual raises so that salaries remain competitive?

Rate your project's strength in this area as "high" (or better) if you can answer "yes" to most of these questions. If you answer "no" to two or more of the questions, then rate this area as "very low."

Customer Focus

Customer focus has two primary components: (1) customer familiarity, and (2) customer-based priorities. Are you thoroughly familiar with the customer? Are most of the members of your project team familiar with the customer? Is your executive management team familiar with the customer? Equally important, have you seen evidence that executive management wants the customer's needs to come first?

As above, if you can answer "yes" to these questions, select one of the higher strength ratings.

Historically Based, Relevant, Predictive Data

Is historical data available that you can use in calculating productivity rates, estimating product size and complexity, estimating total hours to build the various components of the system, and planning a schedule of activities with estimated durations? If so, was that data collected from the current project and from highly similar, recently performed or completed projects? If the answer is "no" to either of these questions, rate the strength of this area as "very low."

Modern Support Environment and Tools

Do you consider the project to be using a modern environment and productivity tools? This includes easily available tools that are both relatively recent and quite robust. "Modern" does not mean the absolute latest technology. Indeed, if some of the tools are extremely recent (such as a beta-test release of a version 1.0 tool), you will want to rate this as one or two steps weaker than if the tools are modern but have well-established track records.

Project Brevity

Generally, you can use the following scale. If you are somewhat close to a boundary, choose whichever level of strength seems most appropriate to you:

- Less than 2 months — Very high
- 2 to 6 months — High
- 6 to 12 months — Medium
- 12 to 18 months — Low
- 18 months or greater — Very low

These categories are just an example. If your team routinely does projects of two to three years duration, and the current project is planned to be only seven months, then you would likely rate this relatively short duration project as a "very high" strength.

Requirements Stability

How stable will the requirements be? Does the customer thoroughly understand what he or she is asking for? Do you have a history of working with this customer and therefore know that the requirements will be stable? Have prototypes been developed to help ensure that the customer agrees with the user-interface and user-interaction requirements?

If you anticipate that less than 5 percent of the requirements will change during the life of the project, then rate this area as a "very high" strength. If you expect that more than 20 percent of the requirements will change, consider this a "very low" strength.

Strategic Teaming

If you do not anticipate a need for strategic teaming, then this area may not apply to your project. However, if you need one or more capabilities that are not available from within your company, do you have established strategic relationships that allow you to team readily with other companies? Conversely, do you have a list of prequalified teaming partners that you can use? If not, do you feel that you can successfully find a teaming partner if it becomes apparent that one is necessary?

If you can answer the first of these questions "yes," then rate this area as a "very high" strength. Otherwise, the more "no" answers you have, the weaker this area is.

Team Cohesiveness

How cohesive is your project team? An important part of team cohesiveness is team longevity—have the team members been working together long? Do they work well under pressure, yet maintain momentum in the absence of pressure? Does the team have a track record of welcoming and rapidly acclimating new project personnel?

Conversely, do you have one or more project members who prefers to work alone? Do some of the project personnel tend to seek or listen to advice only rarely? Have any subgroups formed where only a few members are part of the subgroup and others on the team are largely excluded?

Answering "yes" to the former questions indicates that cohesiveness is a strength; answering "yes" to one or more of the latter questions indicates increasing weakness in this area.

Team Expertise

Does your team have extensive expertise in both the problem domain and the solution domain? Has it built similar systems previously for this customer? Has the team built similar systems for other customers? If you are building an "off-the-shelf" product, has the team built similar products for your company? For other companies? How much expertise does the team have working in the expected programming environment? How much experience does the team have using the planned development tools and software libraries?

Training Support

If "team expertise" is extremely high, then you may not need to provide additional training for team personnel. However, especially on longer duration projects where you expect some turnover, it may be necessary to provide training to the team members. What type of training support is available for your use? Do you have a formal in-house training organization with regularly scheduled classes? Can you arrange for training easily? Does your company have an established relationship with an external training organization or independent training specialists? Does your company have a history of being receptive to providing training to employees?

Again, your team members may not need formal training on your particular project. However, in recognition that requirements and technology are both highly subject to change, having the option to use a training support organization—should training become necessary—is definitely a project strength. Conversely, if your primary option is to resort to mentoring and other informal approaches to on-the-job training, then rate this area less strongly.

Your Expertise as a Manager

Finally, and possibly most importantly, what is your expertise as a project manager? Have you managed similar projects with this team? Have you managed similar projects with other teams, or maybe for other companies? Given your current view of the primary challenges facing your project, do you have an established track record of being successful at overcoming those challenges? How well prepared do you feel for planning, tracking, controlling, and otherwise managing this project?

SELECTING THE BEST LIFECYCLE

Once you've given some careful thought to the relative strengths of your project, you can begin thinking about which lifecycle might be best. Think of a lifecycle as an organizer of activities and events. For most software projects, a lot of the same types of activities occur. For example, requirements need to be defined, a software design needs to be built, code needs to be developed and tested, and software subcomponents need to be integrated. During all of this, training needs to occur, review meetings held, configurations managed.

Major software activities, derived from Institute of Electrical and Electronics Engineers (IEEE) Standard 1074, typically include:

- Project management processes
  - project initiation
  - project monitoring and control
  - software quality management

- Predevelopment processes
  - concept exploration
  - system allocation

- Development processes
  - requirements
  - design
  - implementation

- Postdevelopment processes
  - installation
  - operation and support
  - maintenance
  - retirement

- Integral processes
  - verification and validation
  - software configuration management
  - documentation development
  - training

The purpose of a lifecycle is to organize all these activities in a meaningful, efficient, and effective way, and to help ensure that all important activities are performed. If you begin to suspect that a particular lifecycle approach is making your life more complicated, you are probably right. When used in the appropriate circumstances, lifecycle approaches will help make the project easier to plan, track, and control.

Depending on the strengths and weaknesses of your project—and the specific circumstances affecting your project—a particular lifecycle will likely be much more appropriate than the others. Each lifecycle works very well in the conditions for which it was designed, and works rather miserably under any other conditions.

Processes and activities can occur in a variety of different orders; by selecting an appropriate lifecycle, you establish an order of occurrence that makes the most sense for your project. On most projects, one of the following lifecycles will likely serve your needs:

1. Waterfall
2. Throw-away prototype
3. Incremental build
4. Multiple build
5. Spiral
6. Legacy maintenance

However, if the project is unusual, you may find that you prefer to take ideas from one or more lifecycles and design and implement your own lifecycle model. This approach is discussed below as a seventh option, the hybrid lifecycle.

Selection of the most appropriate lifecycle for your project is subject to a variety a factors, not the least of which is your own familiarity with managing a project that is following that lifecycle. Lifecycles are best chosen when you have a clear understanding of the strengths and weaknesses of your project. Figure 4 suggests areas where you should have clear project strengths that complement the different characteristics of the seven lifecycle approaches.

Figure 4
Project Strengths That Complement Lifecycle Approaches

	Waterfall	Throw-away Prototype	Incremental Build	Multiple Build	Spiral	Legacy	Hybrid
Appropriate Processes	●						●
Capitalization		●					
Customer Focus				●		●	
Historical Data						●	
Modern Support Environment		●	●	●			
Project Brevity	●						
Requirements Stability	●						
Strategic Teaming				If applicable		If applicable	
Team Cohesiveness			●				
Team Expertise					●		
Training Support							●
Expertise as Manager							●

Waterfall

Arguably the first widely accepted lifecycle, the waterfall lifecycle is essentially a linear ordering of the major software development activities. A simple example of a waterfall lifecycle (see Figure 5) is:

- feasibility analysis,
- planning,
- requirements specification,
- design development,
- coding,
- unit testing,
- integration testing,
- system testing,
- deployment, and
- maintenance.

The general assumption behind this lifecycle is that events affecting the project are predictable, tools and activities are well-understood, and, as a rule, once a lifecycle phase is done, it remains done. While you may occasionally need to correct or update an output from a prior lifecycle phase, in general:

- When the planning is done, the planning phase will not need to be revisited.
- When the requirements are specified, you can send the requirements analysts elsewhere.
- When the design is done, you can move the designers to a different project.

Figure 5
Waterfall Model

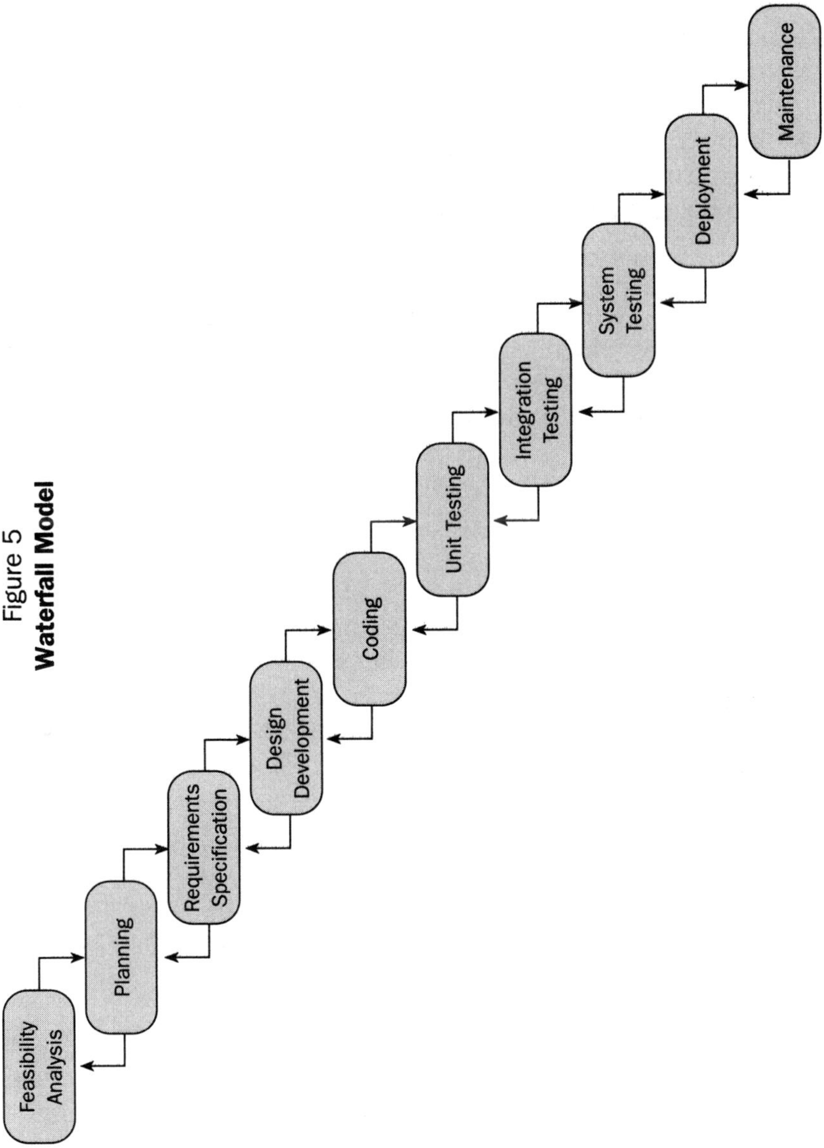

The waterfall lifecycle is highly effective for short-duration, well-understood projects with extremely stable requirements. To use it, put your activities in sequential order and execute them one at a time. No activity can commence until its predecessor activity is complete. By following a waterfall lifecycle, you can avoid the far too common problems of commencing code development before the design is complete, commencing design before software requirements are complete, or commencing any of these before planning is complete.

When selecting a lifecycle, consider the waterfall lifecycle as your lifecycle of choice. Then, try to find a reason why waterfall won't work. If you cannot find any problems with using it, then follow the waterfall. It has the advantages of being simple, easy to understand, easy to plan and track, and highly effective for short-duration, well-understood projects.

Throw-Away Prototype

In software development, it is sometimes very difficult for people to agree on some of the most critical issues. For example, requirements are often vague, and entire subsections of the requirements may be completely unknown. This is sometimes characterized by a customer (or manager) who asserts, "I'm not sure exactly what I need, but I'll recognize it when I see it."

When the requirements are vague, highly uncertain, or otherwise subject to extreme volatility, consider using the throw-away prototype lifecycle.

Although widely misunderstood and misused throughout the software industry, the throw-away prototype lifecycle has a very important purpose: It provides sufficient insight to all interested parties, including customers, developers, and managers, so that requirements can be clearly defined and understood. That's it. This lifecycle has no additional phases. When the requirements are understood and agreed upon, this lifecycle model, and this part of the project, are complete. The prototype is used as a reference for the documentation of requirements, or the prototype can be baselined and used as an executable requirements specification.

Throw-away prototyping is almost the reverse of a waterfall. In essence, this lifecycle is intended to handle those situations where you truly have to build something before you can understand the requirements thoroughly and commence detailed planning properly. However, you want to build as little as possible, and build as quickly as possible. After all, this is not the "actual" project. Instead, this is a preliminary activity designed to resolve major uncertainties in the objectives or requirements of the actual project—uncertainties that must be resolved before the actual project can commence.

By far, the single greatest problem with the throw-away prototype lifecycle model is that the prototype is built, but then management, the customer, or both decide not to throw it away. This is a perfect setup for disaster.

When software prototypes are built, they are typically waived from all the usual constraints placed on normal software development. That is, the coding standards are waived, the inspection process is waived, quality assurance oversight is waived, etc. Additionally, a significant portion of the prototype is simply faked. File input/output operations, screen updates, calculations, and communications may all have major aspects that are fake. After all, the purpose was not to build the system, but to understand the requirements. The prototype doesn't have to work; it simply needs to aid in identifying and understanding requirements.

Consequently, trying to turn a prototype into a robust, fully functional, high-quality system is to attempt to force quality as an afterthought, and to attempt to compensate with patches, fixes, workarounds, and other compromises for a software core that doesn't work. The system is going to fail; the only question is when.

Numerous variants on the throw-away prototype lifecycle are intended to produce, if not a completely reusable prototype, at least parts of a prototype that can be reused in the actual project. Some of these variants are discussed below. None is referred to as a prototype lifecycle. If you intend to keep some or all of the developed software, do not call it a prototype.

If you intend to prototype, ensure that everyone understands that none of the prototype should be reused in the actual system. The risk is far too high.

Incremental Build

Incremental build is in some ways similar to a throw-away prototype, but the system is constructed much more carefully. Incremental builds allow you to develop the system a piece at a time, and test each piece as it's developed. Increments may depend on prior or future increments. If the increment needs data from a future increment, then that part of the system is either "stubbed out" so that, at the moment, no data is expected, or it is covered by a throw-away module that temporarily fakes the existence of the future increment.

Incremental builds allow project personnel to understand the various system components and their interactions. They usually allow testing to begin earlier and to be spread over a longer period of time. This lifecycle approach is also an excellent way to decompose the development of a large, high-risk system into the development of a succession of smaller, lower risk subsystems.

An example of an incremental build lifecycle (see Figure 6) is:

- feasibility analysis,
- planning,
- requirements specification,
- design development, increment 1,
- coding, increment 1,
- unit testing, increment 1,
- integration testing, increment 1,
- design development, increment 2,
- coding, increment 2,
- unit testing, increment 2,
- integration testing, increment 2,
- design development, increment 3,
- coding, increment 3,
- unit testing, increment 3,
- integration testing, increment 3,
- system testing,

Figure 6
Incremental Build Model

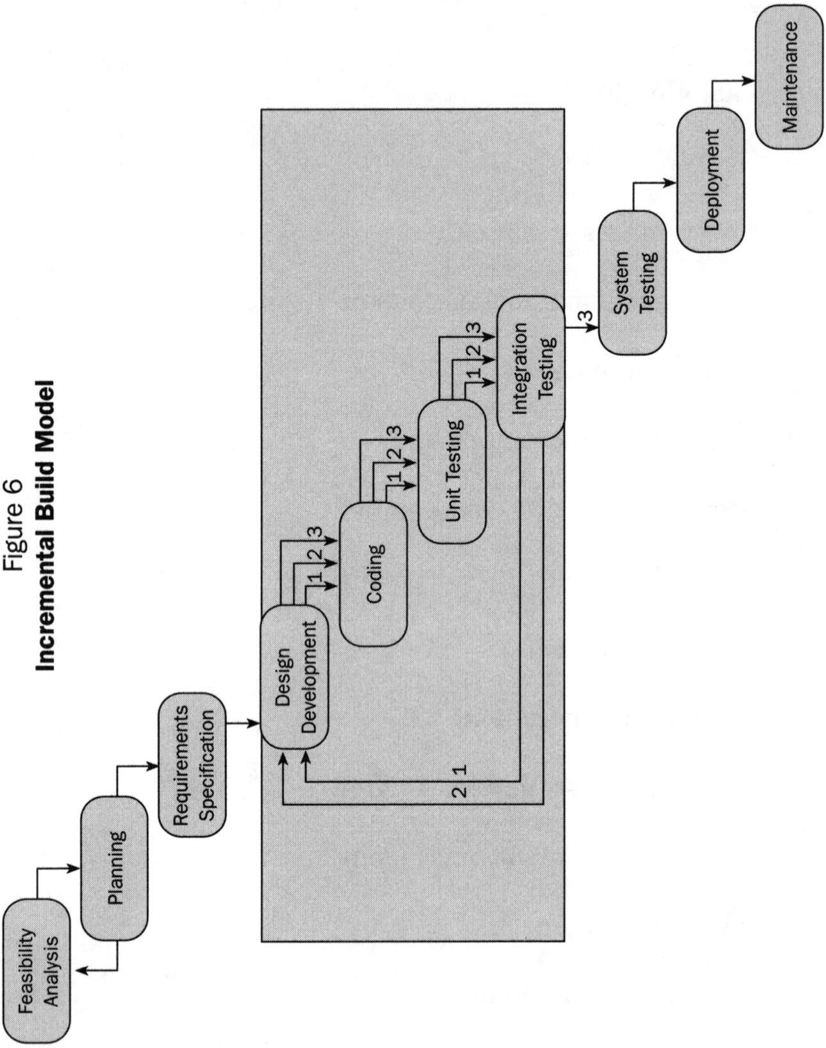

- deployment, and
- maintenance.

As indicated in the example, one of the advantages to the incremental build lifecycle is the opportunity to defer some of the design decisions until later in system development. Typically, after the first increment has been built, you have considerably more insight into system details than you did prior to starting the first increment. These insights can be useful when developing the design for the next increment.

Although not shown in this example, another option is to increment the requirements specification phase. However, it is almost always better to define requirements before commencing any design and development. If requirements are that uncertain, consider starting with a throwaway prototype or, alternatively, using a spiral lifecycle.

Multiple Build

The multiple build lifecycle is very similar to an incremental lifecycle, with one critical exception: Functional pieces of the system are being delivered to the customer. These pieces may temporarily be stand-alone, with the intent being to integrate them during a later build. Or the pieces may be an integrated set of partial functionality that contains an increasing number of features with each build, and that becomes fully functional with delivery of the last build.

An example of a multiple build lifecycle (see Figure 7) is:

- feasibility analysis,
- planning,
- requirements specification,

Figure 7
Multiple Build Model

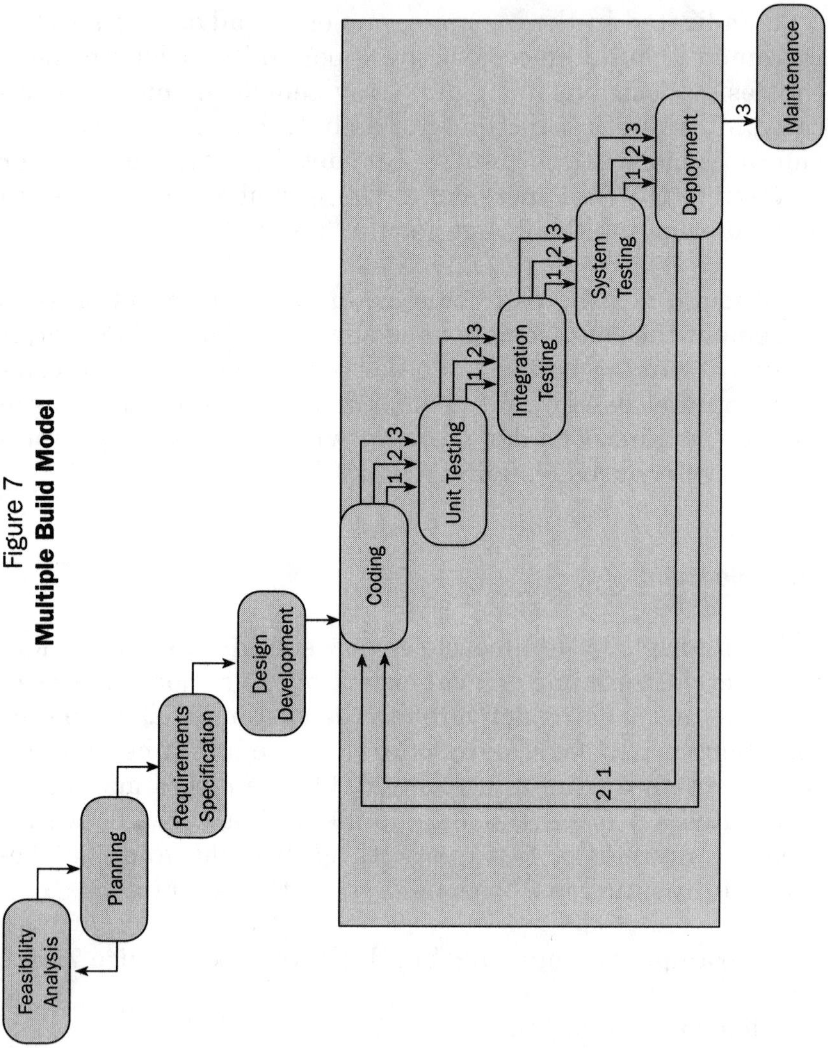

- design development,
- code and unit testing, increment 1,
- integration and system testing, increment 1,
- deployment, increment 1,
- code and unit testing, increment 2,
- integration and system testing, increment 2,
- deployment, increment 2,
- code and unit testing, increment 3,
- integration and system testing, increment 3,
- deployment, increment 3, and
- maintenance.

Generally, the development of subsequent builds requires that changes be made in previous builds. For this reason, the previously delivered builds are usually not corrected or maintained in the field. Instead, the corrections are made within the baselined development software, and an entire new system is delivered to the customer with the release of each build.

In the preceding example, the design phase is shown as being completed before developing, testing, and delivering the various builds. This is because the multiple build lifecycle typically involves customer input into the total number of builds, the functionality to be contained in each build, and the expected delivery time for each build. It is almost impossible to make such decisions and commitments without both the customer and the development group having reasonably good insight into not only what the problem is (i.e., the requirements), but also how that problem is going to be solved (i.e., the design). However, if the customer is willing to be flexible on functionality within specific builds and the dates the builds are needed, then the design phase can also be approached via multiple passes or builds.

Spiral

The notion of a spiral model is relatively simple: You keep cycling through the same set of lifecycle phases until product development is complete. Figure 8 depicts a spiral lifecycle.

Each cycle through this sample spiral is characterized by four phases: plan (phases 1, 5, and 9), design (phases 2, 6, and 10), build (phases 3, 7, and 11), and evaluate (you probably see the pattern by now). Generally, planning is conducted at two levels. An overall spiral plan indicates the total number of cycles and the total number of phases within a cycle. There is also a detailed plan, but only for the current phase of the spiral. This approach helps eliminate the common problem of attempting to develop detailed plans that reach so far into the future that the likelihood of the plan being accurate effectively approaches zero.

You should include as many phases per cycle as appropriate for your project. For example, if field testing and customer reaction are important, you may want to add more phases per cycle, such as:

1. Evaluate alternative solutions
2. Plan
3. Design
4. Build

5. Test

6. Field

7. Assess results

Figure 8
Spiral Model

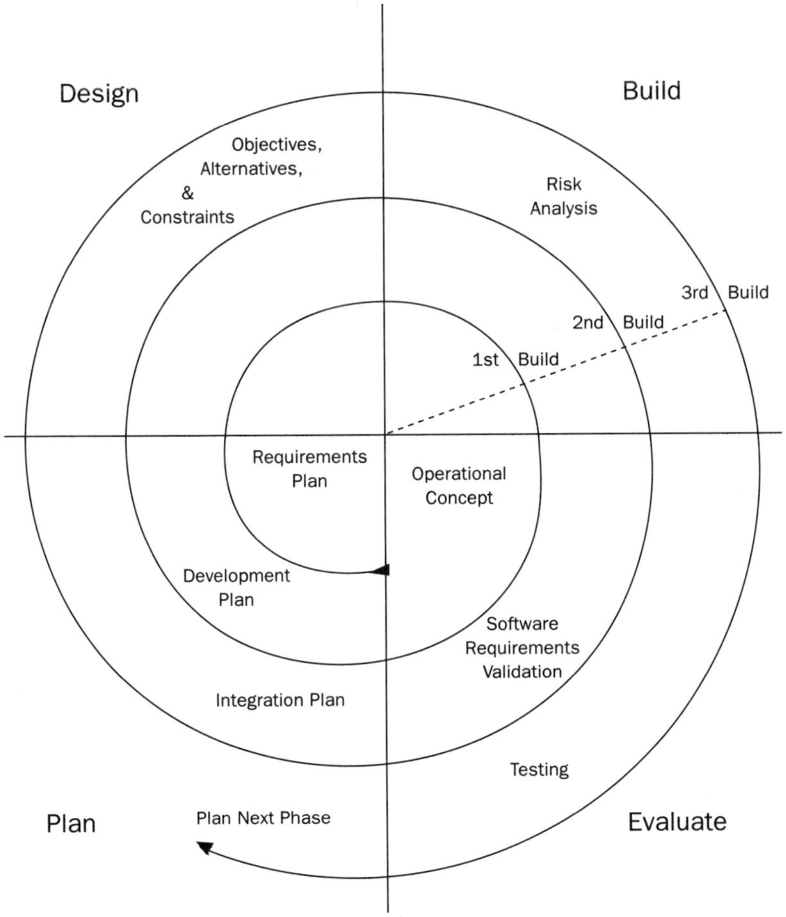

The spiral lifecycle can be very effective when the customer (or your executive management) truly does not know what the final product should look like, and a prototype will not answer the question. This could happen, for instance, when you need to assess the reaction of real customers using initial functionality before you decide what additional functionality would increase marketability.

A special variant of the spiral lifecycle is the *risk-driven spiral*. This lifecycle is effectively identical to the spiral model (and was, in fact, the original spiral model). However, when using a risk-driven spiral, the purpose of each cycle is to attempt to develop whatever part of the system currently presents the highest risks.

For example, when starting the first cycle, you, as project manager, ask yourself: "What part of this system scares me the most?" That's the part you develop and test. When you are done with that cycle, you ask yourself the question again: "What, at this stage, scares me the most?" Then you design and build that part of the system.

The advantages to this approach are twofold. First, it reduces risk faster than any other lifecycle option. Second, if the project is going to fail, it will usually fail with the least amount of money and time invested. As a result, the time and budget available may still be sufficient to investigate a completely alternative solution.

Legacy Maintenance

Legacy maintenance differs from pure development mostly in that a maintenance project is usually characterized by a succession of parallel microprojects. For example, a typical maintenance plan will allocate a certain number of resources dedicated to fixing software defects, implementing minor improvements, and, when there is nothing else to do, testing the legacy system to find any latent defects before the customer does. These resources usually work their way through a backlog of change requests and problem reports. Their turn-around time is significantly influenced by the backlog. If there is already three months of work servicing existing problem reports, then a new problem report (all else being equal) will take three months plus to implement.

As a project manager, your primary activities involve tracking the backlog of work, working with a change control board to evaluate and prioritize change requests, and working closely with configuration management personnel to ensure that fixes are not accidentally overwritten and that older versions of subcomponents are not accidentally reintroduced into the system.

From one perspective, you have a single lifecycle phase: Implement change requests. However, each change request is similar to a miniature project. Someone will need to analyze the problem and propose a solution. The effort and impact associated with that solution will need to be evaluated. One or more modules may need to be redesigned, and code will need to be developed. Unit and integration testing will need to be done. All of this may occur, if the change is small enough, within a single day.

In performing legacy system maintenance, most of the change requests can be implemented using waterfall lifecycles; the duration is short, requirements are stable, and the solution is well understood. However, you can use any lifecycle necessary, depending on the characteristics of the change request. For example, if a specific change request looks like it will require a team of ten developers attempting to discover a technological breakthrough, then you may want to develop a dedicated plan for that effort and associate it with a risk-driven spiral lifecycle.

The legacy maintenance lifecycle can be viewed as an ongoing succession of miniature projects that all have their unique project characteristics and that all should be evaluated on an instance-by-instance basis.

For this lifecycle model to be successful, it is essential that you have customer input into the importance of implementing the various change requests. A change that can be implemented by one person in four days is vastly different from a change that requires a team of five for the next three months. But, the three-month effort may be essential and the four-day effort a waste of time.

Generally, when doing legacy system maintenance, customer priorities and preferences are a key input for determining how best to apply your team.

Hybrid

The hybrid lifecycle is, as the name implies, a combination of two or more lifecycle models. For example, you may want to commence a project using the throwaway prototype lifecycle, then use a few cycles of the spiral model, and eventually transition to a waterfall model.

SELECTING THE BEST ENGINEERING METHOD

In addition to selecting a lifecycle approach for the project, you will also need to identify the one or two best engineering methodologies for project technical personnel to use. Typically, you select the engineering methodology concurrent with, or subsequent to, selecting the lifecycle method. This is done at the very beginning of the planning phase because the engineering methods can have a significant impact on the character of the activities detailed in the project plan.

As with selecting the best lifecycle for the project, selecting the best engineering methodology is something that you should revisit regularly as the project unfolds. Especially on multiyear projects, you may occasionally find that the engineering method best suited to last year's development efforts is not the best method for this year's efforts. Hence, as the needs of the project shift, you will want to examine regularly the efficiency and effectiveness of the software engineering methodology.

There are numerous engineering methodologies and hybrid combinations of methodologies. For our purposes, we will focus on the following four engineering approaches:

1. Functional decomposition
2. Object-oriented
3. Human-usage based
4. Software engineering hybrid

As with lifecycle selection, a clear understanding of project strengths can aid in the selection of an engineering method. As shown in Figure 9, you should strive to have at least the indicated project strengths if you are anticipating using one or more of these engineering methods.

Figure 9
Project Strengths That Complement Engineering Methods

	Functional Decomposition	Object-Oriented	Human-Usage Based	Hybrid
Appropriate Processes				●
Capitalization		●	●	
Customer Focus			●	
Historical Data				
Modern Support Environment		●		
Project Brevity				
Requirements Stability	●			
Strategic Teaming			If Applicable	
Team Cohesiveness	●			
Team Expertise		●		
Training Support				●
Expertise as Manager				●

Functional Decomposition

Functional decomposition was one of the earliest formalisms of software development and continues to be a highly efficient way to develop some software systems. The basic idea is to take an overall system and decompose it to progressively smaller pieces until any given piece can be readily understood and implemented. In some environments, each decomposition must divide into at least three pieces but not more than seven pieces. This approach often leads to a more orderly decomposition.

Functional decomposition works very well on small- to medium-sized systems, and can work well even on very large systems. The primary advantage of functional decomposition is that it is quite easy for designers and developers to conceptualize the system in terms of the functions that the system will provide.

However, this approach also has a few disadvantages. First, as the system becomes bigger, the number of problems relating to the interfaces between subsystems tends to increase. To leverage the services provided elsewhere in the system, developers working on one part of the system may start making function or procedure calls to other parts of the system. However, the developers working on those other sections may find a need to change parameters being passed or services being offered, thereby "breaking" the code of anyone calling those routines.

Designers and developers can attempt to avoid such tight coupling between various subsystems, but doing so can lead to increased redundancy. That is, several subsystems may be implementing nearly identical functionality. This is both time-consuming and inefficient.

As a project manager, you will likely plan to use a functional decomposition methodology whenever you consider your overall project risk to be relatively low. This might occur when the project duration is short, the expertise on the project is high, or other risk factors discussed previously are largely absent.

Object-Oriented

Object-oriented methodologies were developed, in part, as a response to some of the problems encountered when attempting functional decomposition. The general philosophy behind object-oriented software engineering is to hide implementation details. Software services are encapsulated within objects. As a developer, all I have access to are the published services offered by an object. I have no access to any of the internal functions, procedures, subobjects, or data structures.

This has the clear advantage of allowing the developer of a software object complete freedom to change the internal implementation details of that object without having an adverse impact on any other software in the system. Because others do not have access to the object's internals, those internals can be changed as needed. The only aspect of an object that needs to be stabilized is the interfaces to its published services.

While, in principle, the object-oriented approach seems superior to functional decomposition, in practice, object-oriented principles can lead to problems. One major problem is that if an object does not publish a service that you need, you must convince the developer of the object to add a new published service—or you may find yourself developing a similar object but with increased functionality.

Additionally, keeping track of all the available objects and the services they offer can become both complicated and time-consuming on larger systems. Ironically, this is highly conducive to developers simply implementing the object and services they need rather than trying to figure out if someone else has already done so. This, of course, leads to an explosion in the number of objects within the system, making this problem aggressively self-perpetuating.

When you are planning a project, you will likely select an object-oriented approach whenever you and the project team are both experienced in this software methodology. Additionally, since requirements volatility is conducive to significant changes in the source code, you might select an object-oriented approach to reduce the repercussions of those changes.

Human-Usage Based

Another set of methodologies you may want to consider is those designed for the construction of human-intensive systems. A significant proportion of these systems is dedicated to implementing the human interface. The intent of these methodologies is to ensure that the system development effort is always focused on the needs of the end user.

As with the other approaches, a human-usage based approach affects every lifecycle phase of the software engineering effort. Requirements are typically derived from a set of scenarios describing in detail how humans will be interacting with the system. Consequently, the design documents usually are also closely tied to, and traceable to, the usage scenarios. Hence, development often proceeds by incrementally building and testing closely related sets of user functions.

Note that nothing about human-usage based systems prevents the use of functional decomposition or of object-oriented methodologies. However, neither of those approaches is designed specifically to focus on the human interface or the interactions between the system and its users.

Arguably, the increasing use of Web-based environments and technologies is shifting attention—and risk—back toward issues relating to human factors. When a majority of the risks associated with developing a system can be tied directly to human factors, you should choose an engineering method designed to minimize those risks.

Software Engineering Hybrid

The preceding discussion somewhat simplifies the issue of selecting the most appropriate engineering process by treating each approach individually. In practice, the needs of a project will typically be rather complex—especially on larger or longer duration projects. Consequently, it is not uncommon that some parts of a system are built using one engineering methodology while other parts are built using a different engineering methodology. This is not only appropriate, but on some projects, attempting to force the use of a single engineering methodology across the entire project may be wholly inappropriate.

Adherents to particular methodologies (and especially the authors who publish the books describing those methods) tend to think that their particular approach is, of course, the "best" approach for building software. In practice, the best approach for larger projects tends to be discernible only at the subsystem level. Further, a mixed or hybrid combination of multiple approaches may be most effective.

The advantage to using a single engineering approach is that you can typically go to a public source and easily provide project personnel with documentation or instruction on how you expect them to perform their work. Alternatively, when you need to use a hybrid methodology, you must take the time to describe, or at least outline, the engineering methodology so that all project personnel understand your expectations regarding how to build the system.

3 Developing Plans

"Everyone is trying to find 'the best' people. This is a complete waste of time."

On a typical software project, development of the project plans tends to occur in multiple passes. On larger projects, different segments of the plan may be assigned to different people for development. Your role as project manager will be to integrate the various plans into a complete and integrated set of planning documents. On smaller projects, you will likely personally develop most or all sections of the plan, possibly with reviews and comments provided by topic area experts.

DEVELOPING PRELIMINARY PLANS

In developing the project plan, you will regularly be revising, adjusting, and revisiting the various sections as more of the project details are discussed, documented, and communicated to others. On each pass through the plan, you will:

- add missing material,
- revise existing material,
- identify and resolve internal inconsistencies, and
- identify and prioritize remaining planning activities.

As you add content and details to the plan, near-term details will be easier to capture than more distant ones. For example, the parts of the plan covering the next three to six months will typically include more detail than the parts covering months twelve through eighteen.

One of the first determinations you must make when undertaking preliminary planning is whether or not the project is even feasible. Once feasibility has been established, project initiation and preliminary planning can be undertaken.

Feasibility Analysis

Prior to or concurrent with preliminary planning, a high-level analysis is conducted of the overall feasibility of the project. Often, someone else has completed this analysis and executive management has already approved and funded the project. However, if this has not already been done, you should allocate some of your preliminary planning time to understanding the feasibility of the project.

One objective of feasibility analysis is to ensure that none of the expectations associated with the project is far beyond historical precedence. For example, if expectations are that you can, using the same team and in the same time frame you previously used, deliver a system that is ten times larger and far more complex than the prior system you built, those expectations render the new project essentially infeasible. However, if 95 percent of the new system will be implemented using commercially available software and you only have to build half the software that you built on your prior project, then the system may well be feasible.

In principle, when you start project planning, the inputs are the high-level requirements for the software system, and the outputs are the estimates of how long it will take and how much it will cost. In practice, there are often expectations that the project should be completed at or below a certain budget and on or before a certain date. Such expectations can be incorporated into your feasibility analysis. There is no use spending two months developing a detailed plan for an estimated two-year project, only to find out that management expects the entire project to take less than half a year.

When performing a feasibility analysis, carefully assess expectations regarding each of the following:

- maximum cost,
- maximum overall calendar duration,
- maximum personnel resources available,
- maximum computational resources available,
- limitations on training,
- limitations on salary levels,
- limitations on ability to hire external personnel,
- limitations on ability to select internal personnel,
- need for technology breakthrough,
- need for research breakthrough,
- limitations on modern tool acquisition or usage, and
- need for early proof of project success.

In addition to ensuring that the project is feasible given prevailing expectations, you will need to ensure that there are no known requirements that, even at this early stage, can render the project infeasible. For example, there may be requirements related to system cycle time, processor types, and bus types that allow you to assert that the system simply cannot be built as specified. A fair amount of detective work may be involved in reaching this determination, as any obviously conflicting requirements would usually have been caught before this stage.

Project Initiation

Project initiation consists of the set of one-time activities you need to perform to commence more detailed project planning activities. This may include formally approving the project planning budget or assigning support resources to assist you with the planning activities.

Ideally, at this stage, you will have an approved statement of work or an approved product description (you may have previously been working with draft versions). If you are quite fortunate, you may even have been provided with an approved high-level requirements specification.

The primary purpose of project initiation is to serve as an initial gate that helps ensure that:

- those sponsoring or funding the project have approved the initial release of funds and the accrual of expenditures, and

- those responsible for planning and management of the project tentatively agree that the project appears feasible.

Preliminary Planning

Preliminary planning consists of determining the structure and organization of the project plan, and then documenting within the plan any currently known project goals, requirements, constraints, milestone dates, resource needs, risks, and any other planning-related information that you already know.

At this point, don't worry about style or polish. Instead, start using the project plan as the primary repository for all information related to the project. Eventually, your plan will have sections covering most or all of the following areas:

1. Purpose and scope of the project
2. Goals and objectives of the project
3. Listing of all acronyms used in the project plan, and an explanation of those acronyms
4. Listing of all supporting documentation or published works referenced in the plan, and a brief description of their content
5. Summary description of the product's customer characteristics and needs
6. External or internal standards with which the project must comply
7. Description of the lifecycle or lifecycles selected for the project and a rationale for the selection
8. Any documented procedures, methods, and techniques for managing, developing, maintaining, or supporting the software, the software project, or project-related artifacts. This may include descriptions of the processes for:
   - software size estimating
   - software effort estimating
   - software planning
   - project tracking and oversight
   - configuration management

- quality assurance
- subcontract solicitation management
- subcontract acquisition management
- requirements management
- software design
- software development
- software inspection
- software integration testing
- system testing
- system deployment
- problem or change request tracking and management
- status reporting
- technical documentation development
- user documentation development
- training material development.

9. Tools that will be used to support these procedures, methods, and techniques, and the rationale for their selection and use

10. Detailed listing and supporting descriptions of all software and related products to be developed

11. Size and complexity estimates for all software and related products

12. Work breakdown structure

13. Resource breakdown structure

14. Estimates of the project resource requirements

15. Estimates of the project costs

16. Estimated use of critical computer resources, including those in the
    - development environment
    - in-house test environment

- field test environment
- customer environment.

17. Project schedule, including major milestones and reviews, resource requirements, and critical path analysis

18. Identification, evaluation, and management of the project's risks

19. Documentation of the project's software engineering facilities and any additional support tools.

This list is fairly comprehensive, and is excessive for smaller projects. However, for any sections that you are thinking of eliminating from your plan, be sure that you will not inadvertently introduce disproportionate risk into your project. As a general rule, you should opt for making certain sections quite brief, rather than eliminating them altogether.

During preliminary planning, you should generally lay out the entire plan, even though most of it will be blank. As you proceed with developing the intermediate plan, you will continually be expanding and integrating the growing collection of material.

DEVELOPING INTERMEDIATE PLANS

As you develop the intermediate plan, you will be documenting your initial version of the project organizational structure, the project staffing profile, the tools you will need, work and resource breakdown structures, and any other information that will help you construct the eventual detailed plan.

Remember, even at this stage, the plan needs to be highly flexible. Don't try to get things perfect. Excessive effort in any given part of the plan tends to cause excessive "ownership," which can lead to defensiveness and a reluctance to change elements of the plan as more information becomes available. The intermediate plan (or plans—you will likely make several passes at building the intermediate plan) simply represents a draft version of the plan at a given moment in time. You will continue revising the plan as you integrate the various components.

Initially, however, it is fairly common to develop some or many of these pieces in isolation (and in parallel), and to reconcile differences or inconsistencies between the pieces during a subsequent pass.

Project Organization

You have a variety of choices for organizing your project. Keep in mind that your company may impose certain elements of this organization. For example, your company may have a culture of using matrix management. If so, you may find that you are responsible for the technical progress of the project while someone else is responsible for the business progress of the project.

Notwithstanding project organizational constraints that your company imposes on you, you will still have some discretion over the details of how your project team is organized.

Generally, projects are formed to support one of four overall business paradigms:

1. Product-oriented
2. Market-oriented
3. Function-oriented
4. Matrix-oriented

Product-Oriented Project Organization

Product-oriented projects are organized so that the same team performs the majority of the activities necessary to develop and deliver the product. Different people on the team have different specialty areas. For example, the team may be composed of two requirements analysts, two design specialists, six developers, two testers, two documentation developers, one technical editor, and a configuration management specialist. The team is generally kept together throughout the duration of the project.

On smaller teams, it is very helpful to have people who demonstrate a variety of skills. For example, you might have a technical editor who is also quite proficient at developing training material. Multipurpose team members make it easier for you, as the project manager, to distribute work evenly.

Market-Oriented Project Organization

Market-oriented projects (which can be called customer-oriented if your customer is large enough) are organized so that they are highly responsive to nontechnical objectives, constraints, and considerations. In addition to the technical personnel typical on a product-oriented team, the market-oriented team includes nontechnical personnel and delegates a significant amount of authority to a subset of these nontechnical personnel. Projects that are managed by nontechnical personnel, or projects whose managers are directed by nontechnical personnel, are likely following a market-oriented paradigm.

This type of project organization works well when requirements are unknown, competition is extremely aggressive, or there is a need for very fast reaction times to factors external to the project. Of course, to whatever degree those factors are unpredictable or chaotic, the project likewise will be unpredictable or chaotic.

Function-Oriented Project Organization

Function-oriented projects are organized to allow personnel to focus on whatever they are best at doing. In this paradigm, there is a requirements group, a design group, a documentation group, a test group, and other groups for whatever functional specializations are necessary. Therefore, if you are the project manager for the code development team, your team consists entirely of software coders. If documentation needs to be developed, another group does it. Likewise, when integration or system testing is needed, a different group carries it out.

The advantage to this approach is that it allows people work within a group where they can find help and advice easily. The disadvantage is that intergroup conflict—and a corresponding decrease in overall efficiency—are quite common.

Matrix-Oriented Project Organization

Matrix-oriented projects strive to use two different organizational paradigms with the objective of maximizing the strengths of both while minimizing their weaknesses. For example, a company may be using a hybrid of product-oriented and function-oriented paradigms. Hence, every project member has two managers: one responsible for getting product on the street, and one responsible for ensuring, for example, that the documentation group is used as efficiently and effectively as possible. As long as the decision-makers remain in agreement, the project proceeds well. When project personnel start receiving conflicting assignments from their dual managers, chaos ensues.

In practice, matrix management usually works best when the delegation of who has final authority on what types of decisions is clearly documented. In this environment, managers make joint decisions as long as they can come to consensus quickly. In the absence of rapid consensus, one of the managers has the authority to make the final decision.

There are, of course, numerous variations regarding project organization. If you are unsure which organization would work best on your project, use the product-oriented paradigm. A team of people who are all working together, sharing complete responsibility for development of the product, and led by a single, competent project manager, has excellent potential for being a highly successful team.

Project Staffing

Variance in productivity ratios in software development may be one of the most extreme in any industry. Productivity ratios as high as 28 to 1 have been cited. Put differently, what takes one programmer an entire year to do can take another programmer less than two weeks. Hence, staffing your project with appropriate personnel is one of the most important actions you will take.

When it comes to project staffing, you usually will find yourself in one of these four situations:

- Project personnel have been assigned to you by executive management, and you have no choice.
- You can swap existing project personnel with other personnel within the company.
- You can augment internal project personnel by hiring additional resources from outside the company.
- No resources are available and you must hire everyone from outside the company.

In all but the first of these situations, you will need to make staffing decisions. Your selection of a project organization already tells you something about the types of personnel you need. If your project is product-oriented, you likely need multitalented people. If it is market-oriented, you need people who can be highly flexible and who don't get frustrated easily. If it is function-oriented, you need specialists and people who like repetitive work. If it is matrix-oriented, you need personnel who are highly capable of self-management, conflict management, and conflict resolution.

In any event, you will be looking for people who are in very high demand. Accordingly, these people are very hard to find and attract.

Options for finding people to staff your project include any combination of the following:

- placing a recruitment ad in your company newsletter,
- placing a recruitment ad in one or more local newspapers,
- soliciting referrals from existing company personnel,
- participating in a job fair,
- posting openings to the internet,
- posting openings to the placement departments of local colleges and universities, and
- retaining a search agency.

Other techniques include calling people you have worked with previously and casually asking them if they might be interested in a bit of a change.

Many companies encourage employee referrals. When successful, this results not only in a new hire, but also in an unofficial mentor. The employee who made the referral has a vested interest in the success of the referred employee. The newly hired person likewise does not want to disappc referring employee.

When staffing the project, remember that there is strength in diversity. Typically, the best team is one that has a mix of senior people and junior people, generalists and specialists, veterans and new hires. This mix usually offers you the greatest flexibility when distributing various types of work to the team. It also avoids the high costs associated with a team of senior, veteran personnel as well as the high risks associated with a team of junior new hires.

Environment and Tools Estimation

During intermediate planning, you also try to define the environment the project will require and any supporting tools that will be needed. Environment decisions range from the physical location of the team and the square footage of space required, down to the types of software you will need to install and the types of computers that project members will need to access.

Examples of the types of activities you need to consider supporting with tools include:

- project planning and tracking,
- configuration management,
- software size estimation,
- defect tracking,
- software design,
- integrated software development,
- software testing,

- team communication (such as e-mail), and
- internet/web access.

Most of these tools will be software-based. On larger projects, you should consider specialized vertical applications, such as a dedicated software size estimation tool. On smaller projects, conventional word processing, database, and spreadsheet software will likely meet your needs in most of these areas.

Many companies have a standardized particular set of tools. As a project manager, you will need to select whatever tools you want to use from the company-approved list. Although this constraint has the advantage of simplifying tool training and support, it has the disadvantage of potentially missing some of the latest tools (due, for example, to a slow cycle time for evaluating new tools and updating the approved tool list). Some companies allow the use of nonpreapproved tools, if the project provides a documented justification or supporting rationale.

When considering tools, you will always face the decision between buying a more mature tool that is missing the latest features, or a leading-edge tool that does not yet have an established track record. Since the software tool industry is highly competitive, vendors get into feature wars with their competitors and products tend to evolve rapidly. Because of this rapid product change, track record is no guarantee that the latest release is free of defects.

However, two of the most important tool selection factors are also among the easiest to determine: (1) your own familiarity with the tools you intend to use, and (2) your team members' familiarity with the tools you are expecting them to use. Typically, a tool with fewer features, but that you know how to use, is more beneficial than a tool with extra features that you have no idea how to use. This is especially true on short duration projects. On larger projects, you can afford a greater learning curve because you can amortize the benefits of learning the new tool over a longer period of time.

Work Breakdown Structures

As you are deciding how to organize your project, and the types of tools that you will need, you can also begin documenting the overall work to be performed. This can be achieved relatively quickly and easily by developing a work breakdown structure (WBS). However, one of the difficulties involved in building a WBS is that you need at least a very high-level idea about how you are going to build the system. In other words, you need a preliminary design. But the design effort is still in the planning stages, and a design doesn't yet exist.

As discussed, planning proceeds by making multiple passes through various sections and updating material in parallel. You will also find that some elements of planning require you or others to commence with some of the engineering activities, such as developing a very preliminary conceptual design. Needless to say, later in the project, you will likely need to change certain aspects of the design. Indeed, the design may end up substantially different from your first expectations. However, this is usually not a major problem if you make it a regular practice to update your plan systematically so that it remains consistent and compatible with all other project documentation. If you later find that the design needs to be changed, you will need to adjust the WBS (as well as other aspects of the plan, such as resource assignments and the schedule of activities) to ensure that everything is in agreement and is completely up to date.

A WBS is a decomposition of the entire project effort into progressively smaller pieces. You continue this decomposition until you have sufficient information to support detailed tracking of the project's progress. As an example, consider Figure 10, a diagram of a partial work breakdown structure.

Figure 10
Partial Work Breakdown Structure

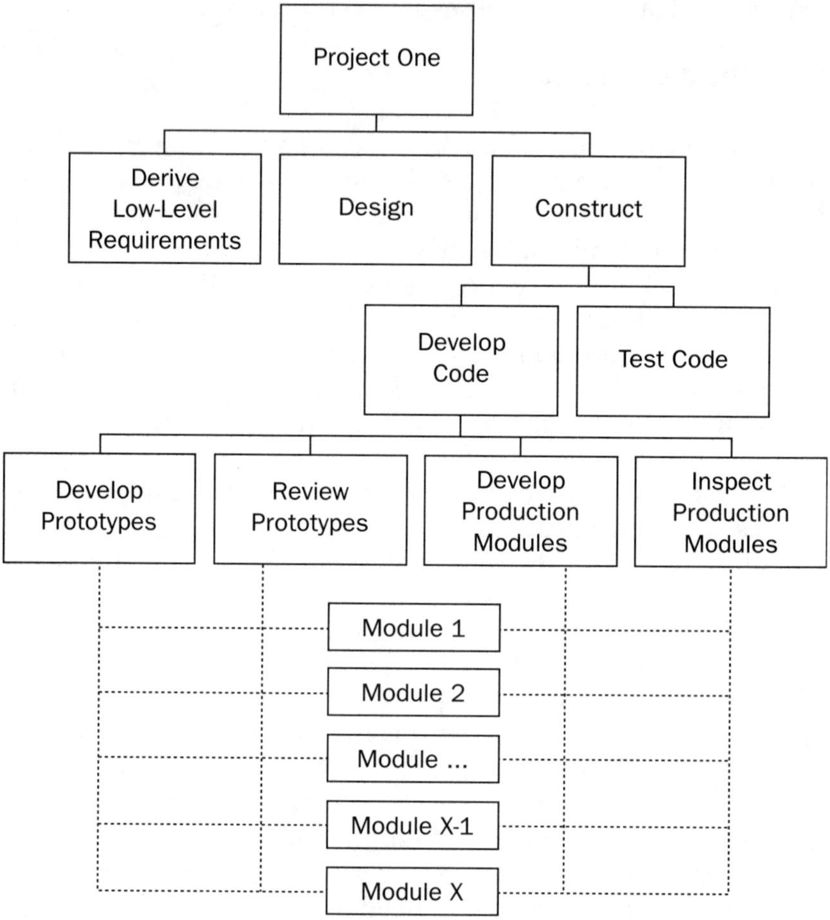

In this example, the WBS shows a simple decomposition of activities to progressively lower levels. One of the characteristics of a WBS is that a charge code (or accounting code) will be allocated to each of the boxes. When detailed planning occurs, you will be associating size and effort estimates for each of the lowest level boxes. You will also be calculating an associated cost for each of the lowest level boxes. The cost of a higher level box is simply the sum of the boxes attached underneath it. When the WBS and associated estimates are approved, the estimated costs become the project's budget.

In this example, dotted lines are used to simplify the diagram. The dotted lines indicate that each of the named modules ("module 1" through "module x") will have activity associated with developing the prototype, reviewing the prototype, developing the production module, and inspecting the production module.

However, note that the "test code" box does not have any boxes underneath it. This indicates that, as far as you are concerned, once testing starts, you do not need any status information until testing has been completed. If you want additional insight into the progress of the "test code" activity, you will need to decompose that activity into subactivities. For example, you could attach the following boxes to "test code":

- test core features,
- test support features,
- conduct performance tests, and
- conduct abuse tests.

This approach would allow you to determine, for example, that core and support features have completed testing, the performance tests have started but are not complete, and the abuse tests have not yet started.

The structure and content of the WBS should clearly show any activity that you consider important. For example, the WBS shown in Figure 11 highlights the need for planning analysis, deployment, and maintenance in addition to the major software engineering activities.

Figure 11
Work Breakdown Structure

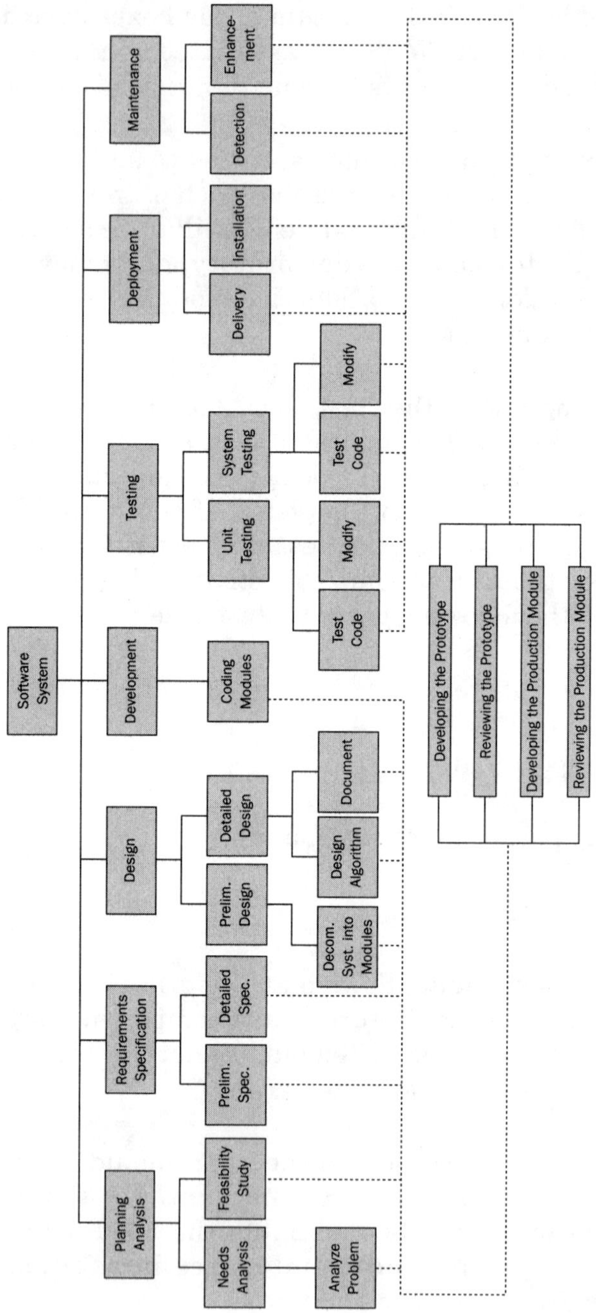

One of the most important questions to answer when developing a WBS is, "How many boxes do I need?" The answer is that you need to keep adding boxes until you no longer care about progress inside the lowest level boxes. A very important principle, referred to as "binary accounting," is that there is no such thing as a lowest level box being 50 percent done. At the lowest level, a box is either 0 or 100 percent done. There are no other options.

Higher level boxes in the WBS are calculated with a percent complete as a function of the percentages associated with the lower boxes. As a simple example, if a box has ten subboxes, and three of the subboxes are 100 percent complete and the others are 0 percent complete (even though all seven might be well underway), then the percent complete of the parent box is 30.

As a general rule, on shorter duration projects (four to twelve months), consider decomposing the activities until each lowest level box represents about one or two weeks of work. For longer projects, the lowest level boxes might represent work expected to last one to four weeks. Remember, when you stop the decomposition, you are asserting that you will not need any additional information regarding the status of that activity other than (1) it has started, and (2) it has finished.

On a short project, a two-month box is very high risk. Work could continue for two months without you having any idea that the work is seriously behind schedule. Only after two months, and after the inability of the people performing the work to assert that they are done, would you begin to learn that the group is in trouble.

Conversely, decomposing boxes to the point where one box represents two hours of work and another represents four hours of work, is almost assuredly excessively detailed.

Resource Breakdown Structures

A resource breakdown structure is similar to a work breakdown structure. However, resource breakdown structures focus on the organizations, divisions, programs, projects, teams, and individuals who will be performing the work.

A common problem with resource breakdown structures is the issue of a given person reporting to someone but not having the same level of authority that other people who report to that person have. For example, a resource breakdown structure may show a secretary reporting to an executive manager. Several project managers also report to the executive manager. With regard to diagrams of resource breakdown structures, most companies employ a rather confusing convention of solid lines meaning one thing, dotted lines meaning something else, double lines indicating yet another relationship, etc. In short, the organizational relationships of who manages whom, who reports to whom, and who supports whom become highly confusing.

When you develop a resource breakdown structure for your project, keep it simple and clear. The most important relationship to document is who has authority to tell someone else what to do. It is far less important to show that person x has a secretary, or that person y provides a quarterly report to person x.

Ideally, a resource breakdown structure will effectively duplicate the abstraction levels of a work breakdown structure. For example, if the work breakdown structure shows four levels of product abstraction (that is, the smallest instances of a work package are only four levels removed from the overall system), then it is helpful if the resource breakdown structure shows a similar decomposition. That is, for this example, the individual software engineers, or the smallest teams, are only four levels removed from the top of the overall development organization.

Detailed Requirements Analysis

It is both regrettable and ironic that all the previously described actions take place before you perform detailed requirements analysis. In theory, none of these should happen until requirements are understood, accepted, and agreed upon. In practice, requirements tend to appear and shift throughout the entire life of the project simply because your customer's problems and opportunities tend to shift at least as fast as technology does.

Hence, as part of intermediate planning, you will need to revisit the existing requirements regularly and evaluate their relevancy, objectivity, completeness, consistency, and testability. Of course, you must also ensure that all elements of your project plan (including preliminary design assumptions) are consistent with and reflect your latest understanding of the current requirements.

DEVELOPING DETAILED PLANS

At some point in the planning process, you will realize that you've moved beyond the stage of intermediate planning and have commenced with the development of detailed plans. There is no clear boundary between the two. Indeed, on some projects, the intermediate plans may contain considerably different types of information than on other projects. With regard to preliminary and intermediate planning, you work with developing whatever information is initially available to you.

However, eventually (and usually relatively quickly) you need to start analyzing issues relating to the size of the system being built, the estimated costs, the expected schedule of activities, and the remaining details necessary to complete the software project plan.

Estimating Product Size

Estimating product size is one of the most difficult tasks to perform accurately. Regrettably, size estimates have a huge influence on cost, effort, and schedule estimates. If the size estimates are wrong, a variety of other key project estimates will also be wrong.

Size estimates are made using a variety of units, including:

- thousands of source lines of code (KSLOC),
- function points,
- objects,
- screens, and
- unique graphical elements.

Software sizing techniques can vary from formal, database-driven, historically derived size estimates, to the moderately informal Delphi estimation technique, to the highly informal guessing by a project manager that "this product will likely be twice as big as the last one we did."

The Delphi technique is a good compromise between having hard data and making guesses. Properly used, this technique can be applied quite effectively to software sizing. The Delphi technique is typically used to answer questions that cannot be answered. For example, suppose you want an answer to the question, "What will the Dow Jones average be two years from now?" Nobody knows. But suppose you still need an answer? You can use the Delphi technique.

The Delphi process is simple. Ask a variety of knowledgeable people to develop their own best answer to your question. When they are done, have them meet in a group where each individual presents, without interruption, his or her answer and what it is based on. Everyone listens to everyone else. Typically, there are no discussions regarding what is wrong or right; people just state their position, and then sit down and allow the next person to present. Next, you end the meeting and ask each person to reassess his or her answer and, if they like, to revise their rationale. After they have worked individually to develop what they now consider to be the most accurate answer, they meet again. This meeting is handled identically to the first. Everyone simply states their latest opinion on what the answer is, and why they arrived at this answer.

Almost always, the group will start to close in on an answer that approximates consensus. In principle, each person is listening to all the others, becoming smarter, and developing an answer that is probably becoming more accurate with each iteration.

The process is complete when the group is more or less in agreement, or when you think that subsequent iterations will not have much influence on the answers you are given.

Since many consider accurate predictions of software size to be essentially impossible, the Delphi technique can be quite useful. To use it for software size estimations, identify a group of people who you think are capable of making relatively good guesses regarding possible software size. Ask them to study any known information and to estimate the size of modules, objects, subsystems, or other system components. Then follow the process described above. When the smallest estimates are at least 75 percent of the average and the largest are below 125 percent of the average, you may have an average that is good enough to use. For larger Delphi groups, you can establish a rule where you eliminate, for example, the two smallest and two largest numbers before you apply the 75 percent-125 percent test.

Estimating Project Effort

When estimating effort, you need to account for a variety of factors. These factors include:

- Software size
- Software complexity
- Team experience with the problem domain
- Team experience with the solution domain
  - programming language
  - development environment
  - support tools (configuration management, diagnostic, etc.)
- Application of productivity tools
- Use of in-progress product and process quality evaluations
- Intended quality thresholds during postdevelopment testing

In evaluating these factors, one of the key problems you will encounter is determining how you weight their relative impact. Most software cost estimation tools assert that if the results end up being wrong, then you should just adjust the coefficients until they yield accurate results. To do this successfully, you need to determine the relative correlation between estimation inputs and resulting outputs. Of course, a major problem is the existence of nonlinear and nonarithmetic relationships between inputs and outputs.

Additionally, even when historical data is available, software development rarely offers the luxury of repeating near-identical projects. The cumulative impact of numerous new factors introduces variables that reduce predictive confidence to unreliable levels.

If you are highly uncertain about your effort estimates, consider using a multiple-build lifecycle. For example, you can develop the first build of the system and get it into customer use. You now have a wealth of actual data relating to the size of the software delivered, as well as the time, effort, and cost required for development. This allows for considerable improvement to any subsequent estimates. You are using real data gathered early in the project and will be making subsequent deliveries using essentially the same parameters.

This scenario presumes that subsystems generally have similar characteristics. That is, you cannot do the simplest subsystem first and the most complex subsystem last and expect early data to be predictive of the remaining effort. Instead, consider trying to be a bit easier than average for the first and second subsystems so that you can overcome the learning curve costs in relatively low impact areas.

Then develop the third and fourth builds around subsystems that represent the most risk and difficulty. By taking this approach, you avoid pushing high-risk areas into the end of the development schedule, where you have the least time to recover. This leaves the final builds to be of moderate difficulty. Theoretically, the average of the earlier performance and productivity data should be reasonably representative and allow for relatively accurate revised predictions and, if necessary, mitigation actions. This potentially allows you to take significant corrective actions when you are only about halfway through the project. Using a more traditional approach, projects are often 80 to 90 percent of the way through their original plan before the manager clearly understands how much trouble the project is in.

Scheduling Milestones

As you continue with detailed planning, you will need to develop a schedule showing major project milestones and indicating, in detail, when the various activities will occur and who will be performing them. A simple method for developing this schedule is to build a precedence network.

To build a precedence network, you start with a list of activities to be performed. These activities are the lowest level boxes from your WBS. For each activity, you estimate its duration. Duration is derived from your size estimates, effort estimates, and availability of resources during the period for which you've scheduled the activity. For each of the activities on the list, you indicate any predecessor activities. The predecessors for any given activity are any activities that must be complete before the given activity can start.

For example, consider the following list of activities:

Activity	Code	Duration	Predecessors
Requirements	**A**	**12**	**None**
Design	**B**	**9**	**None**
Test Plan	**C**	**10**	**A**
Documentation	**D**	**10**	**B**
Coding	**E**	**24**	**B**
Risk Analysis	**F**	**10**	**A**
Test Lab	**G**	**35**	**C**
Tech Editing	**H**	**40**	**D**
Marketing	**I**	**15**	**A**
Integration	**J**	**4**	**G, H, E**
User Evaluation	**K**	**5**	**I, F, J**

Once you have this list, the next step is to build a precedence network showing activities as nodes and with lines connecting each activity to its predecessors. For each activity, add a number indicating its duration (typically, this is in calendar days).

Figure 12 shows an example of a precedence network for this list of activities.

Again, each node represents an activity and each activity has an estimated duration (both shown within the circles). Above the circles for each activity are two numbers:

- earliest start date, and
- latest start date.

(Note: There are also two boxes shown on the network. These are the "start" and "end" boxes. They do not represent activities, and do not have any associated duration. They are included to simplify the structure and interpretation of the network.)

To calculate the earliest start date for each activity, you start at the beginning of the network and analyze each activity's data. The earliest start date for an activity is the highest sum resulting from adding each of the immediate predecessors' earliest start dates to its duration.

For example, assume activity T has predecessors R and S. Activity R has an earliest start date of 50 days (from project commencement) and a duration of 5 days. Activity S has an earliest start date of 45 days and a duration of 15 days. The soonest that R can be completed is 55 days from project start (50 + 5). The soonest that activity S can be completed is 60 days (45 + 15). Since activity T cannot start until both R and S are done, the earliest start date for T is 60 days.

Another important number shown in the example is the latest start date (shown opposite the earliest start date). The

Figure 12
Precedence Network

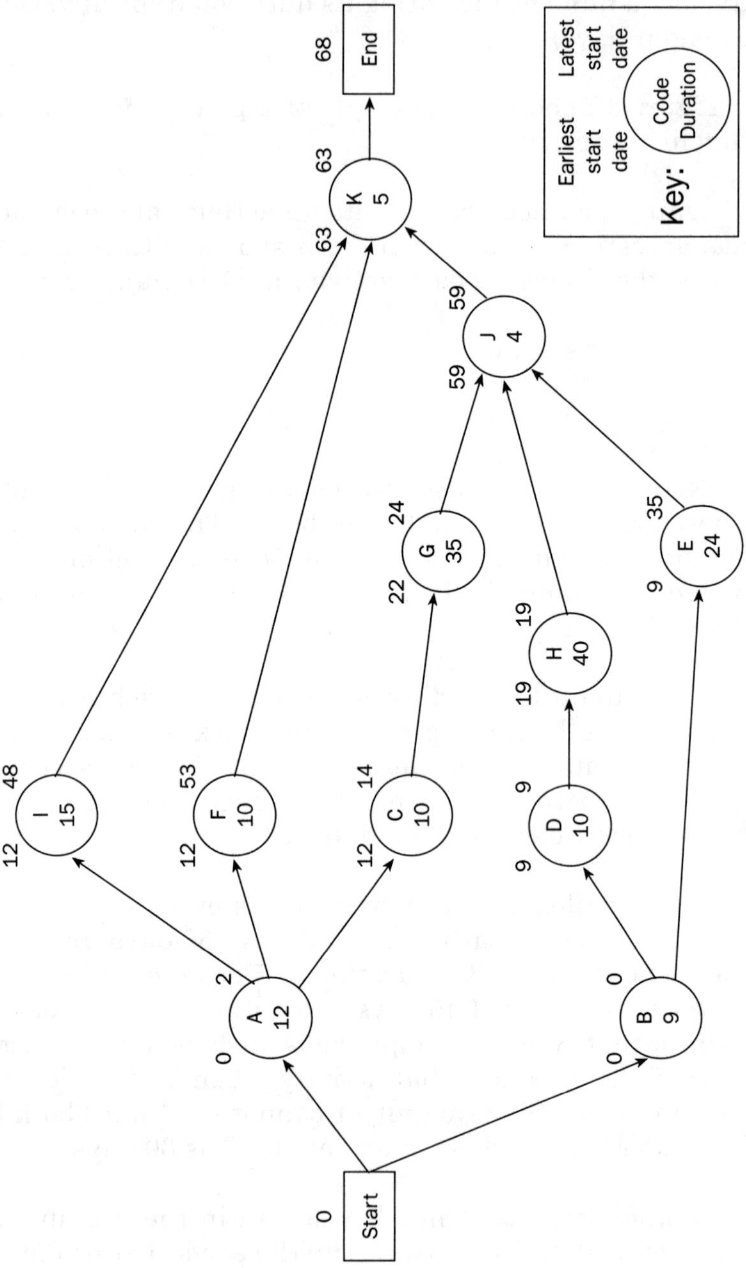

latest start date is calculated in a manner similar to the earliest start date.

To determine latest start date, start at the *end* of the precedence network. Working backwards, the latest start date for an activity is that that activity's duration subtracted from the minimum latest start date of any successor (or later) activity.

Two other numbers that are useful to have are earliest end date (equal to earliest start date plus duration) and latest end date (equal to latest start date plus duration).

After you have calculated earliest start date and latest start date, study the precedence to discover the critical path. A critical path is any sequence of activities where, if any activity is delayed, the entire project is delayed. Finding the critical path is easy. Look for any sequence of activities where the earliest start date and the latest start date are equal to each other. There is always at least one critical path.

In the preceding example, the critical path is: B-D-H-J-K.

The activities on the critical path must be monitored carefully. Be sure that you have sufficient resources for those activities and take any additional steps to reduce the likelihood of any delays. For any activity that is not on the critical path, you have "slack time"—the difference between the activity's earliest start date and latest start date. Slack time within an activity means it can be delayed, or can be late, up to the limits of its slack time without delaying the overall project. However, by definition, the critical path has zero slack time. If activities on the critical path are late or delayed, you will not complete the project on time.

Precedence networks can be built even when activity durations are uncertain. To do so, you replace the exact duration value with a simple equation intended to give an estimated value. A common approach is to estimate, for each activity, the following three values:

A = Likely shortest duration
B = Expected duration
C = Likely longest duration

The estimated duration, D, is calculated using the equation:

D = (A + (3 * B) + (2 * C)) / 6.

For example, you might expect a given activity to take around 20 days. However, you are confident that it has to take at least 15 days, and you are similarly confident that it will be completed within 40 days. Using these values, the estimated duration is (15 + (3 * 20) + (2 * 40)) / 6, or 25.83 days.

Analysis of a precedence network can support a variety of decisions. For example, a bonus may be associated with bringing the project in ahead of schedule, or a penalty associated with the project being late. Since the critical path determines the project's completion date, you can look for ways to shorten one or more activities on the critical path, thereby shortening the duration of the project. However, when doing so, always watch for the emergence of new—or multiple—critical paths.

Scheduling Resources

Once the milestones are scheduled and the activities plotted along a timeline, you can start identifying the resources needed to perform the various activities. Each activity can be characterized by needing support from one or more roles, and each role can be characterized by the number of people needed for that role. For example, a preliminary design activity might require four senior software designers, two junior software designers, and one senior requirements analyst.

Ideally, at this point, you can start attaching the names of project personnel to these roles and activities. If you still have unfilled job announcements, you can simply assign a temporary code to represent the new hires.

As you assign people to activities, you will likely gain a considerably clearer picture of the staffing requirements for the project. Invariably, you will have far too much work for some people, and far too little for others. This is where resource analysis, balancing, and load leveling really become your primary effort.

Leveling Loads

Load leveling is the process of evenly distributing the work across all project personnel so that each team member has about 40 hours of work to do each week. During the initial assignment of resources to activities, it is common to have a single person assigned as full-time support to multiple activities. This is fine as long as those activities do not overlap. However, if two or three such full-time activities overlap, then you've assigned that person 16 or 24 hours worth of work to be done each day the overlap exists.

Sometimes, you can eliminate an overload by taking the overloaded person's name off one of the activities, and substituting the name of an available person who has similar qualifications. Other times, the only way to reduce an overload is to delay one of the activities so that it isn't scheduled to start until the other activity is finished. If you use this approach, be sure the delayed activity does not affect the critical path.

DEVELOPING A RISK MANAGEMENT PLAN

Very few projects even have a functional project plan, much less a risk management plan. However, risk management is critical for project success, and risks are surprisingly easy to plan for, track, and mitigate.

The benefits of risk management are hard to quantify. For example, how do you know when you've spent enough money to make your house or apartment fire-safe? Have you ever bought an extra smoke detector? Have you purchased one or more fire extinguishers? Do you have a chain-ladder to use as a fire escape from the second floor?

Suppose two years go by and you never have a fire in your house. Does that mean you've wasted the money?

The first objective in a risk management plan is to prevent undesirable situations from occurring. The second objective is to reduce any negative consequences when something undesirable does occur. Hence, one highly ironic consequence of successful risk management is that you don't have highly visible problems. But don't be fooled into dropping your risk management activities; the problems are being kept in check precisely because you are actively managing and mitigating them.

A simple way to plan for risks is to develop a "house of risk management." (This technique is virtually identical to the "house of quality"—quality function deployment—technique that is popular in Japanese manufacturing industries.) The first step in building a house of risk management is to identify any significant risks you think you may have on the project. In the following example (see Figure 13), three risks are shown along the rows:

- realtime performance shortfalls,
- volatile requirements, and
- staff lack of expertise.

Figure 13
House of Risk Management

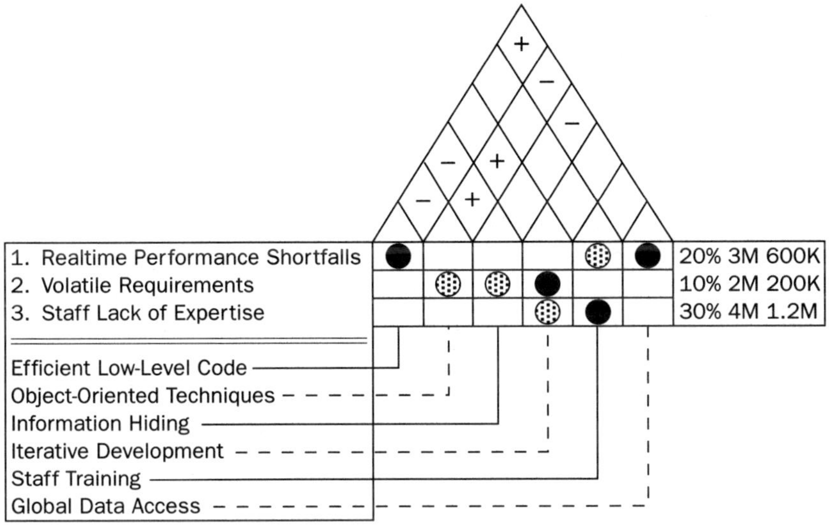

Next, for the columns of the house, you list potential ways that the risks can be reduced or eliminated. In this example, possible solutions are:

- efficient low-level code,
- object-oriented techniques,
- information hiding,
- iterative development,
- staff training, and
- global data access

Inside the house, where the columns and rows intersect, place a marker indicating the degree to which the solutions help reduce the risks. In this example, the black circles indicate that the solution is likely to be highly effective, and the gray circles indicate moderately effective solutions. For example, this house shows that, with regard to managing risks associated with volatile requirements, iterative development would be highly effective, and object-oriented techniques and information hiding would be moderately effective.

Next, you construct the roof of the house, which is used to intersect all the options for solutions with each other. You will find that any given solution will work well in combination with some of the solutions, but may be quite incompatible with other solutions. Put a plus in the roof to show highly compatible solutions, and a minus to indicate highly incompatible solutions. Leave the space empty when the solutions have relatively little influence on each other.

In this example, object-oriented techniques are quite compatible with information hiding. However, information hiding is incompatible with the notion of global data access.

Finally, to the side of the house, add values to indicate your estimate of risk exposure. This is the most difficult part to quantify, but as you'll see shortly, it will be worth trying. Risk exposure is defined as the product of the probability of the undesirable event occurring and the expected cost if it does. For example, if the impact of realtime performance shortfalls is estimated to be $3,000,000 and the probability of that occurring is estimated to be 20 percent, then your risk exposure is $600,000.

Once you've built the house, the obvious question is, what do you do with it? The purpose of the house is to help you analyze risk exposure and make better decisions about the actions you will take, if any, to reduce your risk. Note that in this example, "staff lacks experience" presents twice the risk exposure of "realtime performance shortfalls" and six times the risk exposure of "volatile requirements."

To help analyze your risks and the impact of mitigating them, you may want to develop a risk exposure scatter plot. As shown in Figure 14, the scatter plot has a dollar scale on the y-axis and a probability scale on the x-axis. For each risk on the house, plot it at the appropriate x and y coordinates. The three numbered risks from the house are plotted on the chart.

As shown on the chart, there are curves where your risk exposure is identical along the entire curve. As shown by the

Figure 14
Risk Exposure

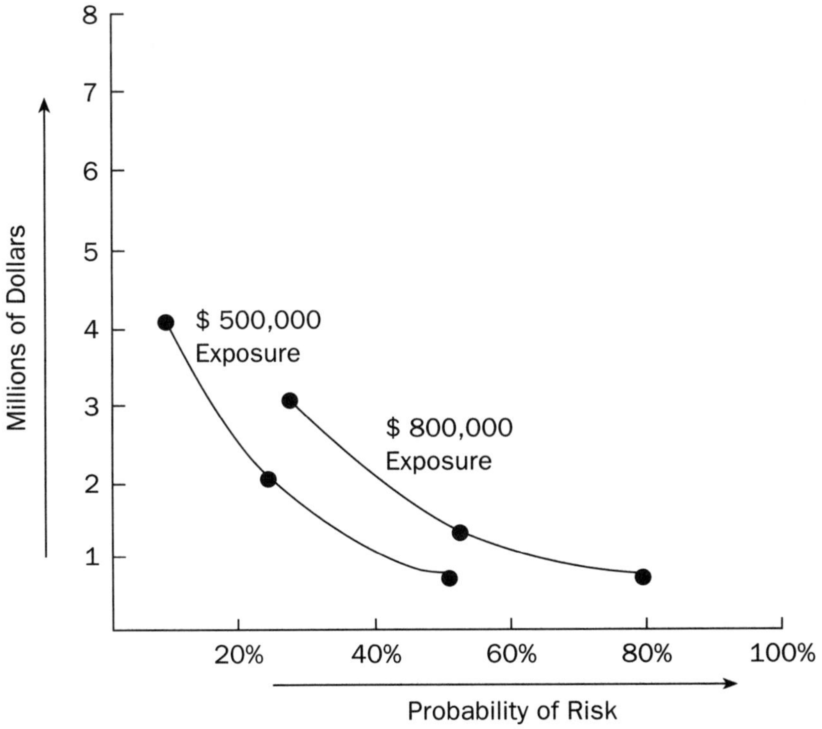

black dots, the following impact and probabilities result in an $800,000 risk exposure:

- $4,000,000 at 12.5 percent probability
- $2,000,000 at 25.0 percent probability
- $1,000,000 at 80.0 percent probability

Also shown on the chart is a $500,000 exposure curve.

Risk exposure is reduced by reducing the probability of the undesirable event occurring, reducing the cost if it occurs, or both.

Suppose, continuing this example, that the project manager decides to reduce the risk of "staff lacks expertise" by implementing the solution "staff training." The manager decides to spend $5,000 on a comprehensive set of video training courses, and budgets $15,000 for in-house technical training. The manager believes that, while this will not eliminate the risk, it will reduce the probability from 30 percent to 10 percent. This reduces a $1,200,000 exposure (30 percent probability * $4,000,000 impact) to a $400,000 exposure (10 percent * $4,000,000).

The project manager has decided that it is worth spending $20,000 to realize an $800,000 reduction in risk exposure. When you see these types of ratios, you can be wrong on your probability estimates, and wrong on your impact estimates, and yet still be making the correct decisions. For instance, if the $20,000 investment only ends up reducing the project's risk exposure by $100,000 instead of the estimated $800,000, it is still an excellent investment.

A simple risk management plan contains, at a minimum, the following items:

- top ten risks, in priority order (that is, ranked by exposure),

- potential solutions for reducing risk exposure, and

- contingency actions to be taken in the event that the undesirable event occurs.

A brief description should accompany each of the risks, as well as each of the solutions. Additionally, each of the contingency actions should be accompanied by its triggering mechanisms. That is, there needs to be some obvious manifestation, or some threshold being exceeded, that indicates that the contingency action must commence.

As with other project plans, you will need to update your risk plan regularly. When you do this:

- Revisit your estimates on probabilities and impacts.

- Add any new risks.

- Remove risks from the top ten list when their exposures fall sufficiently low.

- Update the house and scatter diagrams.

- Discuss the updated risk information and diagrams with your project personnel.

Comprehensive risk management does not need to be time-consuming, expensive, or complicated. Even just a few hours a month may be sufficient to avoid a major project disaster.

ORGANIZING THE PROJECT PLAN

As your plan evolves from the initial plan, through one or more intermediate plans, and finally to a detailed plan, it will progressively include an increasing amount of detailed project information. As new information is added to the plan, some of it will invariably contradict other information. Hence, as the plan becomes more comprehensive, you will need to spend an increasing amount of time ensuring that the internal details of different sections of the plan are all kept consistent and compatible.

Eventually, your plan will contain (or contain references to) documents that include at least some, and probably most, of the following sections:

1. Project's purpose and scope

2. Project's goals and objectives

3. Listing and definition of all acronyms used in the project plan

4. Listing of all supporting documentation or published works referenced in the plan, and a brief description of their contents

5. Summary description of the product's customer characteristics and needs

6. External or internal standards with which the project must comply

7. Description of the lifecycle or lifecycles selected for the project and a rationale for the selection

8. Any documented procedures, methods, and techniques for managing, developing, maintaining, or supporting the software, the software project, or project-related artifacts

9. Tools that will be used to support those procedures, methods, and techniques, and the rationale for their selection and use

10. Detailed listing and supporting descriptions of all software and related products to be developed

11. Size and complexity estimates for all software and related products

12. Work breakdown structure

13. Resource breakdown structure

14. Estimates of the project's resource requirements

15. Estimates of project costs

16. Estimated use of critical computer resources

17. Project schedule, including major milestones and reviews, resource requirements, and critical path analysis

18. Identification, evaluation, and management of the project's risks

19. Documentation of the project's software engineering facilities and any additional support tools

Although issues relating to most of these sections were discussed earlier in this chapter, every section in the planning document is briefly described below from the perspective of establishing and maintaining integrity and consistency throughout the plan.

Section 1: Purpose and Scope

This section briefly describes the purpose of the project. Explain the project in terms of the customer's needs or target market. Explain the scope of the project in terms of where and when the project effort will be complete. For completeness, include examples of features or capabilities that are within the scope of the project, and also provide explicit counterexamples of one or more features or characteristics that are clearly outside the scope of the project.

Section 2: Goals and Objectives

Describe the overall goals of the project. Typically, these can be expressed in the form of two or three separate goals that can be articulated succinctly and clearly. Each goal can then be characterized as representing a variety of objectives that, when accomplished, represent incremental progress toward the goal. Describe each objective and, for each, include the tangible criteria that will be used to determine impartially whether or not the objective has been achieved. Once this material has been documented, verify that the goals and objectives are completely compatible with the project's purpose and scope.

Consider sending out the first two sections of the plan for preliminary review as soon as you have them ready. If you and others disagree regarding the purpose, scope, goals, and objectives of your project, you will want to identify and resolve those disagreements at the earliest opportunity.

Section 3: Acronyms and Abbreviations

Before documenting any later sections, provide a listing—and definitions—of all acronyms and abbreviations you expect to be using in the project plan. Until later sections are actually completed, you often will not be entirely certain whether or not you will be using all the acronyms, so keep the definitions quite simple. As you develop the remaining sections of the plan, ensure that you use abbreviations and acronyms consistently. Whenever you use a new abbreviation or acronym, be sure to return to this section to add the new information.

When the plan is complete, revisit this section and remove all unused abbreviations and acronyms. Also, review and update the definitions to ensure that a typical reader of the plan can clearly understand all abbreviations and acronyms.

Section 4: Referenced Documentation

A plan does not have to include physically all the information needed for its successful understanding and implementation. Instead, it is common for plans to make reference to other plans or supporting documentation.

In this section, provide a full listing of all supporting documentation or published works referenced in the plan, as well as a brief description of their content. As with Section 3, when you start this section, you will be including material that you intend to reference in later sections. As you develop subsequent sections, regularly revisit this section to add or remove references to reflect accurately the sources and documentation that are actually referenced in later sections.

Section 5: Summary Product Description

Use this section to provide a high-level, easily understandable, summary description of the product. This may be accomplished in as little as a few short paragraphs. (Detailed descriptions of the project's products are deferred until a later section.) Include in this section a description of major customer characteristics, and the primary needs of those customers.

Provide sufficient detail in this section to allow readers to understand your motivation and rationale for selecting the applicable standards, project lifecycle, major project processes, and project tools that you describe in the next four sections.

Section 6: Applicable Standards

Your project will typically be subject to a variety of standards. These will include standards that are externally imposed upon you (e.g., if your customer requires that you use software Capability Maturity Model—CMM—Level 3 processes) and standards that you have identified as likely to provide valuable support to your project (e.g., compliance with one or more IEEE standards).

Examples of the types of standards you need to consider for your project include:

- process-related standards,
- product quality standards,
- security standards, and
- company or organizational (internal) standards.

Clearly distinguish between those standards that are mandated on your project by others, contractual agreements, or law, and those standards that you have the option of deselecting later in the life of the project.

Section 7: Project Lifecycle

In this section, describe the lifecycle or lifecycles selected for the project and provide a reasonably detailed rationale for their selection. Describe the major characteristics and activities that will occur within each lifecycle phase. Explain the milestone event or other nonambiguous criteria that will be used to indicate clearly the transition from one lifecycle phase to another.

If you have selected a spiral lifecycle, include a high-level description of any major characteristics that will distinguish one cycle through the spiral from the next cycle.

Section 8: Major Project Processes

Describe any documented procedures, methods, and techniques you are planning to use while managing the project, and while project personnel are developing, maintaining, or supporting the software, the software project, or project-related artifacts.

Processes, activities, or tasks that potentially need detailed descriptions include the steps to be taken for:

- software size estimating,
- software effort estimating,
- software planning,
- project tracking and oversight,
- risk management,
- configuration management,
- quality assurance,
- subcontract solicitation management,
- subcontract acquisition management,
- requirements management,
- software design,
- software development,

- software inspection,
- software integration testing,
- system testing,
- system deployment,
- problem or change request tracking and management,
- status reporting,
- technical documentation development,
- user documentation development, and
- training material development.

This list is fairly comprehensive. However, as with each of the major sections, you will likely be better served by including at least a few paragraphs or sentences describing the simple steps that will be taken in these areas, rather than deleting the section or subsection entirely.

Section 9: Tools

Use this section to document and describe the tools that will be used to support the above procedures, methods, and techniques. For each tool, provide a rationale for its selection and an explanation of its intended use.

Be sure to document (and, over time, to update as required) the version numbers or releases of these tools, and the platform(s) or environments they will be installed and used within. As appropriate, describe the planned licensing arrangements in terms of whether a tool will be purchased or leased, the number of copies, licenses, or "seats" that will be needed, and any other information that helps explain your planned use of the various tools.

Section 10: Detailed Product Description

In this section, develop a detailed listing of the software products and subproducts that will be developed during this project. Also describe any related products, both deliverable and nondeliverable, that you plan to develop. This might include user manuals, training material, design specifications, system migration description, etc.

Generally, describe the purpose of each product, and if applicable, its highest level inputs and outputs. Decompose major products to at least one level of subproducts, and further decompose the larger subproducts to successively lower levels. Describe each subproduct and the purpose it serves within the context of the larger product.

Section 11: Size and Complexity Estimates

Begin this section with a high-level explanation of the technique you are using (or that others are using) to develop the size and complexity estimates. If you are using tools as part of the estimating effort, briefly explain those tools (and verify that you listed them in Section 9).

Next, for each of the products and subproducts described in the previous section, use the techniques described above to develop initial size and complexity estimates. Generally, start with the smallest or lowest level products and estimate their size and complexity. Then, as applicable, use the sum of all related lower level components to estimate the size of a higher level component.

In the event that you will be using multiple techniques and then comparing, merging, or averaging their results, be sure to describe each technique, as well as the method you will be using to merge results or resolve conflicts or inconsistencies between results.

Section 12: Work Breakdown Structure

As described earlier in this chapter, develop a work breakdown structure that shows the activities and subactivities that will be used to develop the products and subproducts described in the previous section. It may be necessary to push the work breakdown structure to greater levels of detail than was needed for the detailed product description.

When you are done with the work breakdown structure, verify that none of the lowest level boxes clearly represents an excessive amount for work (for example, a single box that you guess will likely take six months or more). If you find such a box, decompose it another level.

Section 13: Resource Breakdown Structure

Develop a detailed resource breakdown structure. Explain the roles that will be used on the project, the different types of teams that will be required, and which roles will be needed on each team. Describe the responsibilities associated with the roles and teams, and specify any minimum experience requirements.

Generally strive for a resource breakdown structure that roughly parallels the abstraction layers of the work breakdown structure. The lowest level of the resource breakdown structure should be composed of boxes representing individual project personnel or very small teams. Do not actually associate a person's name with a box. Instead, just associate a single role, a small team consisting of personnel performing the same roles, or a small team of mixed roles.

In Section 17, you will be associating actual project personnel with the roles they will be performing and the activities they'll be performing. Using only role and activity associations in this section allows you to make personnel changes without having to update this section repeatedly.

Section 14: Estimated Resource Requirements

With the work breakdown structure and resource breakdown structure in place, you can now develop initial estimates of the total resources required. You should develop these estimates for each type of role within resource breakdown structure.

Your initial estimates will often be very high level and based on relatively little analysis. However, even during the early stages of the project, you will start to have some idea of whether you need five developers or fifty, whether you intend to have one tester per developer or one tester per ten developers, whether you need ten technical writers or none, etc.

Once the initial resource estimates have been developed, continue developing the rest of this plan. After completing the remaining sections, revisit this section and revise it so that it is consistent with later sections, in particular with Section 17, Project Milestones and Schedule.

Section 15: Estimated Project Costs

Start this section with an explanation of the process, methods, or techniques used for estimating project costs (or include a reference to Section 8, or to external or support documentation that explains how to perform project cost estimation).

Using the size and complexity measures documented in Section 11, estimate the costs of each of the project products and subproducts. Also include the costs associated with project tools and any other known expenses.

For simplicity (and on smaller projects), in lieu of attempting to calculate exact costs as a function of the salaries of individuals on the project, you can pick three or four cost levels (such as very low, low, moderate, and high). Then, associate a different average hourly cost to each of those levels. Finally, estimate hours (typically using size and complexity as inputs) for the work to be performed at the lowest level of the work breakdown structure. Associate an appropriate cost level with the different lowest level work breakdown structure boxes, multiple by the estimated hours, and thereby calculate the estimated costs for each activity. Aggregate these costs at progressively higher boxes until you have total salary costs for the work to be performed during the project. As before, add other costs such as tools or planned training.

Numerous scheduling tools are available for use in calculating costs as part of constructing the schedule. If you intend to use such a tool, then develop Sections 16 and 17 first, and use the cost information derived from the scheduling tool to help document estimated costs within this section.

Section 16: Estimated Critical Computer Resources

Use this section to describe any computer resources you consider critical for your project. Examples of areas where you need to consider the existence of critical computer resources include:

- development environment,

- in-house test environment,
- field test environment, and
- customer environment.

Specific instances of critical computer resources include disk space or hard-drive size, main memory, cache memory, and throughput capacity on various busses or channels.

Section 17: Project Milestones and Schedule

Describe the project's major milestones and then show, in detail, the activities and events that will occur to achieve those milestones. Include all major reviews. Associate resource requirements with each activity. Explicitly show who on the project will be performing which activities, and between which dates.

For most projects, you will likely prefer to use one of a number of relatively low-cost project scheduling and management tools. Also, to facilitate analysis and communication, represent your schedule graphically through the use of Gantt charts, PERT charts, or other diagrammatic techniques.

When you have completed a draft of this section, be sure to recheck and update any affected sections earlier in the plan. By this stage, you will undoubtedly have additional details and insights that you need to include in other sections. Similarly, other sections may need to be revised based on your increased understanding on how the project will progress and on the ongoing changes you make as you strive to develop an efficient and effective schedule.

On longer projects, especially projects using a spiral type of lifecycle, detailed (day-by-day) scheduling of activities is commonly done only for near-term months. As the work being scheduled recedes into the future, activities and their assigned dates are tied only to the nearest week, month, and eventually calendar quarter as the time of that work becomes progressively more distant from the current date.

Of course, as time transpires, you will need to revisit this section regularly and add more scheduling details to those months that are drawing nearer.

Section 18: Risk Management Plan

In this section, document your risk management plan. The plan can be patterned on this project plan (that is, sections that describe "purpose and scope," "goals and objectives," "acronyms and abbreviations," etc.). On smaller projects, this plan may be as brief as a couple of pages. On larger, complex, long-duration projects, you need to consider seriously the need for a comprehensive and detailed risk management plan.

Within the plan, explain how you intend to identify, evaluate, prioritize, mitigate, and manage project risks. (Alternatively, the plan can reference Section 8 or an external document that describes the risk management process.) As described earlier, select the top five or ten risks to be the primary focus of your risk management activities and describe each. Document the probability and impact of each risk and calculate the resulting risk exposure.

Explicitly document in the risk management plan the frequency with which you will be reexamining project risks and updating risk-related material.

Section 19: Software Engineering Facilities

In this section, describe in detail the software engineering facilities. This includes anything necessary for the performance of the overall project. Ensure that this section is consistent with the critical computer resources you described in Section 16, and the tools described in Section 9. If you anticipate needing additional tools to support implementation of the software engineering facilities, describe the role they will play (and add that description to Section 9).

Use this section to discuss anything related to the software engineering infrastructure that is not covered by a prior section. Describe any of the following if you consider it important to the success of the project:

- special hardware,
- network facilities,
- access control,
- security,
- special software, and
- communication facilities.

When you finish this section, check to see that other affected sections are updated if necessary. In particular, ensure that there are no costs associated with facilities that were not included in Section 15.

MAINTAINING THE PROJECT PLAN

The prior section presented the project plan in sequential order, and discussed the plan as though it is written from front to back. However, the reason for first discussing preliminary planning, then intermediate planning, and then detailed planning is to reinforce the idea that plans are not written front to back. Instead, plans are written in the order that you can gather the needed information.

No matter how you arrange a plan, earlier sections will depend on information that is documented in later sections, and vice versa. Hence, there is no order that will guarantee that all inputs needed to complete a given section will be found in earlier sections. When developing the plan, do not hesitate to move around working on different sections in different orders, and regularly return to previously "completed" sections to add information or to make changes so that all sections remain consistent with each other.

Finally, the plan is a living document. Projects often start before an approved plan is in place. However, a sufficient portion of the plan may exist in draft form for work to commence. As a software project manager, you will never be "done" with planning until the project is essentially done. You will always be updating the plan to accommodate changes in requirements, personnel, tools, resources, needs, risks, and opportunities. As with software, you may elect to accrue a set of changes before you issue a proposed new release of the plan. As with the original plan, you will need to circulate subsequent major updates to the plan for review and approval.

Although formal review and approval will likely happen only on a periodic basis, the evolution of the plan is a nearly constant process. You must update the plan and keep it consistent with the latest available information. Although you may at times think you are done with planning and can now move on to the "real work" of project management, resist this tendency. A living project plan is an indispensable part of any successful project. Accordingly, maintenance of the project plan is an indispensable activity that must be performed as a regular part of project management.

Software projects are subject to rapid and significant changes arriving from numerous and diverse sources. Therefore, for the plan—and the project—to be successful, you have to allow adequate time in your schedule to keep the plan current and accurate.

DEVELOPING A STAFFING PLAN

As you are developing the intermediate and detailed plans, you will need to think about the types of skills you need on the team, and any assistance you might need with the various management-related activities. For example, are you going to perform all the configuration management activities yourself, or do you need to staff your team with a configuration management manager? Likewise for requirements management. Will you personally be performing all requirements management activities or do you intend to delegate those responsibilities to a requirements manager? Document these decisions in your project plan and, for larger projects or projects requiring a significant staff increase, consider developing a detailed staffing plan.

As you plan project staffing, you need to consider the required technical skill set. What type of programming experience is needed? What tool skills do you need on the team? Do you need software engineers, just coders, or a mix?

As you look for answers to these questions, you must also consider your ability to find and retain the types of people you are planning to use. Even during early planning stages, you should be considering the overall cost impact of paying for the types of skills you expect to put on the team.

Project Roles

The following set of roles is neither the minimum required nor an exhaustive list. Instead, this list covers the majority of the types of roles you should at least consider having on your team. You should include or exclude roles depending on the specific characteristics of your project, and in light of your own experience and skills.

An important principle to remember when staffing the team is that you, personally, do not need to be capable of doing everything. However, the resources on the team, in combination with your abilities, must be capable of doing all required work.

Some of the roles described may exist above your management level. This depends on the size of the project and on the preferred project structure within your company or organization.

As you review this set of roles, remember that several of these roles can be assigned to one person. These are not necessarily full-time positions, and many of the roles are quite compatible with each other. However, be careful to avoid losing an oversight role as a result of combining it with a performance role. For example, the project senior manager has oversight over all the other management roles on the project. If, on a given project, the project senior manager, project manager, and project software manager are all assigned to the same person, then who conducts the oversight? As a rule, someone not performing that activity must conduct oversight of a given activity.

Project Senior Manager

The project senior manager monitors the strategic direction of the project to ensure that (1) progress is consistent with the overall project plan, and (2) goals remain consistent with strategic business or executive goals. Generally, the project senior manager has simultaneous responsibility for multiple projects and is not involved in the day-to-day details or management of the project.

The project senior manager conducts both periodic and event-driven reviews. Periodic reviews occur at planned regular intervals, such as monthly or quarterly. Event-driven reviews occur when major events occur. These include any of the major milestones shown in the project plan, as well as any other predefined triggering events. Examples of thresholds you might define as triggering a senior management review include:

- Project staffing is at or below 50 percent of the planned level.
- The customer has requested a major change in the project's requirements.
- The project's costs are at or above 125 percent of planned costs.
- The project will be turned over to a new project manager in one month.
- The project was turned over to a new project manager one month ago.

Project Manager

The project manager is responsible for all resources on the project. Focused on just a single project, the manager's primary responsibilities include tracking the progress of the various groups involved in the project, and negotiating commitments and compromises between these groups. The project manager is also responsible for resolving any issues that result from disagreements between groups within the project, or between project groups and external groups. For issues involving groups external to the project, if the project manager cannot broker a resolution, the issue is raised to the level of the project senior manager.

Software Manager

The software manager is responsible for all software resources across the entire project. On very large projects involving hundreds, or even thousands, of software developers, there is one project software manager. Clearly, the software manager may be a third, fourth, or higher level manager. In such situations, other managers plan and track portions of the software effort, and these lower level managers report their status and progress to their immediate managers.

Conversely, on smaller projects, the software manager may be the first line manager, to whom all project software personnel report. The software manager generally has responsibility for performing, or overseeing, all the activities described in this book.

Configuration Management Manager

The configuration management manager has responsibility for ensuring that:

- software and software-related products are uniquely identified, controlled, and available,
- changes to software and software-related products are controlled, and
- the status and content of software baselines are communicated to those who need such information.

Configuration management is crucial on any software project. However, the formality and tool support for configuration management activities can vary significantly between small projects and large projects. On smaller projects, the configuration management manager may not be managing any project personnel, but instead personally performs all configuration management activities. The configuration management manager may be providing support simultaneously to multiple projects.

Software Quality Assurance Manager

For the software quality assurance manager to perform his or her responsibilities properly, he or she really should not work for you. Ideally, this manager works for the same organization that you work for. Your goal is to get high-quality software delivered in a timely manner. The software quality assurance manager's goal is to ensure that you are taking the proper steps to meet your goal.

This is a key point that nearly all project managers miss. The software quality assurance organization is really trying to help you. That long list of software defects and process violations may not feel like help, but if you are seeing that list before executive management sees it, then the software quality assurance manager most certainly has your best interests in mind.

Software Requirements Manager

Nearly all projects need someone to manage the software requirements. This can be a matrixed responsibility, and may require very little effort. However, since requirements drive the entire project, someone needs to be assigned the responsibility to pay attention to (shifting) requirements.

As project manager, you may legitimately decide that requirements management is your responsibility and, hence, you will be carrying out the associated responsibilities. Conversely, you may find that the effort related to project planning, tracking, oversight, control, and management is sufficiently demanding that you need to delegate the authority to someone else to serve as the software requirements manager.

Domain Experts

You will need domain experts of two general types: problem domain experts and solution domain experts. Experts in the problem domain understand your customer's needs. For example, if you are automating a medical system, you need experts in the functionality and use of medical systems. Likewise, if you are building a software system to support traffic control, you'll need one or more experts on traffic flow management.

Solution domain experts understand the tools and technologies you'll be using to implement the system. If the system requires multi-tier networking, active web pages, and a complex relational database, and if you plan to implement the system using an object-oriented language and a third-party package of library routines, you will need expertise in each of these areas.

Regrettably, it is common on software projects to undertake projects without having sufficient expertise in the problem domain. Many software developers, especially junior ones, believe that as long as they have experience in a programming language or environment, they can program nearly anything. Theoretically, this is true. In practice, however, this attitude is highly conducive to the development of systems that fail to meet the needs of the marketplace—or of the intended customers.

Domain Consultants

On smaller projects, it may be impractical to staff the project with full-time experts in the various areas where you need expertise. In such cases, you should consider augmenting the team with one or more part-time domain consultants (problem, solution, or both). These consultants can help transfer knowledge and thereby help your project staff overcome the more difficult obstacles they encounter.

The disadvantage to using consultants is the general impression that they never seem to be around when you really need them. Additionally, if you use multiple consultants and their areas of expertise overlap, you may find yourself hearing contradictory advice and having to reconcile inconsistencies.

However, if you can find the right types of consultant and use them as a regular part of the team, you can often reduce overall project costs.

Mentors

When staffing your project with domain experts, strive to ensure that at least some of them are capable of working as mentors. This should also be one of the criteria you use for selecting consultants. Although junior people are always learning from senior people (and sometimes vice versa), not everyone makes a good mentor. Having some mentors on the project will improve the likelihood that junior people will learn quickly.

Technical Leaders

Among the project's senior personnel, you should have one or more who have both an aptitude for and an interest in performing a few management functions. You can rapidly move these personnel into positions as technical leaders.

The role of technical leader can vary significantly among companies, so when you discuss this role with existing or potential project personnel, be sure you both clearly understand the duties associated with this role, and its corresponding responsibilities and authority. Of particular interest to most technical personnel is the likely ratio between time spent performing management activities and time spent performing technical activities. Some technical personnel have very little interest in moving into management positions, and they can become quite frustrated if they feel they are not getting sufficient time to work on technical issues.

Team Leaders

Team leaders differ from technical leaders in that they usually head teams where one or more people on the team have more technical expertise than the leader does. This is fairly common and doesn't create a problem if the team leader has the right set of skills. In this context, technical decisions are made either by individuals on the team or by consensus among multiple team members.

As with the technical leaders, you need to ensure that the team leaders clearly understand the scope of their responsibilities.

Software Specialists

Although it may not seem like it after reading the above descriptions, the majority of your team will consist of software specialists. You will need software personnel who are proficient at every lifecycle phase in your project. As you staff the project team, ensure that you have a combination of senior, intermediate, and junior software specialists.

You need a mix of different levels of specialists to be able to minimize both risks and costs simultaneously. That is, your senior people are expensive, but they are better able to ensure that problems are kept to a minimum. When problems occur, the senior personnel help ensure that they are overcome rapidly and effectively. Conversely, junior personnel help reduce project costs.

Avoid having too much of a dichotomy between the senior and junior personnel. If it is substantial, be sure to have one or more layers of intermediate expertise. When the experience levels between two team members become substantial, it can be difficult for the more senior person to understand why the junior person is having trouble. It can also be difficult for the junior person to understand what the senior person is advising. Hence, it will likely be more effective to have senior personnel help, advise, or mentor intermediate personnel, and to have intermediate personnel do the same for more junior personnel.

Administrative Support

Any software project will involve a considerable amount of administrative work. This work includes handling timesheets, filling out travel requests, developing expense reports, tracking and ordering routine supplies, determining the availability of training and arranging for training, and completing a myriad of other activities and forms. Without administrative support, you will likely do much of this work, and pass some of it through to your technical personnel. These options are much more expensive than the cost of administrative personnel. Nevertheless, it is still somewhat rare for any but the larger software projects to have administrative personnel on staff. One reason for this is the ease of determining the cost of administrative support (salary), compared with the difficulty of determining the cost of administrative activities when project technical and management personnel perform them.

If at all possible, add one or more administrative support personnel to the project team. Then, assign them any of the work you are doing that you don't absolutely have to do. Also assign them any work being done by other project personnel that they don't absolutely have to do. You'll find that, fairly quickly, the administrative support personnel have plenty to keep them busy.

Finding Talent

Finding the right talent is a problem. Demand for software skills continues to increase far faster than colleges and universities can produce computer science graduates. As a result, a lot of software positions remain open longer than desired, and salaries paid are higher than planned.

And, of course, everyone is trying to find "the best" people. This is a complete waste of time for the following reasons:

- If every organization is trying to hire only the best talent, the majority of them, by definition, will be unsuccessful.

- The best tend to want a lot more money than most organizations are willing to pay.

- It is still very common to hire people based on a few half-hour or one-hour interviews—and it is almost impossible to identify "the best" in such a brief period of time.

- Many organizations have such a large backlog of unfilled positions that they'll hire anyone with a degree and a pulse.

When staffing your project, you don't need the best. With a few above average people on an otherwise average team, you can have a very successful project. The key is to find whatever personnel you can who meet your minimum educational and experience requirements and then build them into a highly effective team.

An increasingly popular method for finding software personnel is by paying a sizable "finder's fee" to existing employees when they recommend a friend who is hired. This has several benefits. Employees, of course, like the extra money. More importantly, they feel a bit responsible for the person they recommended, so they tend to stay in touch with the new hire, help the person out, and otherwise informally ensure that the new hire is viewed as a success. A similarly important benefit is that the new hire doesn't want their friend to look bad by having made a "bad" recommendation, so the new hire may try a little harder to be productive and make a good contribution.

Depending on your staffing requirements, you may be able to handle all hiring using employee referrals. Otherwise, you can follow the traditional approaches of:

- holding a companywide or divisionwide open house,
- reserving a room or booth at a local job fair,
- running classified ads in newspapers and magazines,
- posting on the major recruitment web sites, and
- conducting on-campus recruiting.

After you've found someone who has expressed an interest in working on your project, you still have the problem of determining whether or not he or she meets your minimum qualifications. For certain very basic skills, some companies are again returning to the notion of applicants having to take and pass a fundamental exam. For certain highly specialized positions, this can be a helpful determinant. However, if you are trying to hire a generalist, developing a reliably predictive exam can be very difficult.

A mainstay to virtually any attempt at staffing a software project is the interview process. Most organizations prefer to have an applicant interview with three or more employees. Some organizations favor an initial series of interviews where the applicant meets with technical personnel. Then, if the applicant is successful at that level, he or she is asked to return for a second series of interviews with management personnel.

When interviewing an applicant, concentrate on the person's ability to work as a team member. If a person is willing to be flexible in work assignments, has a history of being able to learn new technology, and has a positive and cooperative attitude, you can likely use that person on nearly any project.

Again, the objective of "finding the right talent" is not about finding the perfect software engineer. Your objective is to find a sufficiently good software engineer. A sufficiently good engineer is one who meets your minimum technical and educational requirements and who is capable of:

- learning—because new technologies and tools are constantly appearing,
- changing—because projects and products never seem to unfold the way they are originally envisioned, and
- becoming and remaining a member of the team.

Balancing the Team

Healthy, effective teams are characterized by diversity. If everyone is an expert, they will tend not to listen to each other, and they may tend to forge ahead with their own approach even when that approach is incompatible with those of others on the team. Conversely, if everyone is junior, they will likely work more closely together, but the primary way they'll learn is through trial and error.

A balanced team is characterized by a combination of different:

- roles,
- types of language experience,
- types of tool experience,
- types of domain experience,

- levels of expertise,
- backgrounds, and
- personalities.

Software development projects often call for a lot of effort in areas not directly related to software. Documentation needs to be developed and maintained, presentations are required, informal training must be conducted, etc. A balanced team will help ensure that whatever it is you need at any given moment, someone on the team will be able to provide it.

Typically, project planning and project staffing occur in parallel. Therefore, as you actually add resources to the project team, be sure to make any appropriate adjustments to the project plans.

Part III

Essentials of Project Control

4 Product Management

"Software project management consists primarily of explaining chaotic, discordant, unrelated, unpredictable, and random events in a manner that convinces others that those events are exactly what you expected and intended."

Simplistically, the role of a software project manager is to plan and manage the software project. The preceding chapters have focused primarily on planning. This chapter (and the next) will focus on issues more closely related to software project management and control.

Of the numerous definitions of software project management, two of the more useful are:

- Software project management is the refined art of doing everything, simultaneously, all the time.
- Software project management consists primarily of explaining chaotic, discordant, unrelated, unpredictable, and random events in a manner that convinces others that those events are exactly what you expected and intended.

The first defines successful project management; the second, unsuccessful project management.

Several different areas that you must manage successfully as part of the software project share the characteristic of being generally related to the management of products as well as to the integration of products being developed on your project. These product management areas are:

- managing software in a systems context,
- managing requirements,
- managing product complexity,
- managing configurations, and
- managing defects.

Additionally, several management activities you perform tend to be globally necessary across the entire project and any of the products being developed. These activities include:

- ensuring quality,
- tracking progress using earned value management, and
- using product measurements and metrics.

The underlying intent of these activities is to ensure that your focus remains on finishing the project by delivering product.

As with the material on planning, the following material is presented as a sequence of topics. In the interests of clarity, these management activities are separated into discrete topics and discussed individually. However, it would be erroneous to infer that sometimes you are doing one of these activities, and other times you are doing another. In practice, you will be more or less doing all of them all of the time.

MANAGING SOFTWARE IN A SYSTEMS CONTEXT

Some software projects are, essentially, pure software. If you need to develop a mass-market product to run on a widely installed platform, then you likely need to concern yourself only with software-specific issues.

Alternatively, you may be working on a project involving, for example, avionics software that will help fly aircraft; navigation software that will access global positioning satellite data and help a team of backwoods hikers stay on their intended trail; or medical software that will display rotatable, three-dimensional pictures of the chambers of the human heart. If so, then software is only a part of the product. Hence, the problem that needs to be solved is a systems problem, and not just a software problem.

One of the most significant distinguishing characteristics of technology-intensive systems is, simply enough, whether or not software is a component of the system. If so, then everything is different.

Put another way, some systems need to be intelligent, while other don't. If you don't need intelligence, then you don't need software. Purists will argue that highly intelligent behavior can be implemented entirely in hardware. And they are correct. But no one has yet built a circuit board that is capable of redesigning and dynamically rerouting its circuits to, around, and between other electrical components. In a matter of minutes, you can upload new software to a rover on Mars, but if you want new hardware, you are going to have to launch it and wait a year or two for it to arrive.

The primary problem with managing software in a systems context is that no matter how "small" the software component is, if it doesn't work, typically, the entire system fails. Consider the space shuttle. Published data indicates that the software running on the shuttle consists of about 10,000 source lines of code (10 KSLOC). As of today (this qualification would not be necessary if we were not talking about software), shuttle software is about as close to perfect as any software on the planet.

But think about its size—a mere 10 KSLOC. There are software entertainment games on the market that dedicate far more lines of code just to the opening game sequence. The actual game may involve hundreds of thousands—or even millions—of lines of source code. And these are merely games. From one point of view, most experienced programmers consider 10,000 lines of code to be a trivial challenge. But ask any of them if space shuttle software is trivial and the problem becomes clear. Even if the "thinking" part of the system is by all other standards trivial, "faulty thinking" is essentially equivalent to system failure. And if you are working on an incredibly spectacular system, you end up with an incredibly spectacular failure.

As the software project manager, you need to realize that if 25,000 hardware engineers are working to produce the right hardware, and you are managing 20 software engineers who are trying to make that hardware perform intelligently, then almost no one is going to pay any attention to what you are doing. Your project is tiny. It is, compared to the hardware effort, outright trivial. When 25,000 people are building the system, how much influence can a mere 20 software engineers have? As numerous historical projects have already proved, they cannot ensure the success of the project, but they can certainly ensure its failure.

MANAGING REQUIREMENTS

Requirements management is an entire engineering discipline unto itself. Hence, this subsection will highlight some of the key concerns that you, as software project manager, need to address.

Requirements definition is one of the most challenging objectives in software systems engineering. And this relates only to the original capture of requirements. When you add the fact that requirements nearly always change—and some requirements change both rapidly and substantially—it becomes clear that requirements management is both a continuous and a critical project management function.

The most reliable approach for ensuring that you are building the right software products is to ensure that you have a highly effective and efficient requirements management and maintenance process. Maintenance is crucial, since even a highly effective and skillful approach to documenting original requirements can easily be negated by ongoing requirements volatility. Hence, regardless of the accuracy and clarity of original requirements, in light of the volatility universally associated with software requirements, the requirements maintenance process is often more important than the original capture process.

To ensure successful management of requirements, you need to address each of the following questions:

- Who has responsibility for managing requirements?
- What process will they follow?
- What tools will they use?
- Do they need any additional training?
- Who will double-check their work?

Who Has Responsibility for Managing Requirements?

You need to assign someone (or some team) explicit responsibility for managing requirements. The amount of effort required will typically vary as a function of which lifecycle phase the project is in. However, as noted, the need for managing requirements never disappears—it persists until completion of the project.

It is acceptable, and not uncommon, for the software project manager to assume responsibility for maintaining requirements. However, do not undertake this additional responsibility lightly. Activities associated with requirements management must be performed correctly and in a timely manner. Otherwise, the system design, and the system itself, may evolve out from—and away from—the documented requirements. As this happens, project personnel (including yourself) rely progressively less on documented requirements and progressively more on each other. Eventually, the documented requirements are ignored—with the intent that the requirements specification will be updated after the software is built, which generally doesn't happen. As a result, the requirements for the system degenerate into everyone's mental picture of the requirements, and, for all practical purposes, you no longer know, or have control over, what is being built.

If you accept responsibility for personally managing requirements, be sure that you have the experience, training, and time to perform the necessary activities. Otherwise, assign the responsibility to one or more personnel on the project.

What Process Will They Follow?

Once you've assigned responsibility for managing requirements, the next step is to decide what requirements management process to use. Your company or organization may have a standard process to follow, or you may decide to use one of a number of published methodologies for requirements management. Alternatively, you may elect to follow a hybrid requirements management process that is tailored to the unique needs of your project.

Whichever alternative you choose, be sure to provide the requirements management personnel with a documented process to follow. This process should explain all the activities you expect to occur as a regular part of identifying, capturing, updating, revising, and deleting requirements. The process needs to explain clearly who has the authority to do what, when reviews and approvals are required, and who has responsibility for conducting reviews and authority for granting approvals.

What Tools Will They Use?

Requirements are often documented in a word processor, and no other tools are necessary for performing requirements management. Alternatively, some very sophisticated requirements management tools support the construction of complex and detailed requirements specifications, and help ensure the integrity, consistency, completeness, and testability of requirements.

You and the requirements management personnel need to examine and discuss any tools that can be used to help make requirements management activities both efficient and effective. Considerations for tool requirements include the:

- expected stability of the requirements,
- percentage of requirements that can be known at project commencement,
- overall number of requirements, and
- degree and extent of cross-references required between requirements, design specifications, and test cases.

If you anticipate developing one or more prototypes to help elicit or refine requirements, then consider any tools that will be necessary for the construction of those prototypes. These tools may include:

- screen builders,
- code generators,

- screen animators,
- input recorders, and
- test data generators.

When considering tools, be especially attentive to the learning curve involved in developing proficiency at using the tool. Requirements management begins at the earliest stages of the project and very little time may be available for learning a tool. Delays resulting from an inability to capture and document requirements tend to cause delays in virtually all other work on the project.

Do They Need Any Additional Training?

Once you've identified the people who will perform requirements management, the process they will be following, and the tools they will be using, you can analyze the need to provide them with any additional training. Also determine the best time to provide that training. Typically, "just in time" training is most effective. This way, when project personnel have completed their training, they can start applying what they've learned almost immediately. If training significantly precedes the planned time to commence requirements capture, try to accelerate the prerequirements management schedule so that requirements management can commence sooner in the life of the project.

Requirements management activities can vary significantly from one lifecycle phase to another, or from one cycle around a spiral lifecycle process to another. For example, you may build one or more prototypes during the early stages of requirements management, but later in the project you may transition to requirements capture and management using an in-house developed relational database. Training for the former will be significantly different from training for the latter. Hence, examine training needed to support requirements management throughout the entire project. For longer duration projects, be sure to allow for the possibility of personnel turnover.

Who Will Double-Check Their Work?

As you will see during the discussion on software quality assurance, a fundamental technique for reducing project risk is to ensure that all critical processes have a backup or "safety net" process that ensures that the primary process is occurring as planned, and is working as intended. Therefore, as part of identifying and preparing project personnel for requirements, you need to determine how you will monitor the effectiveness of the requirements management process. At a minimum, you will need to have planned, regular meetings with your software requirements manager. During these meetings, you check the status of the requirements and respond to any issues that have arisen.

In addition to status and review meetings, you should have software quality assurance personnel regularly check the execution of the requirements management activities. They should verify that all activities are in accordance with the documented requirements management process, and, on larger projects, the documented requirements management plan.

MANAGING PRODUCT COMPLEXITY

Any software developer with two years of experience can write extremely complicated code. The problem is that it seems to require at least five years of experience before programmers understand how to write elegant, simple code.

Software product complexity is directly related to the difficulty that a programmer will have while trying to change or update the software without inserting defects. The more complex the software, the greater the likelihood that touching it for any reason will introduce defects.

The primary techniques available for managing software complexity include:

- designing for simplicity,
- structured formatting,
- extensive commenting,
- support documentation, and
- software elimination reviews.

Designing for Simplicity

Complex designs invariably lead to complex code. Hence, one of the earliest opportunities to reduce system complexity is the beginning of the design phase. Depending on the type of system being constructed and the development approach being used, any of the following are candidates for simplification:

- data structures,
- data flows,
- control flows,
- objects,
- schemas,
- screens,

- error propagation,
- message handling, and
- security.

Remind the design team regularly that simplicity is essential for successful development of the system. Ensure that part of the design walkthrough or review process is dedicated specifically to finding and eliminating unnecessary complexity. Pay close attention to ongoing maintenance of design documents. Typically, when design documents are updated, it is to add design constraints or information. Hence, design—and the corresponding software systems—tend to become progressively larger and more complex over time. Almost always, the objective is to add something. Rarely is anything removed. Therefore, when new design elements are developed to replace old design elements, ensure that the design team removes the old design elements.

Structured Formatting

Even in the earliest days of the software industry, the value of using style and formatting conventions was obvious. While software engineers may debate which conventions are best, nearly all prefer to adhere to some type of convention. While simplifying the format of software does nothing to reduce the complexity of the logic, it can improve software readability substantially. Since complexity is defined in terms of a person's ability to understand the software, improving the readability—and hence the understandability—of software contributes directly to reducing complexity.

Style and formatting conventions should not be limited to software code. Requirements specifications, design documents, user manuals, and virtually all other software-related artifacts can be rendered more readable through a consistent approach to formatting the information or material.

Extensive Commenting

As with style and formatting conventions, extensive commenting of software directly improves its readability. In the days of rather arcane assembly languages, it was sometimes necessary to comment every line of code. With higher level languages, it is typically sufficient to comment primarily with "header-block" descriptions that are part of each software unit, such as a module, object, function, procedure, routine, or subroutine. These descriptions often provide details on the software unit's:

- purpose,
- inputs,
- outputs,
- error messages, and
- revision history.

Having this information included for every software unit helps any developer understand the functionality of the software more clearly and rapidly, and helps ensure that any changes or updates are made without inserting defects.

Additionally, the revision history contributes to understandability by helping programmers with debugging software. Revision history usually includes, for any changes made to a software unit:

- date of the change,
- name of the developer making the change,

- purpose of the change (this may include a reference to a defect report),
- description of the change, and
- location of the change and the specific lines of code or algorithms affected.

When a stable piece of code has been enhanced recently, and now the code is executing unreliably, the most likely source of the defect is the recent change activity. Hence, developers performing software debugging can concentrate initially on the revision history. They can then focus specifically on the software units that have been changed recently. This can help them find and correct the recently inserted defect quickly.

Commenting software not only enables developers to understand the software better, but it also helps them understand what has happened to that software over time.

Support Documentation

Support documentation occurs in numerous varieties as a function of who needs to be supported. For example, user manuals are support documentation for end users, installation instructions are support documentation for the technical support group, and design documents can be viewed as support documentation for developers.

In addition to design documents, other documentation can be developed to help programmers understand the overall structure and implementation of a software system. This additional documentation may include:

- software architecture overview diagrams,
- system functionality overview diagrams and descriptions,

- software schema layouts,
- naming conventions, and
- standard abbreviations and acronyms.

When developing support documentation for software developers, remember that the primary objective is to improve the developer's ability to understand, comprehend, build, and maintain the software system. Be careful that the support documentation does not become so complex and confusing that it actually starts to make the system more confusing to the developer. For example, naming conventions can become so restrictive that data or module names start becoming meaningless or confusing—exactly the opposite of what you're trying to achieve. Additionally, architecture diagrams (or any technical diagram) can become so covered with different types of lines, arrowheads, and shapes that they become nearly unintelligible.

As a general rule, if you notice that the developers are not following, referencing, or otherwise using the support documentation, it is often for a very good reason.

Software Elimination Reviews

As mentioned earlier, software systems tend to become progressively larger and more complicated. This occurs because the vast majority of enhancements and corrections is accomplished by adding more code.

Moreover, most programmers experience a certain amount of paranoia when they delete apparently useless or unnecessary code. After all, can you really be completely confident that the code is unnecessary? Even when developers are replacing an old routine with a new one, they sometimes like to leave the old routine in place (maybe with a minor change to its name so that no other routines actually invoke it) and wait to see if their new routine really is better. If the new routine fails dismally, the reasoning goes, it'll be simple to revert to the original routine and try again. Of course, just because the new routine seems to be working now doesn't mean it will continue to work next month, so some developers reason that the safest approach is not to delete the old routine at all.

Obviously, this type of thinking leads to an increasing amount of completely unnecessary code within a system. Even worse, it can lead to programmers spending time studying—and trying to fix—code that is not being executed.

Numerous tools and development environments are available to detect and warn you about uncalled routines and unreachable code fragments. Environments that support single-step code execution likewise help ensure that programmers work on fixing only code that is truly part of the executing system. However, even with such tools, the general tendency for programmers to resist deleting code persists. And this tendency contributes directly to systems becoming steadily more bloated, complicated, and difficult to understand.

As project manager, you need to schedule software elimination reviews periodically. These reviews consist of a team of developers inspecting a subset of the system with the objective of identifying and removing unnecessary code and unnecessary complexity. You can improve the ability and willingness of developers to identify and remove code substantially by:

- Having current detailed design documents. (If they are not called for in the design, they should not be part of the software code.)

- Having a reliable configuration management process. (If it turns out that essential code was deleted, it can be retrieved easily from the prior version of that code.)

MANAGING CONFIGURATIONS

The objectives of configuration management are simple. They are to ensure that:

- software and related products are all identified uniquely,
- access to software and related products is allowed only to authorized personnel,
- two or more individuals or teams do not inadvertently attempt to change the same files or products simultaneously (which would lead to the loss of one set of changes), and
- any version of the software that previously existed can be recreated at any future date.

Configuration management does not need to be complicated or expensive. On small projects you, as project manager, can establish a dedicated file directory on the network that only you can access. As software modules (identified in your software plan) start becoming available, you move (not copy) files into a subdirectory under the configuration management directory. This subdirectory will hold all the files, for example, for version 0.1 of the system.

When integration testing commences, only the files in the 0.1 folder are tested. While testing is occurring, you create a new subdirectory named, for example, 0.11. You copy all files from 0.1 to the 0.11 folder. If defects are encountered, then you assign the rework to someone on the team, and you copy the file from the 0.1 folder to the developer's machine. When the developer indicates that rework is complete, you move (not copy) the file into the 0.11 folder.

You may go through several cycles and eventually arrive at, for example, a 0.24 folder that has software that is functional and thoroughly tested. You may then want to create a baseline consisting of all the files in this folder. You name the baseline folder 1.0, put everything into it, and then never change the content of that folder. If software defects are later found in the 1.0 release, you repeat the cycle by creating a version 1.01 folder, etc.

Change Requests

An integral part of the configuration management process is the change request process. Change requests have a variety of different names, including:

- trouble reports,
- software problem reports,
- engineering change forms,
- customer request forms, and
- incident reports (or test incident reports).

The purpose of each of these is essentially the same: to document either a perceived problem or the perceived need to make a change to the system. You and your project personnel can evaluate this change request to determine the:

- likely benefit of making the change,
- likely impact the change will have on other parts of the system,
- likely cost (both in dollars and time) of implementing the change, and
- priority or importance of making this change relative to the importance of work already planned or in progress.

When properly implemented, each baseline of the system is equal to a prior version plus the revisions resulting from an identifiable set of change requests. This allows anyone to know exactly the contents of any given baseline and exactly the differences between any two baselines.

To achieve this result, you must observe a critical rule: No changes can be made to the software without a documented and authorized change request. Keep in mind that even a comprehensive change request form can be very simple to use. You might, for example, have a change request form containing the following fields:

- Date of submission
- Submitter's name
- Submitter's e-mail address
- Type of change (select one)
  - Problem
  - Maintenance
  - Enhancement
- Recommended priority of change (select one)
  - Low
  - Medium
  - High
  - Critical
- Description of deficiency
- Description of recommended change

The submitter fills out these fields. Then, when you receive the change request, you fill out the following fields:

- Date of receipt
- Estimated effort (staff hours)
- Estimated completion date
- Disposition (select one)
  - Returned for additional information
  - Rejected
  - Deferred until at least (provide date): __________
  - Approved
- Disposition by: ______________________________
- Status
  - Pending evaluation
  - Under evaluation
  - Scheduled for rework
  - In rework
  - In test
  - Closed
- Assigned priority (select one)
  - Low
  - Medium

  - High
  - Critical
  - Not applicable
- Actual effort (staff hours)
- Actual completion date
- Date closed
- Closed by: ______________________

You can achieve comprehensive configuration control on your project simply by using something similar to this form (see Figure 15) and the previously described configuration management process. At any given time, you will know the status of all change requests, and those submitting the requests will know the status of their request (e.g., rejected, approved, in rework). Moreover, you will be managing the impact of change requests carefully relative to resource availability and commitments you've already made within the project plan.

Configuration Control Board

On larger projects, you may need to establish a configuration control board (CCB). As project manager, you will likely chair the CCB. The purpose of a CCB is to convene a group of people on a regularly scheduled basis to evaluate and make decisions regarding all pending change requests and to review the status or progress of all outstanding change requests.

You will want to include senior technical personnel on the CCB. They can assist you in estimating the time, cost, and technical impacts of implementing the change requests. You will also want to include one or more representatives from

Figure 15
Change Request Form

Date of submission: ____________

Submitter's name: ____________ Submitter's e-mail: ______________

Type of change: Problem ____ Maintenance ____ Enhancement ____

Recommended priority of change: Low ___ Medium ___
High ___ Critical ___

Description of deficiency:

Description of recommended change:

Date of receipt: __________ Estimated effort (staff hours): __________

Estimated completed date: ____________

Disposition: Returned for additional information _____ Rejected ___

Deferred until at least (date): _____ Approved ___

Disposition by: _______________

Status: Pending evaluation _____ Under evaluation _____
Scheduled for work _____ In rework _____ In test _____
Closed _____

Assigned priority: Low _____ Medium _____ High _____
Critical _____ Not applicable _____

Actual effort: _________________ Actual completion date: __________

Date closed: __________________ Closed by: _____________________

the customer organization, who will be able to assist you in evaluating the probable benefits of implementing the change. If a considerable number of change requests is originating from test groups, you will want a senior testing person on the CCB. That person will be able to provide additional explanation regarding the circumstances and conditions under which problems are encountered.

Periodically, a change request is sufficiently large that implementing it will require revisions to nonsoftware project artifacts. For example, the requirements specification might have to be revised and the project plan updated. For this reason, the CCB is often the source of change requests. In this example, one change request is made for revising the requirements specification and a separate change request is made for updating the project plan. Having separate change requests simplifies tasks such as assigning priority, estimating impact, and determining an estimated completion date.

Remember, configuration management involves controlling changes not only to software but to all important project artifacts. The requirements specification and the project plan are two of the most important artifacts on the project. Therefore, they should certainly be placed under configuration management, and no changes should be permitted unless they are initiated by an approved change request. Not surprisingly, change requests originating from the CCB are usually approved immediately.

Successfully managing each project artifact, and controlling those artifacts as part of a succession of system versions, are critical to project success. Configuration management is about change control. Change is a common occurrence on virtually all projects. If you don't control the change process, you lose control of your project.

MANAGING DEFECTS

The objective of defect management is to deliver software that meets or exceeds required quality objectives. One of the distinguishing characteristics of software systems is that, unlike some other systems, software can be 99 percent perfect and 100 percent useless. A system that takes a second to destroy all its data accidentally every two minutes is, arguably, working perfectly more than 99 percent of the time.

Although the ultimate objective is software that is 100 percent defect-free, the sheer magnitude and complexity of software render this goal effectively unachievable. So as a practical matter, our real objective is to develop software that is as good as we can possibly make it.

The first step in managing the construction of high-quality software is to follow management and engineering practices that are designed to prevent the insertion of defects. The second step is to presume that the first step won't work, and to design the software architecture itself in a manner that facilitates the diagnosis of software quality (see Appendix A for additional information). The third step is to assume that neither of the first two steps is working, and to use a software inspection or review process to find latent defects. And the fourth step, of course, is to assume that some defects remain undetected after the other three steps, and therefore to perform systematic and comprehensive testing of the software product.

An integral piece of this process is software reviews and inspections. You should be sure that at least the following four types of software reviews occur on your project:

- management software reviews,
- senior software reviews,
- software walkthroughs, and
- software inspections.

Management Software Reviews

Management software reviews involve you taking some time to check the software being developed on the project.

You might, for example, ask project personnel to e-mail a source code file to you once a week for whatever module they are working on. The advantage to management reviews is that if someone is developing code in a style that does not comply with project standards or, in your opinion, represents an unnecessarily risky approach, you can detect that very early in the process and redirect the developer. An indirect advantage is that you will have considerably more insight into actual progress than you would typically get from just reading a weekly status report. Management software reviews tend to be the fastest (in terms of lines of code scanned per hour) and the least formal type of review.

Senior Software Reviews

Senior software reviews involve one or two senior people reviewing the software developed by someone who is junior to them in one or more technical areas. For example, a programmer with five years of software development experience will review the code developed by someone with two years of experience.

It is also common to have someone review someone else's code because they are more senior in a particular important area. For example, a programmer with eight years of software development experience may have been using a new language for only the last six months. You might have that code reviewed by a developer who has only two years of development experience—but both years were spent developing the new language.

As with the management software reviews, these reviews are highly informal. They depend extensively on the expertise of the person doing the review, and may or may not involve the use of documented coding standards. However, these reviews can be highly effective in detecting poor design and discovering defects early in the software development process.

Software Walkthroughs

A software walkthrough is a somewhat formal process that consists of several software engineers meeting to examine and discuss a software artifact. Typical meetings will range from thirty minutes to two hours. The preferred approach is to distribute the walkthrough material several days in advance of the meeting. This allows all reviewers the opportunity to familiarize themselves with the software, and to find defects before the meeting. However, in some organizations, the material is simply distributed at the beginning of the meeting and reviewers are given ten to thirty minutes to conduct individual reviews.

During the meeting, the author explains the purpose of the software component, and presents a systematic section-by-section explanation of the software. The reviewers are given time to examine each section for defects and for code that is potentially defective. When uncertain, the group discusses the code, examines related areas, and makes recommendations to the author regarding corrections or alternative approaches.

As the walkthrough progresses, the author marks up a hard-copy list indicating where defects (or potential defects) have been identified. The author also documents recommended fixes or alternative implementations. The meeting is over when the entire software component has been reviewed, or when the group agrees that the remainder of the review will need to be rescheduled for another day.

After the review, the author studies the recommendations, reexamines the code, and makes whatever changes the author believes are necessary.

Software walkthroughs usually require more hours to perform for the simple reason that more people are involved. The advantage of walkthroughs is that the group dynamics can often lead to the discovery of subtle defects that a single reviewer might have overlooked. Additionally, this process contributes to the sharing of experience among the team members, and to a general consistency in software design and implementation conventions.

Software Inspections

The last tool you need in your defect management toolchest is a software inspection process. Software inspections are highly formal processes that consist of following a set of well-defined activities supported by well-defined roles. The typical inspection consists of the following activities:

- coordination,
- planning,
- overview,
- preparation,
- inspection meeting,
- rework,
- follow-up, and
- causal analysis.

The following roles are involved in performing these activities:

- coordinator,
- moderator,

- key inspector,
- regular inspector,
- reader,
- scribe,
- author,
- remote inspector, and
- guest.

Some roles are optional, and most activities require only a subset of the participants.

Coordination

The coordination activity is performed, of course, by the coordinator. Coordination consists of supporting moderators as they plan for inspections and look for inspection resources. From initial planning through rework and follow-up, a single inspection can easily span several calendar weeks. On larger projects, multiple inspections with overlapping schedules are often conducted. The coordinator's job is to relieve you as the project manager from tasks relating to the logistics and details of ensuring that all the inspection-related activities are occurring efficiently and effectively.

Planning

The planning activity is carried out primarily by the moderator. Planning begins with the receipt of inspection material (such as software code) from the developer or author. The moderator evaluates the size of the material to ensure that it can be inspected within a two-hour period (inspections exceeding two hours tend to become very tiresome and inefficient).

The moderator contacts developers and asks if they can participate on an inspection team. The ideal team size, including the moderator, is about four or five. The moderator assigns the roles of key inspector, scribe, and reader to various members of the team (some team members may have multiple roles). The moderator then packages the material to be inspected with any relevant standards or reference materials, attaches a cover sheet indicating the amount of time budgeted for each person to prepare for the inspection, and the date, time, and location of the inspection meeting.

Overview

The optional overview activity consists of bringing together the entire inspection team and explaining to the members the purpose and context of the item to be inspected. The reader, not the author, presents the overview, to reduce the risk of the author inadvertently "selling" the structure and content of the artifact and thereby biasing the inspection team. The objective of the overview is to prepare the team for the preparation (individual inspection) activity, and to answer any initial questions that inspection team members might have. Overview meetings usually run about ten to thirty minutes.

Preparation

The preparation activity commences when the inspection team participants receive the inspection packages. Each person individually inspects the material and develops an inspection preparation log that documents, for each defect found:

- defect type,
- defect severity, and
- defect location.

During preparation, it is important that inspectors not attempt to "fix" the defects or spend time working on solutions. Their objective is to focus on finding defects. Typical preparation time for a two-hour inspection meeting can vary from one to four hours. However, inspectors may need several days to a week of calendar time to find sufficient time in their schedules to conduct the individual inspections.

Inspection Meeting

Everyone but the coordinator attends the inspection meeting. The optional role of remote inspector is used for anyone who you want to conduct an individual inspection, but who cannot attend the inspection meeting. The optional role of guest is for anyone who wants to participate in the meeting, but who really does not yet have the credentials to participate as an inspector. Guests are asked to observe, and not actively participate in the meeting.

The inspection meeting commences with a brief review of who will play which roles. The moderator opens the meeting and when preliminaries are done, turns the meeting over to the reader (not the author—who is an optional attendee). The reader then takes the inspection team through the inspection material one section at a time. Each inspector uses his or her prepared inspection log to announce defects found in the section being discussed. All inspectors reinspect and discuss the material. The reader coordinates these discussions and leads progress through the material. The group must reach consensus that something is a defect before it is entered on the inspection meeting defect log.

The scribe develops the inspection meeting log and gives it to the moderator at the end of the meeting. The moderator then asks the team whether a full or partial reinspection is required. The greater the number of defects, the greater the likelihood that a reinspection is needed.

Rework

During the rework phase, the author makes changes to the code (or inspection material) to address the defects listed on the inspection meeting log. An extremely important rule for inspections is that the author is authorized to make only those changes required to address the logged defects. The author is not authorized to make any other changes to a software item. Once an author turns something over to the inspection process, the author no longer owns that item—the inspection team does.

Follow-up

Once the rework is done, the author contacts the moderator. The moderator meets with the author and examines both the inspection meeting defect log and all the changes the author has made. The moderator checks that all defects listed in the log have been addressed. The moderator also verifies that no unauthorized changes were made to a software item. As a practical matter, if the author discovers a defect after the inspection meeting, the author informs the moderator, and the moderator adds the defect to the defect log, thereby allowing the author to make additional alterations to the software item legitimately.

If the inspection team had previously decided that a reinspection was necessary, the moderator recommences this entire sequence by initiating another inspection planning activity.

Causal Analysis

The above activities typically occur as a linear sequence of activities. Causal analysis, however, is not performed in conjunction with inspection meetings. Instead, causal analysis is associated with an overall inspection process.

Causal analysis meetings typically occur on a regularly scheduled periodic basis, such as monthly or quarterly. The purpose of these meetings is to bring together any available personnel who have been participating in the inspection process to discuss probable causes of defects as well as possible process improvements to reduce the incidence of defect insertions. The inspection coordinator brings defect metrics that show defect types arranged by frequency. Typically, the group tries to think of ways to reduce the incidence of the most frequently occurring defects; this approach usually leads to the greatest improvements in software quality.

Planning and Tracking Defect Management

As stated earlier, comprehensive management of software defects is one of the most important skills you need as a project manager. Defect identification and removal should be occurring throughout the entire software lifecycle. So how do you ensure that your project is developing the highest quality software? Do you conduct formal inspections on everything the team builds? Almost certainly not. That's why it is crucial to employ a variety of software review techniques.

While formal inspections are typically the most comprehensive defect identification technique, they also can be the most time-consuming, resource-intensive, and expensive technique. Therefore, as project manager, you will need to decide which review techniques are most appropriate for the various components you are developing.

As a general rule, the higher you risk exposure, the more effort you need to put into defect identification. For example, if a subset of your system is controlling a laser eye surgery device, you will want to have that software inspected thoroughly, maybe multiple times. However, the patient billing subsystem can likely be put through software walkthroughs. The subsystem that allows access to web sites can be put through senior software reviews. At a minimum, everything else can go through management software reviews.

Remember, the objective of managing defects is not simply to remove the highest number of defects. The objective is to deliver a system that meets or exceeds your customer's quality requirements. Since some defects are far more troublesome to your customer than others, you must manage your budget, time, and resources in a manner that ensures to the greatest degree possible that any latent defects are comparatively innocuous.

ENSURING QUALITY

Ensuring software quality is the primary purpose of establishing a software quality assurance person, team, or organization. In many companies, software quality assurance is considered synonymous with software integration and system testing. This is quite erroneous. Although testing is part of the quality assurance process, it is, arguably, one of the less important parts. The philosophical rationale behind this assertion is that quality must be built in to the system and ensured throughout the entire project lifecycle. If done perfectly, there would be no need to test software at the end of the development cycle, since it would have no defects by that stage. Of course, flawless software systems remain more of a dream than a reality. Hence, practically speaking, testing is an indispensable part of the quality assurance process.

The purpose of software quality assurance is to ensure that:

- all project activities are occurring according to plan,
- all plans and project activities are consistent with defined processes,
- all processes, activities, and software products comply with applicable standards, and
- software products satisfy the needs of the customer.

Ideally, a software quality assurance organization exists independent of your project. This group represents the interests of executive management and should be double-checking the activities and products associated with your project. This includes checking on your management artifacts as well as your execution of, and adherence to, defined planning and management processes.

When properly implemented, software quality assurance performs a critical support function by helping you detect and resolve problems at the earliest opportunity. Of course, you are detecting and resolving problems as a routine, daily part of your management activities. However, anything that software quality assurance finds is something that has either been undetected by you or something for which your resolution actions have not yet been effective. In either event, this is very important information for you to know.

In the absence of an external, independent quality assurance function, you will need to implement these actions internally on your project. Your approach should be similar to the approach used for software configuration management. That is, the areas you need to address include:

- Who has responsibility for software quality assurance?
- What process will they follow?
- What tools will they use?
- Do they need any additional training?
- Who will double-check their work?

If you decide to perform the software quality assurance activities yourself, by definition, there will be no protection at the management level of the project. No one will be performing the software quality assurance function on the management activities you perform or the plans and other project artifacts you produce. Considering the importance of successful management activities and products, not having a double-check process at your level is highly risky.

With regard to who will double-check the quality assurance process, this is the classic problem of who polices the police. Certainly not the software project manager. Anything you do to monitor software quality assurance internal to your project is essentially a routine part of your management tracking and oversight responsibilities. The oversight you do as a manager is the initial checking process, not the double-checking process. One option is to bring in an external person occasionally to investigate the plans, procedures, and activities associated with software quality assurance.

Additionally, from one perspective, you can think of the software integration and system testing process as part of your double-check on the software quality assurance organization. In principle, effective software quality assurance will translate into comparatively fewer defects found during post-development testing.

TRACKING PROGRESS USING EARNED VALUE MANAGEMENT

As you manage requirements, product complexity, and defects, you will simultaneously be tracking closely the progress of work and the costs associated with that progress.

As you were building the project plan, you developed a work breakdown structure. Accounting codes were associated with each box in the work breakdown structure (at least at the higher levels) and costs were estimated. Once approved, these costs represented the budget for the work associated with the various boxes.

As the project advances, two major activities are constantly occurring:

- product is being built (or services provided), and
- costs are being accrued.

As discussed in the section on work breakdown structures, you need to decompose the work to a sufficiently small time period where, for any given lowest level box, you do not care about percentage completion. Put differently, work units (boxes) should be small enough that all you need to know is whether or not the work unit is finished. The work in each box is assigned via a work package. For any given work package, you do not need to know, and are not interested in, if the work is 25 percent done, 50 percent done, etc.

As project manager, three of the most important items you need to monitor are:

- value of the product built to date,
- cost of the product built to date, and
- project's performance against the intended schedule.

One simple method is to use earned value management. This system was developed by the Department of Defense (DoD) and released in 1967 as part of DoD's cost/schedule control systems criteria.

Earned value management is based on tracking three values:

- budgeted cost of work scheduled (BCWS),
- budgeted cost of work performed (BCWP), and
- actual cost of work performed (ACWP).

To calculate the BCWS, sum all the budgeted costs for work packages that were planned to have been completed by a given moment in time (regardless of whether or not the work was actually done). Remember, use binary accounting principles and include only those activities whose planned completion dates are on or before the target date.

To calculate the BCWP—also known as the earned value—sum all the budgeted costs for all completed work packages. Again, do not include partially completed work packages.

To calculate the ACWP, sum all the actual costs associated with all completed work packages.

As a result of calculating these values, you can now determine your project's:

- cost variance, and
- schedule variance.

The cost variance is the difference between the BCWP and the ACWP. If the actual costs exceed the budgeted costs, you are spending more than you had planned. To determine the percent of the variance, simply subtract the BCWP from the ACWP and divide the difference by the BCWP. Positive numbers represent cost overruns. For example, if the BCWP is $100,000 but the ACWP is $150,000, you have a cost variance of $50,000 and a cost variance percent of 50 percent.

Similarly, schedule variance is the difference between the BCWS and the BCWP. If the BCWP is greater than the BCWS, the project is running ahead of schedule. If the reverse if true, the project is behind schedule. Identical to the steps taken in determining cost variance percentage, the schedule variation percentage is the schedule variance divided by the BCWS.

With these numbers, it is also simple to calculate an estimated cost at completion (ECAC). If the project has, for example, a BCWP of 25 percent but an ACWP of 50 percent, the ECAC will be twice what was originally budgeted.

Cost, value, and schedule are just three examples of the type of data that software project managers need to gain insights into the overall effectiveness and efficiency of the project's processes, as well as the overall progress of the project's products. However, you can increase the insights provided by tracking and analyzing these three valuable numbers by augmenting this data with additional measurements and metrics.

USING PRODUCT MEASUREMENTS AND METRICS

Before discussing management principles associated with measurements and metrics, some definitions are necessary. The difference between measurements and metrics is simple. Measurements all have unit values. The following are examples of measurements:

- lines of code,
- total defects,
- failure count,
- number of objects,
- number of screens,
- number of data files,
- mean time between failures,
- total training hours, and
- average time to close a defect report.

Metrics combine measurements using formulas or algorithms. Examples of metrics are:

- defect density,
- failure rate,
- productivity rate, and
- staff turnover rate.

Some measurements are closely related to products, some to processes, and some to individual people. Many metrics overlap two or all three of these categories. In software development, the absolute minimum metrics you should track are:

- size,
- cost,
- schedule,
- quality,
- value, and
- risk.

Each of these areas has already been discussed. However, with regard to metrics, you need to decide exactly how you want to quantify this data, and whether you want to track multiple kinds of metrics within a single metric area.

For example, with regard to tracking product quality, any of the following measurements and metrics could be useful:

- total defects discovered to date,
- total defects found during inspections,

- total defects found during integration tests,
- total defects reported from the field,
- defect density,
- ratio of rework hours to development hours,
- defect detection rate, and
- average rework time per defect.

All these metrics can be derived from a very small set of measurements and data (e.g., defect originator, date found, hours to fix, software size).

Collecting metrics takes time, so don't bother collecting any metrics that you do not need. Revisit regularly the metrics you are collecting and verify that they continue to provide you with information that helps you control the project.

With all measurements and metrics, be extremely careful to use a constant unit of measurement. For example, what is a staff month? It could be:

- 173.3 hours (40 hours per week times 52 weeks divided by 12),
- 160 hours (figuring 4 weeks in a month), or
- 168 hours (figuring 21 working days in a typical month).

Similarly, what is a line of code? It could be:

- every line ending with a linefeed,
- every line containing a statement terminator,
- every line in a file excluding the comment lines,

- every logical statement, or
- every logical statement plus every variable declaration.

Combining data using different units will ruin your data set. Therefore, it is best to avoid such complications by using the simplest or smallest unambiguous unit. For example, you can completely avoid the notion of staff-months and instead use staff-hours. With lines of code, you need to pick whatever definition best supports your efforts at estimating and tracking software size and effort. Then, be sure to communicate clearly to project personnel exactly what you expect when you want them to report the size of the software they are working on.

MAINTAINING PRODUCT FOCUS

Throughout this chapter, management principles and activities have been discussed with an emphasis on developing and controlling the products that the project is producing. The intent of this emphasis is to ensure that the focus remains on finishing the project by delivering product.

However, when you are confident that sufficient attention is being directed to the software products, you can turn your attention to managing software processes. Indeed, a key premise behind the Software Engineering Institute's (SEI) software Capability Maturity Model (CMM®) is that the quality of a product is a direct reflection of the quality of the process that produced that product. Process management is the subject of the next chapter.

5 Process Management

"Process support technology should never be allowed to interfere with project success."

The combination of management and engineering processes being executed on a project makes that project unique. From this perspective, literally, no two projects are identical. Project processes can range from completely ad hoc to those that are formally designed and supported by detailed step-by-step instructions.

Software engineers have historically worked in environments that had no, little, or confusing processes. Traditionally, the only companies that developed well-defined processes were those with sufficient vision to see the positive return on investment that would result, and those that preferred to hire inexperienced college graduates and train them on the in-house approach.

Using inexperienced personnel can be a successful model if the in-house approach is well-documented, detailed, and supported by considerable training and an organizational tolerance for an extended learning curve. Putting inexperienced personnel into the middle of an ad hoc, undocumented process is highly conducive to project failure. Even well-documented processes must be managed deliberately and carefully.

Managing the development of project products was discussed in Chapter 4. This chapter focuses on the less tangible but equally important function of managing the project's nondevelopment processes. Key concepts include:

- managing software processes in a systems context,
- managing your project staff,
- managing negotiations with affected groups,
- managing process support technology,
- managing process complexity,
- managing interactions with customers,
- managing interactions with executive management,
- using process measurements and metrics, and
- managing the acquisition of software subcomponents.

You will then be ready to turn your attention to controlling your project control activities.

MANAGING SOFTWARE PROCESSES IN A SYSTEMS CONTEXT

Process management in a systems context is considerably different from process management in a software-only context. In the software-only case, you essentially own your processes. You often have considerable liberty to tailor the processes at will, and to adjust them to the specific circumstances and needs of your project. However, in managing software projects as part of a larger systems engineering project, your processes are usually much less flexible. In particular, you need to be careful that you do not change any element of your process that might alter:

- process artifacts and products you need as inputs from other projects, personnel, or customers,

- timeframe in which you need those inputs,
- process artifacts and products you are producing as outputs for other projects, personnel, and customers,
- timeframe you've planned for providing those products,
- status information you provide to or receive from other projects, and
- participation of yourself or your project personnel in the support or review of other projects.

From one perspective, systems engineering is about teams of people working together as a unified, coordinated, and successful organization. The processes used on your project must be—and must remain—compatible with all the various processes being used anywhere in the overall systems engineering project.

MANAGING YOUR PROJECT STAFF

Managing software engineers is challenging, in part for the following reasons:

- Software development is a highly intellectual activity, and tends to attract highly intelligent people.
- Software development is a highly creative activity, and hence, attracts highly creative people.
- Intelligent people and creative people fundamentally don't understand each other.

Several techniques can help you ensure that your project personnel are motivated and work together as a team. These include:

- Involve the team in decisions.

- Acknowledge and leverage individual expertise.
- Compensate appropriately and creatively.
- Provide management-level information.
- Ensure that skills are upgraded regularly.
- Plan and manage the project so that overtime is minimized.

Involve the Team in Decisions

As manager of a group of software engineers, your people skills will be at least as important as—and often more important than—your technical skills. Software developers typically don't respond well to being given orders. Hence, it is worth the extra time to solicit input from the team, consider their input, negotiate alternatives, and generally build consensus that the project is doing the right thing, is building the right products, and is headed in the right direction. If your normal style is to involve the team in any decisions you are making, then on the rare occasion when you simply have to order them to go in a specific direction (due, for example, to the urgency of the decision or to a persistent lack of consensus), they will be far more likely to comply.

Acknowledge and Leverage Individual Expertise

Within any skill group, there are always differing degrees of talent. Some people will be less proficient, others more. However, skill areas often have somewhat natural limits that represent the degree to which a "highly proficient" person exceeds the work of a "slightly proficient person." For example, if a slightly proficient stone mason can build 10 linear feet of a stone wall per hour, then maybe a highly proficient stone mason can build 20 linear feet per hour. Or maybe 40 feet. But, no stone mason is going to build, for example, 200 linear feet in an hour.

As another example, maybe a slightly proficient waiter can adequately service 10 tables simultaneously. Maybe a highly proficient waiter can service 20, or 30. Or maybe even 50 (doubtful). But, a single waiter cannot simultaneously service 200 tables adequately.

As extreme as these proficiency ratios seem, they are less extreme than the differences between the most productive and the least productive software developers. Productivity ratios as high as 27 to 1 have been reported.

As a rule, your highly productive software engineers will know that they are highly productive. Their only question is whether or not you recognize their contribution. Unless you explicitly recognize and acknowledge the contributions they are making, they will typically conclude that you have no idea who is doing what on the project. Highly productive personnel tend to prefer working for managers who recognize and reward their productivity. If this doesn't happen on your project, they will find a project where it does happen.

Compensate Appropriately and Creatively

Compensating software personnel appropriately is extremely difficult due, in part, to the extreme variance in the productivity and quality of work that different programmers will demonstrate. Nevertheless, you must make a concerted effort to ensure that your maximum producers are compensated to your maximum ability.

Many software managers find the whole process of determining salary increases to be so difficult that they give all project personnel raises that fall within a percentage point or so of the average. A manager may know, for example, that Jerry is 10 times as productive as Mike. Presume the average raise is 5 percent. The manager decides that Mike is still struggling and decides that he will get a 3 percent raise. Well, logically, Jerry should then get at 30 percent raise. But very few organizations allow such raises (sometimes it's even a violation of policy), so Jerry instead gets a 7 percent raise. Jerry knows his relative productivity, knows the average raise is 5 percent, and considers his raise to be an insult.

However, there are steps you can take to compensate creatively. While salary is very important, other actions enable you to send a clear message that you recognize and appreciate someone's contribution. These actions include:

- replacing their computer with the latest monster box,
- allowing them to work a flex-time schedule,
- allowing them to work from home occasionally,
- giving them a small budget for the preapproved purchase of whatever software or books they feel they need,
- paying for them to attend high-interest classes,
- sending them to conferences, seminars, or workshops,
- moving them into an office with a door they can close, and
- telling them on Friday that you really appreciate their effort, and they can go ahead and take Monday off.

While none of these is equivalent to a 30 percent raise, each one sends a very tangible message that the employee's extra productivity and effort are recognized and appreciated.

Provide Management-Level Information

One of the distinguishing characteristics of most software development teams is that they tend to include intelligent people. Such people typically prefer to be informed about important developments. They also strive to understand management's major objectives, issues, and concerns.

When working with a team of software developers and other technology professionals, you can show respect for their potential contributions by providing them with management-level information that would otherwise not be available to them. By doing so, you send the message that you clearly understand and acknowledge that:

- they are intelligent,
- they can use as much information as you can provide them,
- they will work smarter as a function of being more informed, and
- they can provide you better advice as a function of being more informed.

Managers often tend to withhold management-level information from their project team from a sense of insecurity. "After all," reasons the insecure manager, "if I release such information, someone on the project may have a brilliant idea that had not occurred to me."

Conversely, the successful manager prefers to encourage, hear, acknowledge, and reward the brilliant idea, regardless of its source.

Ensure That Skills Are Upgraded Regularly

Virtually all high-technology professionals, especially those implementing software, fully appreciate the incredible pace at which new skills become valuable and old skills become valueless. Therefore, one of the most important rewards that technology professionals seek is the opportunity to learn the latest tools, methods, processes, and technologies.

One of the best methods for ensuring skill upgrades is to be certain that you have no single points of failure. Put differently, ensure that for every critical resource you have, you also have someone else in training as a backup or replacement resource. This not only provides you with extra protection against the unexpected loss of key personnel, but it also provides both a motivation and a means for helping personnel who are highly proficient in one area to start developing proficiency in another area.

Plan and Manage the Project To Minimize Overtime

With regard to their manager, one of the most classic quotes favored by software engineers is, "A lack of planning on your part does not constitute an emergency on my part."

Occasionally, when overtime is required, software engineers are aware of the truly unusual circumstances that necessitate the need for overtime. More commonly, the software engineers have watched a series of events that, unless management was aggressively proactive, would require massive overtime. Hence, software engineers often consider overtime work to be work that was clearly avoidable if the project was being managed effectively. Required overtime is, from a software engineer's perspective, a predictable result of poor management.

Nearly all software professionals are both willing and happy to work overtime hours. However, overtime they work at their discretion and initiative is completely different from overtime mandated by a management organization operating with no, outdated, or unrealistic plans.

MANAGING NEGOTIATIONS WITH AFFECTED GROUPS

Affected groups include any group whose activities, decisions, or responsibilities are affected by your actions and decisions. Examples of affected groups include:

- documentation support,
- training organization,
- systems engineering,
- quality assurance,
- test group,
- marketing,
- sales, and
- proposal teams.

Some affected groups will clearly be working in a support capacity. For example, if your project needs a thousand copies of a user manual to be reproduced and prepared for shipping, that work might be done by a shipping and receiving support group. However, just because that group is working in a support capacity does not mean that it must accommodate every preference you have or request you make. Support groups usually are supporting multiple projects. If each of several projects is insisting on full-time support during the same window of time, then clearly one or more of the projects will be required to change its plans.

Generally, managing the interactions of your project and your project personnel with affected groups is best accomplished though diplomacy and negotiation. On projects of significant size or complexity, it is typically impossible to assert that the needs of Group A always prevail over the needs of Group B, the needs of Group B always prevail over Group C, etc. Instead, as a practical matter, sometimes the needs of one group must come first and at other times the needs of a different group must come first. The likelihood of your project's needs prevailing over those of affected groups depends in large part on your ability to communicate—and substantiate—the:

- urgency of your needs, and
- magnitude of adverse consequences if those needs cannot be met.

That likelihood also depends on the circumstances of the affected group, including:

- magnitude of the adverse impact on the affected group of attempting to comply with or support your needs,
- number and severity of the constraints the affected group is already under, and
- ability of the affected group to negotiate relief from existing constraints.

Again, diplomacy is your most effective technique.

Occasionally, you may be successful in bludgeoning an affected group into submission. However, in such cases you can be absolutely positive that the affected group will have a very long memory.

MANAGING PROCESS SUPPORT TECHNOLOGY

One of the most important principles you must protect regarding process support technology is that the purpose of using such technology is to increase the likelihood that your project is successful. Process support technology should never be allowed to interfere with project success.

This point is stressed because software engineering environments can become highly automated. Over time, such automation may accidentally lead to excessive process complexity and to process inefficiencies.

As with software designs, technology that is simple to use is almost universally better. Simpler technologies typically involve:

- less required training,
- less confusion among project personnel regarding how to use the technology,
- less likelihood the technology will interfere with the use of other technologies, and
- less likelihood of mistakes arising from misuse or misunderstanding of the technology.

As with any software technology, when managing process support software, you should adhere to a few key principles:

- Avoid unnecessary installation of the newest release. If the current release does everything you need, stay with it.

- Beta-test any new process support software in a dark, quiet corner of your project and verify usefulness before you commit the entire project.
- Ensure that project personnel are adequately trained to use the process support software.
- Avoid a 1.0 release of anything.

MANAGING PROCESS COMPLEXITY

One measure of the complexity of a process is the total number of rules the process embodies. More rules usually mean greater complexity.

Process-related policies convey the primary or highest level rules. In virtually all organizations, projects are expected to remain in compliance with applicable organizational policies. However, policies are usually kept sparse, especially those relating to technical issues on development projects. Therefore, it is generally true that policies are not a source of complexity.

On the other hand, project management and engineering procedures can be a source of considerable process complexity. This is particularly true in older or larger organizations where procedures have been updated numerous times. Each new update typically adds more process requirements, and each such addition increases the potential for inconsistencies among the various procedural requirements.

Processes tend to become increasingly large, bureaucratic, and complicated with the mere passage of time. The reason for this is simple: No process is perfect. Hence, during the performance of any given process, problems will invariably arise.

Generally, executive management does not like problems. So, when a problem occurs, management has a natural tendency to take steps to ensure that the problem doesn't occur again. These steps are almost always characterized by additional actions that must be taken, additional reviews that must occur, or additional approvals that must be sought. In essence, management almost always "fixes" problems by adding more rules. But even with the additional rules, new and unexpected problems will arise. Again, regardless of how many rules are added, the process will never be perfect. Therefore, problems inevitably continue to occur and processes invariably continue to get bigger and more complicated.

To manage process complexity, you need to take actions similar to those discussed in the section on managing product complexity. That is, you need to analyze the processes you are using periodically and ask the following questions:

- Are there any multistep activities where the number of required steps can be reduced?

- Are there any multisignature approvals where the number of signatures can be reduced?

- Are there any multiple reviews occurring that cover the same general material and that might therefore be consolidated into a single review?

- Are there different reporting requirements where the contents of the reports are similar and the differences are mostly in formatting and style?

Since processes become more complicated naturally, the most direct means for managing process complexity is to analyze the process periodically and systematically for any opportunities to reduce the number of requirements or rules.

MANAGING INTERACTIONS WITH CUSTOMERS

On some software projects, you will never get close to the customer, so there will be no need to manage customer interactions. However, if you or your project personnel will ever interact with the customer, then you must take steps to manage those interactions.

The easiest way to ensure successful customer interactions is to understand the needs of your customer thoroughly. This includes understanding all your customer's needs, not just those documented in the contract, the product requirements specification, or the product features list. To get a true sense of your customer's needs, put yourself in the customer's position. Consider, for example, the following questions your customer will likely try to answer:

- Have I accurately described what I need?
- Can I afford this approach to addressing my needs?
- Is there anything I can do to reduce costs?
- Will development staff turnover:
  - threaten the quality of the products I need?
  - threaten my timetable for receiving them?
- Are there problems that I'm not aware of?
- What is the #1 objective of this development group?

If you think of yourself as someone purchasing a software system, you will likely seek answers to most or all of these questions. As the software project manager, you need to ensure that your customer's answers to these questions are of a type that increases the customer's confidence that you are taking all the steps necessary to ensure the maximum product value delivered for the least cost. In particular, be sure that:

- Your customer can accurately answer, "What is the #1 objective of this development group?"
- Your customer will like the answer.

Clearly, you need to achieve a balance between your customer's need for a high-value, low-cost product and your company's need to destroy the competition and make huge profits. Fortunately, the most reliable method for beating the competition is to offer excellent value at low cost. From this perspective, the needs of your customer and the needs of your company are often far more aligned than it commonly seems.

MANAGING INTERACTIONS WITH EXECUTIVE MANAGEMENT

Unless you are the company president, you will have one or more layers of management above you. At a minimum, the next highest level of management will be expecting regular updates and status reports regarding:

- progress of your project,
- costs incurred,
- amount of product developed or value earned,
- number of defects found,
- number of latent (unfound) defects, and
- other quantitative information regarding the relative progress and probable success of your project.

More likely, you will be providing this type of information regularly to your immediate manager and periodically to management personnel one level above your immediate manager.

The notion of managing your interactions with executive management is completely consistent with the notion of taking active and progressive responsibility for that interaction, versus adopting a submissive, passive posture and relying on senior management to ensure the success of your interactions.

Think of executive management as just another type of customer. They too want to be sure that their money (your budget) is well spent. They too want to avoid negative surprises.

However, you will also need to be attentive and responsive to certain needs that are usually unique to executive management. For example, executive management:

- may have legitimate strategic or political objectives that supersede immediate business objectives,
- may have immediate, crucial tactical objectives that supersede long-term business objectives,
- may not entirely understand, or be interested in, technical arguments and may therefore prefer a business-oriented approach to any discussion,
- may, in a period of management responsibility transition:
  - defer making decisions in the interests of allowing its successor to have an early influence, and
  - accelerate making decisions in the interest of have the greatest impact possible, and
- may say things that are completely unintelligible to you.

If you intend to take responsibility for managing your interactions with executive management, none of these considerations should present a significant challenge for you. You can anticipate and plan for these possible developments, and plan the steps you will take if one or more of them occur.

The common denominator for all these issues is the fact that the needs of executive management will sometimes be in conflict with what you perceive to be the needs of your project and the needs of your customer. When such conflict occurs, there is usually only one of three possible outcomes:

1. You clearly communicate your position and diplomatically negotiate a successful compromise.

2. Your arguments are vague, wandering, and unnecessarily aggressive, and executive management simply rejects your request.

3. In light of unprecedented overriding priorities, no one will listen to whatever it is you are trying to say regardless of how well you present it.

Of these three possible outcomes, the only one you need to pay attention to is the outcome where your performance was not convincing. Although not taught in most software project management courses, to be successful as a software project manager, you need to be successful at managing your interactions with executive management. And if you want to be successful at that, be sure that you are quite capable of:

- writing terse and convincing rationales for decisions you would like the executives to make,

- presenting project status and issue briefings succinctly and effectively,

- recognizing a reasonable compromise when one is offered to you,
- negotiating a delay in an impending adverse decision so that you can provide more accurate and compelling data to the decision-makers (the premise being that additional data is potentially available that could influence the decision-makers toward a more favorable decision), and
- achieving your objectives via a completely different approach.

Keep in mind that, as insulting as it sounds, nearly all executive managers take the position that with regard to the company's business objectives, they know far more than you do. This is quite reasonable since it is almost universally true. Therefore, as you present your arguments, you will need to be sufficiently convincing that you can overcome a rather persistent attitude that you are not aware of—and therefore do not understand—the major issues related to your project.

Again, to be most convincing, don't look at your project from your point of view. Instead, look at it from the perspective of the specific executive manager (or managers) with whom you are meeting.

USING PROCESS MEASUREMENTS AND METRICS

Whenever you are engaged in any activities related to managing the processes on your project, you can be more effective if you are better informed. In addition to managing the project by carefully tracking cost, value, and schedule, you can use a variety of process-related measurements and metrics while you track the project's progress. However, you must approach this area of metrics quite carefully for the simple reason that process metrics are very powerful. Used properly, process metrics can contribute to powerful good; used improperly, they can contribute to powerful harm.

One of the difficulties inherent in process measures is that it is difficult to measure process without implicitly measuring people. Generally, people don't like to be measured. Your project staff will be wondering about, if not outright asking, the following questions:

- Who will be seeing this information?
- What will this information be used for?
- How might this information potentially be misinterpreted?
- Why is this information necessary?

Who Will Be Seeing This Information?

Anyone working on a project naturally wonders about the types of measurements being taken and who will receive the resulting information. The expected distribution of information can have a significant impact on how receptive and supportive project personnel are of the overall metrics initiative. Imagine yourself as a software developer, and consider your reaction to the following (if extreme) example.

Suppose your project manager distributes a memo that announces a new metrics initiative whereby she will be monitoring the duration of phone calls made by project personnel, the numbers dialed out, and the numbers dialing in. She asserts that this information is needed to perform capacity planning for a possible upgrade to the phone system. What would your reaction be?

After a couple of weeks, the manager sends out another memo. This one announces that the data gathering effort is going very well. It also states that she has started routing the individual phone call information to other managers in the division. The intent of sharing this information is to enable the managers to meet periodically and discuss divisionwide capacity planning. Now what would your reaction be?

Finally, a couple of weeks later, the manager distributes a memo announcing that the phone usage data will be posted on the wall immediately outside her office door. The stated purpose of posting the information is to demonstrate that she has nothing to hide from the project technical personnel. How would you react to this development?

Many people would react to this sequence of events with growing concern, and possibly with growing resistance and resentment. The problem is clearly one of data access. After the first memo, it seems that only the manager will be seeing the information, and maybe summarizing it and sending the summaries to the capacity planning team.

The second memo indicates that now all the managers will be seeing the phone usage data. The problem with this is the increasing likelihood that the data may be misinterpreted. For example, your project manager may know that your software has been deployed at the customer site and is undergoing extensive testing. Thus, your manager understands that you routinely spend a couple of hours on the phone each day providing customer support to numerous end users. However, other managers looking at your phone usage data might simply conclude that you are an irresponsible worker who likes to talk on the phone with friends.

The third memo announces developments that clearly increase the likelihood that uninformed or partially informed people, from rank-and-file to executive management, will be examining the phone usage information and potentially drawing wrong conclusions. These conclusions could negatively affect their perceptions of you, and thus your career potential within the organization.

When you collect process or activity-related metrics or measurements on your project, be sure that the data is:

- summarized whenever possible,
- sanitized so it is not traceable to a single individual, and
- distributed only to those directly responsible for acting on that data.

What Will This Information Be Used For?

As reflected in the example, although the stated objective for collecting the data—capacity planning—seems legitimate enough, the way the data was handled was conducive to it being used for other purposes. Therefore, with any metric or measurement information you collect, be sure that the data is used only for its intended purpose.

One way to reduce the likelihood that data might be misused is to reduce to an absolute minimum the number of people who see that data. For example, as a software project manager, you may decide that you want to make reducing code complexity a high priority for project developers. To support this priority, you buy a software tool that automatically analyzes source code and provides a variety of complexity measures.

You can take several approaches to using this tool and handling the resulting complexity information:

- You can install the tool on your computer, and run random, unannounced analyses of the code developers are creating.

- You can run an analysis of all source code every Friday.
- You can wait until a developer declares his or her code to be ready for analysis, and run the complexity tests at that time.
- You can make the tool available to individual developers, but still run your tests when they have completed their code.
- You can make the tool available to individual developers, and run your complexity checks only after subsystem integration is done and it is no longer possible to trace complexity to individual developers.

Depending on specific project circumstances, this sequence of options generally progresses from the worst approach to the best approach. Although the stated purpose in this example is to reduce code complexity, developers may be concerned that you could use the information during their performance reviews. This introduces an extremely important point: Never let a secondary objective take precedence over a primary objective.

In this example, the primary objective is to reduce code complexity. For you to use complexity information during the annual review, you will need to collect the information in a way that it is clearly traceable to an individual developer. As previously discussed, this is less than ideal.

The best example approach presented is where you provide the developers with the tools they need to analyze the complexity of their own code, and you ask them to make every reasonable effort to keep complexity to a minimum. When the developer is the only one seeing and using the information, he or she will have no motivation to distort or hide that information. All developers can participate in the ongoing analysis and reduction of complexity without fearing misuse of the information. They are helping you achieve your primary objective.

Alternatively, if developers know that you are collecting complexity information that you can trace directly to the developer, they may concentrate less on actual complexity reduction and more on how to look good whenever you run your complexity checks. When this happens, your secondary need of having data to use in the annual performance review takes priority over your primary need to reduce code complexity.

The next section provides additional examples of how your handling of metrics can cause project personnel to manifest unintended and undesirable behavior.

How Might This Information Potentially Be Misinterpreted?

Possibly the single greatest challenge with regard to implementing a process-focused metrics program is to ensure that the numbers are providing you with a complete picture of what you are trying to measure. If you are achieving only partial insights, it is very easy to infer an inaccurate understanding from a particular set of numbers.

Some of the most popular metrics currently in use are dangerous. They are dangerous because they all share a common characteristic: They leave out an important part of the overall picture. Some examples of these metrics are:

- amount of code produced per unit time,
- defect detection efficiency,
- years of experience, and
- programmer average defect density.

Amount of Code Produced Per Unit Time

This metric, often referred to as productivity, is quite popular. If the data is computed by taking all the software developed across the project during a given period of time, the metric is relatively useful. However, this information is often collected at the level of individual programmers. This is both unnecessary and dangerous.

As stated, the distinguishing characteristic of a dangerous metric is that it misses important, relevant information. In the case of the productivity of an individual programmer, when you concentrate on the size of product produced per unit time, possible missing elements include:

- complexity, and
- multiple responsibilities.

Software can range from trivial to exceedingly complex. For example, Mary is one of your more senior developers. She also has a talent for handling extremely complex code. Hence, whenever you are handing out work packages, you routinely give Mary the hardest, most complicated work. Mike is a junior developer and new to the team. Until you know his capability, you routinely give Mike all the easiest assignments. Then, senior management gets hold of the productivity data, sees that Mike is more productive than Mary, and gives him a nice promotion. Big problem.

Another potential problem is gathering productivity data on people who are handling multiple responsibilities. Some of your project personnel may have additional responsibilities that prevent them from dedicating full-time attention to code development. For example, one of the developers may be responsible for fielding technical support calls, another for mentoring and helping new hires, and a third for coordinating and planning all the software inspections occurring on the project. In each case, the developer's apparent productivity is lower—possibly significantly lower—than his or her actual productivity.

Defect Detection Efficiency

Many organizations have verified the value of conducting software inspections. Once inspections are occurring, it is not uncommon to measure the amount of time spent looking for defects, as well as the number of defects found. The general notion is that if you can find defects more quickly, you are being more efficient. Superficially, this makes sense.

However, if you track this data in a manner that allows you to see the detection efficiency of individual inspectors, the following can easily happen. Mary and Jim have each been given a budget of six hours to inspect a software item. Mary spends one hour going through the code and finding the obvious defects. She finds twelve. Then she spends the next two hours carefully studying the code and looking for subtle defects. She finds five. Finally, she makes one more, very thorough pass and spends three hours looking for the extremely obscure defects. Sure enough, she finds two more.

Jim, however, is in a bit of a hurry. He knows he doesn't have the time to use the entire six hours in his inspection budget, but figures he should at least make one pass. So he sets aside an hour and inspects the code. Like Mary, during the first hour, he finds the obvious twelve defects.

Mary's defect detection efficiency is eighteen defects found over six hours, yielding an efficiency of three defects per hour. Jim found twelve defects in one hour, yielding an efficiency of twelve defects per hour.

If you lecture Mary too severely about how long it takes her to find defects, she has a very easy solution available: Find the easy, obvious stuff, and then stop looking.

Although nearly all companies conducting software inspections identify, track, and log defects by type, location, and severity, virtually none characterizes a defect in terms of obscurity. However, without a notion of how hard a defect is to find, the notion of tracking an individual inspector's defect detection efficiency is almost useless and, even worse, discourages inspectors from taking the time to ferret out the obscure defects.

Years of Experience

Years of experience is a common measurement that is used throughout the software industry. Projects use it as one of the criteria for determining whether someone is potentially qualified to perform a particular type of work. Human resource departments use it as part of the employee hiring process. Government agencies frequently use it to help define the minimum requirements for someone to fill a specific labor category.

The problem with this metric is that, alone, it is a very poor predictor of someone's performance. A programmer who has spent ten years developing really bad code is, in all likelihood, still a really bad programmer. Years of experience, as a metric, overlooks the quality of those years. In some environments, you can learn a lot in three months. In other environments, can you can spend an entire year and learn very little. Time is not the predictor; it's how much experience and learning you have acquired. However, time is much easier to quantify, and hence is a far more popular metric.

As a compromise, you can strive to quantify experience, knowledge, and skill levels using, for example, terms ranging from extremely low to extremely high.

Programmer Average Defect Density

Another dangerous metric is the calculation and tracking of defect density (defects per size) for individual programmers. In theory, this metric should provide the project manager with quantitative insight into a programmer's ability to develop high quality code. In practice, the metric can be horribly misleading. Once again, as discussed in the subsection on productivity (amount of code produced per unit time), the missing factors are complexity and difficulty.

If, for example, Susan is being assigned work packages that, on average, are ten times more difficult than the work packages Mary is being assigned, then the fact that Susan's code has only twice the defect density of Mary's is actually a very positive sign. All else being equal, Susan's code should have a defect density ten times that of Mary's. When difficulty is factored in, Susan writes code that is relatively of very high quality. However, the basic metric of programmer average defect density will erroneously tell you just the opposite.

Why Is This Information Necessary?

When you establish a metrics initiative on your project, all project personnel will naturally wonder why you think the metrics are necessary. You could try explaining the purpose of each metric, how and when it will be collected, who it will be distributed to, who will have discretionary access to the data, and how the metric will be interpreted. Alternatively, you can simply strive to educate project personnel on the need for and value of metrics in general.

The primary motivation for collecting and using metrics is that, by doing so, you progress from being an experience-driven decision-maker to being a *well-informed*, experience-driven decision-maker. There is a huge difference between the two, and the difference is the availability of objective "intelligence." There is a common misconception that metrics inhibit the decision-maker. This is true only if you consider reality to be an inhibitor. Metrics help you and your project personnel understand what is really happening on the project. Hence, all decisions are made based on a better understanding of what is really occurring.

Once project personnel understand, in general, the value of properly collecting appropriate metrics, they will tend to be much less concerned about the need for and use of any particular metric. This assumes, of course, that the collection and use of a metric is, from their perspective, clearly appropriate.

MANAGING THE ACQUISITION OF SOFTWARE SUBCOMPONENTS

On some software projects, you may find that a portion of the software development work would best be performed by a subcontractor. As the software project manager, you are responsible for ensuring that the subcontract arrangement is successful.

Success is characterized by the subcontractor providing software products that are of sufficient quality, and are on time and within budget. The success or failure of any software acquisition contract is closely correlated to the actions taken prior to award. Once the acquisition activities are underway, corrections to the acquisition process tend to be both very difficult and very expensive.

Numerous approaches are available for acquiring software. If you are considering a major acquisition, you will want to add one or more experienced acquisition personnel to your project team.

You can expect the acquisition lifecycle to proceed using most or all of the following activities:

1. Conceptual planning

2. Requirements specification

3. Acquisition planning

4. Solicitation

5. Source selection
6. Initiation
7. Acquisition tracking and management
8. Technology tracking
9. Requirements management
10. Acquisition replanning
11. Evaluation
12. Transition to support
13. Impact monitoring
14. Acquisition close-out

Since the management of an acquisition project is so similar to the management of a software development project, each of these steps is described only briefly. If your project will be procuring a significant amount of software using a software acquisition process, in addition to this material, you should study SEI's extensively detailed software acquisition Capability Maturity Model (CMM®).

Conceptual Planning

Conceptual planning for a software acquisition consists of answering several key questions, including:

- Is the likely solution affordable? (feasibility analysis)
- Do we really know what problem we are trying to solve? (readiness analysis)
- Can we communicate that problem with sufficient clarity? (requirements analysis)

Requirements Specification

With regard to developing a requirements specification, be sure that you or others (other project personnel or experts experienced in requirements specification) can decompose the requirements in a manner that renders them:

- complete,
- consistent, and
- testable.

Acquisition Planning

During the earliest stages of acquisition planning, it is essential to determine the major characteristics of this particular acquisition. For example, you will need to decide:

- Will there be only one winner?
- If not, will there be a pool of winners that compete for task orders?
- Will awards be made to multiple prime teams?
- If not, will an award be made to a single prime team that includes multiple subcontractors?
- Will this procurement be a total award or will it be only for the base year plus additional option years?
- Will this procurement be fixed price? Cost plus? Cost plus fixed fee? Other?
- Will CMM® be used as a factor?

Once you have made these decisions, you must ensure that the acquisition process you intend to follow is defined adequately. At one end of the spectrum, you might just assert that your acquisition processes will be in compliance with the goals and key practices of the software acquisition CMM®. At the other end of the spectrum, it may be useful to develop step-by-step instructions that guide you and other project personnel through the acquisition planning process.

Solicitation

When your acquisition planning documents are complete, you can commence with the solicitation itself. Unless you thoroughly understand all aspects of the problem you are trying to solve and the software solutions that offerors are most likely to propose, you may want to initiate the solicitation with a Request for Information (RFI). Use the RFI to solicit comments or recommendations from those who might be interested in responding to your Request for Proposals (RFP).

You should also consider the advantages of publishing and distributing one or more draft RFPs prior to releasing the final RFP. Draft RFPs allow offerors an opportunity to ask for clarifications and to make recommendations regarding ways in which the RFP can be improved. This feedback helps you write a less ambiguous and potentially more competitive RFP.

Source Selection

During the planning stages, you decided on the selection criteria you will use. These criteria may consist of evaluating various proposal sections and information such as:

- management approach,
- technical approach,

- relevant history of building similar solutions, and
- financial strength of the offeror.

Usually, the evaluation criteria will have an associated weight (percentage factor) that allows certain parts of the proposal to have more impact than other parts. For example, you may allocate a maximum of 40 percent of total available points to the management approach, a maximum of 30 percent to the technical approach, and divide the remaining points among the remaining evaluation criteria.

You may also have planned for certain prequalifiers to be part of the evaluation process. Prequalifiers consist of one or more tests that the offeror must pass before the proposal is accepted into the evaluation process. An example of a prequalifier is an SEI CMM® Level 2 requirement. In this example, any offeror must be a Level 2 software organization or you will not even look at its technical or cost proposals.

You can also use a requirement as both a prequalifier and an evaluation criterion. Staying with the CMM® as the example, you can have a Level 2 requirement as a prequalifier, and also have software process maturity as one of the evaluation criteria. With this approach, all offerors must be at least Level 2, but a Level 3 offeror would receive more points in the process maturity category than a Level 2 offeror.

Initiation

Once you've selected an offeror, you meet with that contractor to ensure a common understanding of the details of the acquisition. Before this meeting, you will want to ensure that your acquisition management team is prepared properly.

Next you develop, often through several iterations and sometimes with the help of the offeror, a detailed statement of work (SOW). This is delivered to the offeror, who then should develop, for your (and the acquisition team's) review and approval:

- software development plan,
- quality assurance plan, and
- configuration management plan.

Once you have approved these plans, the offeror can begin developing the products.

Acquisition Tracking and Management

Throughout the acquisition, you will regularly review the status of the activities and products being developed for you. You will analyze and respond to:

- contractor's performance against the latest approved:
  - software development plans,
  - quality assurance plans,
  - configuration management plans, and
  - detailed schedule of milestones and activities,
- intergroup issues not resolvable at a lower level, and
- product defect density.

Technology Tracking

As your acquisition proceeds, you will need to be attentive to ongoing changes in technology and the opportunities those changes might offer to both you and the contractor. A request for major changes in the technology being developed by, or used on, the acquisition will likely require a contract modification. Nevertheless, you need to answer, on a regular basis, the following questions:

- Do all elements of the current statement of work still make sense?
- Do all elements of the current design and development approach still make sense?
- Is the development environment still using the most appropriate tools and technology?

Requirements Management

One of the impacts of shifting technology is the potential to change either the problem you are trying to solve or the solution being implemented. Hence, when new technologies show potential advantages, requirements may need to be renegotiated. Likewise, if the problem you're addressing starts shifting, renegotiations may be required. Be particularly attentive to any relationships between the requirements on your software development project and the requirements on your software acquisition project. Changes in the requirements of one may involve corresponding changes in the requirements of the other.

Acquisition Replanning

When requirements changes are significant, you will likely need to make changes to your acquisition plan. Additionally, as the acquisition advances, you may see elements of your acquisition tracking, oversight, and control activities that you would like to change. Whenever you need to change how you are managing the acquisition, you should update the corresponding planning documents.

Evaluation

At some point during the acquisition, products will start arriving and you will need to begin evaluating those products. As with all the major activities in the acquisition, the evaluation activities should follow a defined process and be performed in accordance with the plan.

The key goal for the evaluation process is to determine objectively whether or not you've received what you contracted for. The need to use objective criteria is based on the fact that what you receive may not necessarily equate to what you want. However, it may well be completely in compliance with the contract, statement of work, and approved requirements specification. In that case, the product is acceptable (if not desirable). In the event of undesirable product, if the contractor is following an incremental or spiral development lifecycle, you still have the opportunity to revisit requirements, update the contract, revise plans, and increase the likelihood that future products from the acquisition are both acceptable and desirable.

Transition to Support

Once an evaluated product has been accepted, it must be transitioned to the group that will be providing the ongoing support for that product. Frequently, this is either an internal group or a group within the customer organization.

The product support group, by this time, should have the necessary experience, training, and tools to install, integrate, and support successfully the acquired software products.

Impact Monitoring

Impact monitoring is outside nearly all formal acquisition processes. Nonetheless, it is very important that you monitor the impact of both acquired and developed software deliveries and determine whether or not the desired results are being realized (or are at least likely to be achieved). If the software does not seem to be meeting the needs of the ultimate customers or end users, you will need to revisit objectives, goals, and requirements for both your overall software development project and for those software components that you are acquiring via the acquisition project.

Acquisition Close-Out

With the delivery and acceptance of the final acquisition, you can commence with a formal close-out of the acquisition project. Typically, this involves a variety of shut-down actions such as:

- accrual and payment of all outstanding invoices,
- baselining of all deliverables,
- auditing of activities, charges, expenses, and other financial information, and
- any legal steps required to shut down or terminate the contract.

Additionally, you should conduct a post close-out meeting with the primary acquisition personnel to discuss and document lessons learned from the acquisition, and to develop a list of recommendations for anyone involved in a subsequent software acquisition.

CONTROLLING YOUR PROJECT CONTROL ACTIVITIES

The material in this and the preceding chapters has focused on the actions you take as the software project manager to ensure that:

- Your project plan is accurate and current.
- Project personnel are performing their work efficiently and effectively.
- The project and all major relevant processes are being tracked and controlled effectively.

However, periodically you need to step back and examine your own actions and activities, and personally assess your effectiveness at performing your management functions. You do this by examining your project for problems that can be traced to factors that you, as software manager, can influence. As described in the next chapter, you ensure that you are controlling your own management activities properly by examining the quality and consequences of those activities and by diagnosing the effectiveness of your project controls.

Part IV

Essentials of Project Recovery

6 Diagnosing Project Control Effectiveness

"The purpose of diagnostic investigations is to gain early and accurate insight into possible control problems. . . . You are not trying to evaluate the products being built, or the project personnel, or the processes they are following. You are instead concentrating on yourself, your responsibilities, and the actions you are taking."

At this point, you have a project on which you have made considerable efforts to develop a reasonably comprehensive, accurate, and current plan. Additionally, engineering activities are underway, and a variety of other management-level activities (including ongoing efforts at project staffing, requirements management, software quality assurance, staff retention, etc.) have commenced.

As reflected by the first five chapters of this book, you are responsible for a lot. All of it can be generalized into one overall responsibility: It is up to you to control the project. Once the project is underway, the next major challenge is: How can you be sure that your efforts to control the project are working?

DETECTING CONTROL PROBLEMS

Detecting control problems is in some ways similar to detecting health problems. When it comes to your health, vitality is monitored and problems are detected using methods ranging from informal and everyday to highly formal and rather rare. For example, you monitor your health informally on a daily, if not hourly, basis through simple feedback such as the occurrence and disappearance of aches and pains. In addition, you occasionally use somewhat more formal home diagnostic techniques. You may, for example, check your blood pressure weekly. Similarly, when you are experiencing flu-like symptoms, you may start checking your temperature. Beyond this, you may have annual health checkups and, if some type of anomaly is detected, you may require highly specialized testing and diagnostic procedures.

For the software project manager, detecting control problems and performing diagnostics have many parallels to the health example. You are essentially always receiving minor feedback on how well your project controls are working. On a daily, even hourly, basis, you receive numerous indicators confirming that the project is going well or that events are starting to slip out of control. Examples of these indicators include:

- number and types of interruptions you receive,
- frequency and intensity of senior management inquiries into your project, and
- overall level of teamwork, or lack thereof, among your project personnel.

In addition to this informal feedback, you are conducting regular status meetings. These allow you to focus specifically on cost, schedule, and other measurements and metrics that provide more quantitative insight into the overall health of the project. Hence, on a regular basis, you are examining the amount of work completed, number of defects detected, number of problem reports closed during the period, number of new work packages commenced, etc. All these measures provide somewhat informal but reasonably quantitative information regarding project health.

More rarely, you will be conducting milestone reviews. These may occur with senior management in attendance; if so, they allow senior management to express their opinions regarding the health of your project and, as appropriate, to provide direction.

Finally, you can also use highly specialized detection and diagnostic techniques that provide clear and reliable details regarding the health of your project. These diagnostic techniques include comprehensive product evaluations, rigorous process assessments, and other formal quality audits. Quality audits are sometimes performed by you as project manager; when you need true objectivity, they may be performed by the quality assurance organization, members of the software engineering process group, or external experts.

Three different approaches to detecting and diagnosing project control problems are commonly used:

- performing routine project tracking,
- leveraging safety net functions, and
- identifying control problems.

Regardless of which of these approaches you are using at a given moment (during the life of the project, you need to use all of them), remember that the purpose of these diagnostic investigations is to gain early and accurate insight into possible control problems. You take these steps so that you can take quick, remedial action to resolve any possible problem.

For this particular activity, you are not trying to evaluate the products being built, or the project personnel, or the processes they are following. You are instead concentrating on yourself, your responsibilities, and the actions you are taking. You should be performing these general diagnostic activities throughout the life of the project.

PERFORMING ROUTINE PROJECT TRACKING

The effectiveness of your project controls will be revealed to you routinely as a regular part of tracking your project activities. One of the primary reasons for systematic project tracking is to gain the earliest possible insight into developing and potential problems and opportunities. Three standard ways for you to monitor the effectiveness of your project control are to evaluate:

- work package completion percent,
- milestone success rate, and
- trendlines.

Work package completion percent offers the quickest feedback, but gradually developing problems will be hard to see. Milestone success rate is evaluated less frequently, but developing problems are more apparent. Trendlines are both short-term and long-term, but require collecting a series of data points before the trend can be considered revealing. Although they are of relatively less value early in a project, trendlines become very convincing indicators of project control effectiveness during the middle and later phases of a project.

Work Package Completion Percent

Work package completion percent is the ratio of completed packages to those still incomplete, including those not yet started. Since a typical work package for an individual or very small team (two or three people) is usually four weeks or less, on a project of a dozen people or so, you may have one or more packages being completed each week. This allows very detailed insight into project control effectiveness as a function of the changing status of work packages, which is reported during weekly status meetings.

Discrete status changes for work packages include:

- work package available,
- assigned,

- in progress,
- in unit test,
- in integration test,
- in system test,
- on hold,
- completed, and
- products added to baseline.

As discussed in the section on work breakdown structures, any single work package should never be tracked in terms of being partially complete. Instead, use binary status tracking, whereby a single work package is shown as either 0 percent complete or 100 percent complete. With binary status tracking, there are no intermediate stages of percent complete.

Work package completion percent is the number of work packages that are 100 percent complete compared to the total number of work packages. If you planned to have 25 percent of the work packages completed by the fourth month of a project, then comparing the actual number of completed packages at the fourth month to the planned amount provides excellent feedback on your overall project control effectiveness.

Milestone Success Rate

Milestones characterize major targets of progress within your project plan. Generally, a greater number of milestones is better than relatively few. Milestones allow you to verify the progress, or lack thereof, on the project. They represent your commitment to complete certain activities or parts of products by certain dates.

Failure to achieve milestones on their originally planned dates is indicative of ineffective project controls. The most obvious indicator of not achieving a milestone is, of course, needing to slip the date further into the future. If you adjust the date long before the date actually arrives, this typically creates less of a problem. It indicates that you are monitoring the project closely and adjusting plans to accommodate the latest developments. However, if the first clear indication that a date has to slip is the arrival of that date concurrent with an inability to pass the milestone acceptance criteria, this clearly indicates inadequate project tracking and control.

In the former case, you are comparing actual progress to plans, anticipating future events and capability, and adjusting dates as a function of project performance and predictions based on accumulated project data. In the latter case, you thought you were done with a major activity or a part of the system, but you weren't. In either event, adjusting the milestone date requires you to:

- analyze the scope and complexity of defects within the product,
- estimate the number and types of latent defects,
- determine the amount of rework that will be necessary to address known and potential problems,
- determine the resources available for performing the rework, and
- adjust the milestone sufficiently far into the future to allow rework and internal retesting to be completed.

Another way to miss a milestone date is not to have the anticipated features that were originally planned for that milestone. This is characterized by reducing or relaxing the acceptance criteria for a particular milestone. Although in your plans, it will look like you achieved the milestone (that is, the date didn't move), you should still consider this to be a signal of possibly ineffective project controls.

Trendlines

Trendlines give you a graphical depiction of relative values of data over time. Usually, you will plot several trendlines on the same chart, or profile, to facilitate instant comparisons between related values. For example, you can use a project profile to plot trendlines for:

- total hours worked,
- total size of completed product,
- productivity (total size of completed product/total hours worked),
- total defects detected, and
- defect density (total defects detected/total size of completed product).

These five trendlines are all plotted on the y-axis, and time is plotted on the x-axis. Three of the values (total hours worked, total size of completed product, and total defects detected) are simple measurements that either increase from period to period or remain the same. The other two are metrics calculated from the measurements.

Figure 16 is an example of how these metrics might look one year into a project if they've been plotted monthly.

Examining this example, productivity appears to have increased substantially around six months into the project. However, that was soon followed by an increase in defects

Figure 16
Trendlines of Five Plotted Metrics

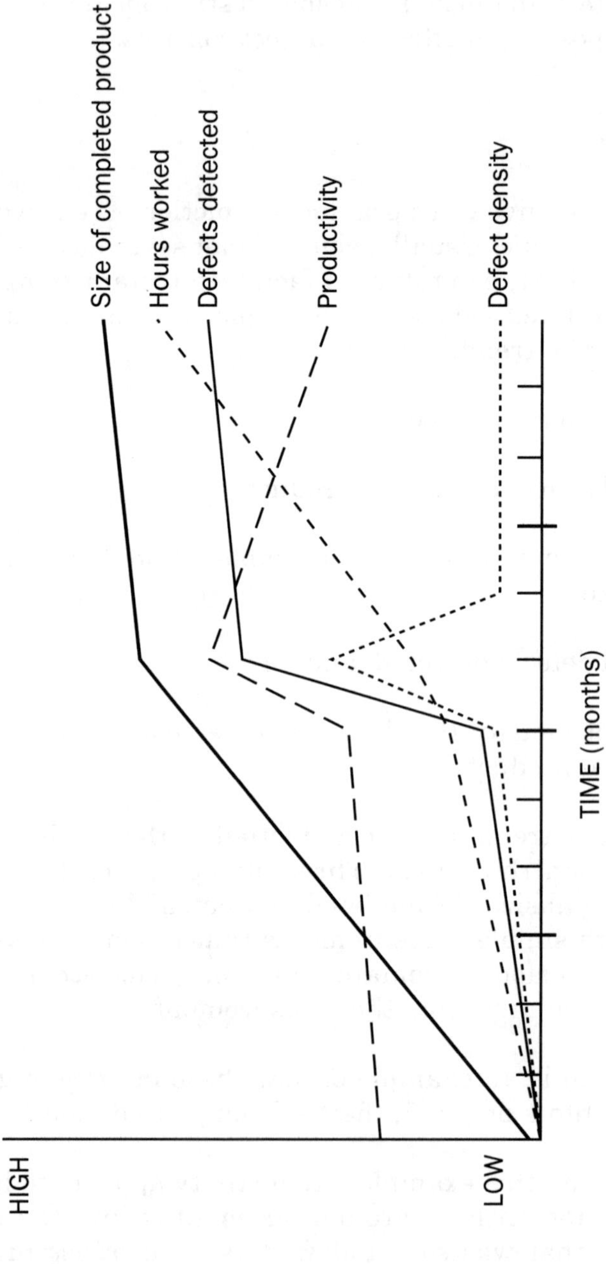

detected and a corresponding increase in defect density. When the project manager noticed this, she incorporated increased use of software inspections. It started taking longer to complete work packages, so the rate at which these packages was being closed was reduced. However, as a result of the inspection process, defect density fell sharply.

As shown in this example, plotting multiple trendlines on the same profile allows comparison of related metrics and a projectwide interpretation of trends as a function of related project activities.

LEVERAGING SAFETY-NET FUNCTIONS

In addition to the activities you perform as a normal part of routine project tracking, you also need to employ backup or safety-net functions to help detect any problems that may otherwise go unnoticed. Safety-net functions protect you from a breakdown in your regular processes. Regrettably, such functions usually look either redundant or unnecessary. For example, since you, as the project manager, are already monitoring the project using the project plan, why should quality assurance personnel check the plan against the actual activities occurring on the project? The primary reason is simply to find anything that you may have inadvertently overlooked, and to bring that to your attention.

Quality audits are safety-net functions in the sense that they are intended to verify that everything that is supposed to happen, actually does happen. They typically rely on a quality framework, such as the CMM® or one or more standards from the IEEE. Additionally, they may employ some type of systematic assessment or evaluation methodology, such as the software capability evaluation (SCE) method developed by SEI at Carnegie Mellon University. Example audit frameworks are described in the following sections, and a sample audit approach is presented. Quality audits not only provide you insights into the effectiveness of your project control, they also provide insights into the effectiveness of the processes and activities occurring on your project.

The Software CMM®

The software CMM® was developed by SEI at Carnegie Mellon University. The CMM is based on a five-level framework. Each level is considered to be a higher maturity software process than the next lower level. Level 5 represents the highest level.

Each level above Level 1 is characterized by a set of key process areas (KPAs). The KPAs, and their associated levels, are depicted in Figure 17.

Each KPA is characterized by several goals, and is defined in detail by a set of key practices. Generally, to satisfy the goals of the KPA, you need to demonstrate how you are satisfying each of the key practices. Key practices make assertions such as:

- "The organization follows a written policy for developing and maintaining. . . ."
- "Measurements are made and used to determine the status of. . . ."
- "The SQA group periodically reports the results. . . ."

The six Level 2 KPAs contain more than 100 key practices. The general premise behind this framework is that the more key practices you follow, the less risk you have on your project.

IEEE Standards

The IEEE has developed a wealth of standards that can be used in performing quality audits. Many of these standards

Figure 17
The Software CMM®

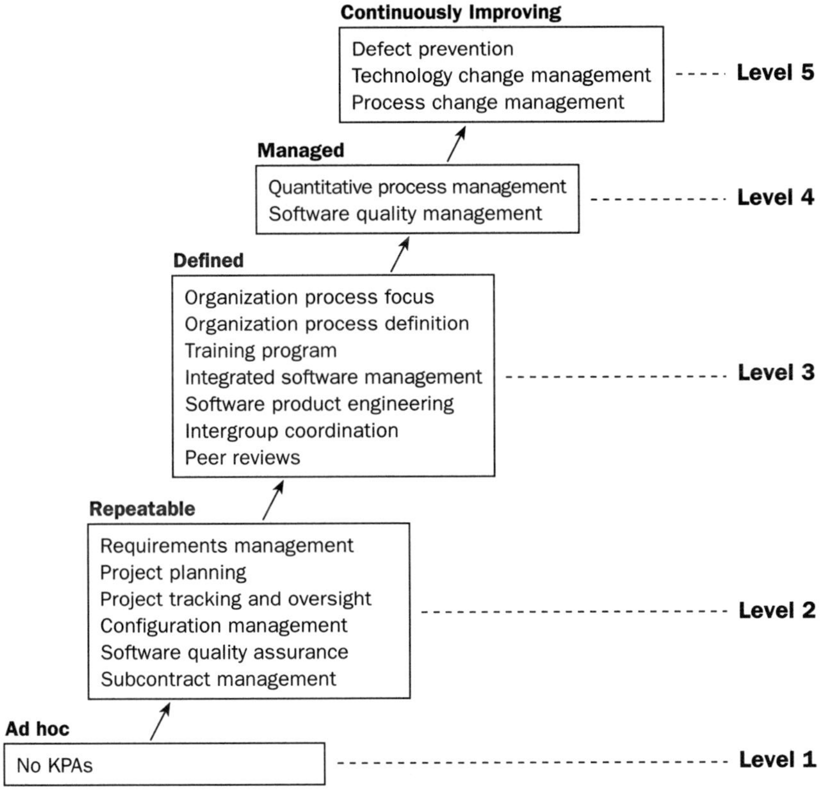

Source: Software Engineering Institute
Carnegie Mellon University

have been through multiple releases and have been revised to keep current with the latest understanding of industry best practices.

The IEEE includes the following standards in its 1997 version of the software collection of standards:

- 610.12-1990 IEEE Standard Glossary of Software Engineering Terminology

- 730-1989 IEEE Standard for Software Quality Assurance Plans
- 730.1-1995 IEEE Guide for Software Quality Assurance Planning
- 828-1990 IEEE Standard for Software Configuration Management Plans
- 829-1983 (R1991) IEEE Standard for Software Test Documentation
- 830-1993 IEEE Recommended Practice for Software Requirements Specifications
- 982.1-1988 IEEE Standard Dictionary of Measures to Produce Reliable Software
- 982.2-1988 IEEE Guide for the Use of IEEE Standard Dictionary of Measures to Produce Reliable Software
- 1002-1987 (R1992) IEEE Standard Taxonomy for Software Engineering Standards
- 1008-1987 (R1993) IEEE Standard for Software Unit Testing
- 1012-1986 (R1992) IEEE Standard for Software Verification and Validation Plans
- 1016-1987 (R1993) IEEE Recommended Practice for Software Design Descriptions
- 1016.1-1993 IEEE Guide to Software Design Descriptions
- 1028-1988 (R1993) IEEE Standard for Software Reviews and Audits

- 1042-1987 (R1993) IEEE Guide to Software Configuration Management
- 1044-1993 IEEE Standard Classification for Software Anomalies
- 1044.1-1995 IEEE Guide to Classification for Software Anomalies
- 1045-1992 IEEE Standard for Software Productivity Metrics
- 1058.1-1987 (R1993) IEEE Standard for Software Project Management Plans
- 1059-1993 IEEE Guide for Software Verification and Validation Plans
- 1061-1992 IEEE Standard for a Software Quality Metrics Methodology
- 1062-1993 IEEE Recommended Practice for Software Acquisition
- 1063-1987 (R1993) IEEE Standard for Software User Documentation
- 1074-1995 IEEE Standard for Developing Software Life Cycle Processes
- 1074.1-1995 IEEE Standard for Developing Software Life Cycle Processes
- 1175-1991 IEEE Standard Reference Model for Computing System Tool Interconnections
- 1209-1992 IEEE Recommended Practice for the Evaluation and Selection of CASE Tools

- 1219-1992 IEEE Standard for Software Maintenance
- 1220-1994 IEEE Trial-Use Standard for Application and Management of the Systems Engineering Process
- 1228-1994 IEEE Standard for Software Safety Plans
- 1233-1996 IEEE Guide for Developing System Requirements Specifications
- 1298-1992 (AS 3563.1-1991) IEEE Software Quality Management System, Part 1: Requirements
- 1348-1995 IEEE Recommended Practice for the Adoption of Computer-Aided Software Engineering (CASE) Tools
- 1420.1-1995 IEEE Standard for Information Technology—Software Reuse-Data Model for Reuse Library Interoperability: Basic Interoperability Data Model (BIDM)
- 1420.1a-1996 IEEE Guide for Information Technology—Software Reuse-Data Model for Reuse Library Interoperability: Asset Certification Framework
- 1430-1996 IEEE Guide for Information Technology—Software Reuse-Concept of Operations for Interoperating Reuse Libraries
- J-STD-016-1995 EIA/IEEE Interim Standard for Information Technology Software Life Cycle Processes Software Development Acquirer-Supplier Agreement

When using standards in support of process audits, you first select the set of standards that you think provides coverage across the processes you consider to be most important. As the IEEE list indicates, there is simply too much occurring in software development to attempt to audit and improve everything simultaneously. This is also the premise behind the five levels of the CMM®: First fix the processes at Level 2, then move on to fix the processes at Level 3, etc.

After identifying, for example, the five or six processes that you consider most important at this time, you can commence with the process audit.

Sample Audit Approach

To audit a process, you generally need to investigate three types of evidence:

- documentation regarding how the process is supposed to be performed,
- plans that demonstrate how a particular project is applying various processes, and
- process artifacts generated as a result of performing the process.

At a minimum, all evidence should be examined for internal integrity with each other. That is, plans should be consistent with the documentation that describes how to perform project activities. Similarly, process artifacts should be examined to ensure that plans are being followed.

In addition to being examined for internal integrity, the evidence is typically compared to a quality framework, such as the CMM®, IEEE, or International Standards Organization (ISO) standards, and evaluated in terms of compliance or noncompliance.

Virtually all quality audits are based on the premise that a set of defined processes exists and is being followed. Hence, an audit usually begins with a comprehensive comparison of the documented process descriptions to the reference quality framework. When the process documentation was developed using the quality framework for guidance, the audit for compliance is typically rather simple. Otherwise, it may require considerable investigative effort to determine conclusively whether or not process information required by the quality framework is missing from the defined process.

The next step in performing a process audit is typically to examine project plans and verify that:

- Plans conform to the defined processes.
- Plans are revised regularly to accommodate changing circumstances.
- Plans are updated to show the achievement of milestones and to document other status and tracking data.

Next, process artifacts are examined carefully to ensure that everything called for within the project plan is actually being done. For example, if the plan indicates that a CCB will be meeting once per month, there should be some evidence that these meetings are actually occurring. This evidence might take the form of:

- CCB meeting announcement memoranda,
- CCB meeting minutes, and
- Documented action items resulting from the CCB.

Similarly, if the project plan indicates that all software components will be inspected before being sent to the integration test group, there should be evidence that the inspections are occurring. As with the CCB process, this evidence may take the form of inspection meeting announcement memoranda or inspection meeting minutes. Additionally, individual defect logs resulting from preparing for the inspections, and documented rework estimates as a consequence of inspections, may be available.

As a general rule, a process that leaves behind evidence of the activities that are occurring is much easier to monitor and audit than a process that does not leave behind evidence.

You have a variety of options regarding who performs the audit. In all cases, you need to ensure that the audit team does not have a conflict of interest. Three possible approaches are:

- internal quality audits,
- external quality audits, and
- self-sponsored quality audits.

Internal Quality Audits

On an internal quality audit, your organization provides the personnel to conduct the quality audit. For example, when the software quality assurance group examines your project, that is an internal quality audit.

Internal quality audits are typically characterized by greater flexibility than external audits. Since the audit is internal, you are more free to interpret the quality framework in a manner that makes the most sense for your specific project. You might, for example, decide to outscope parts of the quality framework that are not applicable to your project. Additionally, with internal audits, you are usually more free to adjust the audit approach to meet your needs at that particular time in the project. For example, you might decide that a relatively simple one-day examination of process evidence will provide you with sufficient insight into process strengths and weaknesses.

Full-scale internal quality audits are commonly performed every one to two years, with smaller internal surveillance audits being conducted every two to four months.

External Quality Audits

External quality audits are conducted by one or more people external to your organization. Since larger companies are often divided into multiple organizations, one organization may be the source of an audit team that examines the processes and products of a different organization.

The distinguishing characteristic of external audits is that the audit team is typically completely free of any potential for conflict of interest. The audit team is there simply to examine the evidence, compare it to a quality framework, and document the results.

Since external audits are often used to compare an organization against a baseline of similar organizations, or against a series of historical audits, much less tailoring is typically done to either the quality framework or the audit methodology. Standardization is necessary to help ensure that the results of multiple audits are comparable, and that differences in results reflect differences within project processes rather than differences within the audit itself.

Since the release of the software CMM®, the government has become more active in performing quality audits. One approach, the software capability evaluation, was developed by SEI and is used by many government teams to assess the process maturity of software contractors. (More on this in Chapter 7.) In some cases, these external audits are conducted prior to a contract award, and a particular minimum maturity level may be a condition for award. In other cases, a minimum maturity level has to be maintained throughout contract performance. If the maturity level falls short of the required minimum, the contractor may lose incentive awards, may be issued a temporary stop work order, or may even lose the entire contract.

Self-Sponsored Quality Audits

As project manager, you always have the option to perform self-sponsored quality audits. Arguably, these are the highest leverage audits you can perform since you can take steps to ensure that the audit provides precisely the types of insights you need. The primary risk of self-sponsored audits is the obvious potential for a conflict of interest. For example, if executive management wants to see the results of the audit, some project managers might adjust the audit so that results look as favorable as possible. Conversely, if you are performing the audit simply for your own insight, and you and the project team are the only people seeing the results, there is much less potential for conflict of interest.

Self-sponsored audits are particularly valuable when you perform them in a manner similar to external audits. That is, once you've determined the quality frameworks (or subsets thereof) that you intend to comply with, and once you've determined the methodology you intend to follow to audit your processes, then you can continue using the same approach for each of your successive audits. This allows you to gain very detailed insights into what is, and is not, happening on your project. Additionally, it provides you very early warning when certain parts of the process start faltering or are otherwise being performed inadequately.

When performing a self-sponsored quality audit, take every reasonable precaution to avoid a conflict of interest. In particular, to the greatest extent possible, strive to conduct the audit as if it is an external software capability audit. This type of audit, and how you can best prepare for it, is discussed in detail in the next chapter.

7 External Software Capability Audits

"Don't torture the audit team."

As the first-line software project manager, your responsibility includes detecting and diagnosing software project control problems. As discussed in Chapter 6, you can use a variety of techniques that range from highly frequent and informal, to relatively rare and highly structured. However, periodically your project may be subject to an external software capability audit (ESCA). A common example of one type of ESCA is the software capability evaluation developed by the Software Engineering Institute at Carnegie Mellon University.

THE PURPOSE OF EXTERNAL AUDITS

ESCAs are performed by personnel outside your project, and typically from outside your company. For example, a government agency may want to investigate, prior to contract award, your organization's ability to produce software reliably. As part of that investigation, the agency may send a team to audit your project's process capability. Similarly, one company may want to investigate the software process capability of another company before teaming with that company or before agreeing to purchase software products and services from that company.

The result of these audits is usually a report that details the software process strengths and weaknesses that were detected on the projects included in the audit. At a minimum, areas of risk or weakness are highlighted and explained. Ideally, you will be provided with a copy of this report and you can use this information as a basis for performing ongoing risk management and process improvement.

EXTERNAL AUDIT APPROACH

To ensure consistency in the audit approach and in the development of results, nearly all external audits are conducted by following a well-defined method and by comparing your software processes and project-related artifacts (such as policies, plans, and standards) to the explicit and implicit requirements conveyed by one or more quality frameworks. Two of the quality frameworks used most often to audit software processes are:

- **Software Capability Maturity Model** (CMM®) developed by the Software Engineering Institute at Carnegie Mellon University (discussed in Chapter 6), and
- **ISO 9000**, developed by the International Standards Organization.

Although ISO 9000 was originally developed as a quality framework for the manufacturing community, a set of guidelines was developed to assist organizations in interpreting and applying the ISO requirements to organizations that are "manufacturing" software. These guidelines are contained in ISO 9000-3.

One of the most widely used types of software audits is the software capability evaluation (SCE). This method, which was also developed by the Software Engineering Institute at Carnegie Mellon University, is nearly always used in conjunction with the Software CMM® quality framework.

ESCAs tend to follow a fairly standard sequence of events. First, you are usually given relatively short notice that your project will be part of an audit. You might, for example, only be given a few weeks' notice. Indeed, in some instances, an audit team may arrive virtually unannounced. However, invariably, logistical and administrative details must be worked out jointly by the audit team and the organization being audited. These details may take a few weeks to stabilize. Examples of the types of details that need to be discussed, negotiated, and jointly understood include:

- the scope of the organization being audited,
- the projects within the organization that best represent organization processes and, hence, are the best projects to be audited,
- the types of evidence the audit team will need,
- the types of personnel the audit team will need to interview, and
- optionally, a "first-impression" investigation of process strengths and weaknesses, typically accomplished through the use of a comprehensive questionnaire.

Once an audit plan is developed, the audit team can begin examining organizational and project-level evidence and artifacts. These include:

- applicable organizational policies,
- procedures and activity descriptions,
- guidelines and templates,
- applicable standards,
- project plans,
- meeting minutes,

- action item logs, and
- status reports.

This list is not even close to exhaustive. The audit team will look at whatever evidence is available, given that the evidence:

- is applicable to the project or organization being audited, and
- potentially supports the audit team gaining insights into the satisfaction of requirements established by the quality framework.

STANDARD RULES FOR EXTERNAL AUDITORS

Essentially, all audit teams need to see proof that the following four rules are true:

1. Your project is following a defined process that complies with applicable standards.
2. You have developed and are maintaining all required plans.
3. The plans are consistent with the defined processes and comply with applicable standards.
4. The activities actually being performed on your project are consistent with applicable plans, defined processes, and standards.

To investigate the degree to which these four rules are true, the members of the audit team will carefully examine all appropriate evidence. Additionally, they will typically need to interview a representative number of organizational and project personnel. These interviews may involve executive management, middle management, first-line management, project technical personnel, project support personnel, functional area specialists, and anyone else who is a potential source of reliable information about the project.

The audit team gathers as much evidence as practical and then examines, organizes, distills, and eventually compares that evidence to the requirements of whatever quality framework they are auditing against (such as the Software CMM®). Finally, they develop a report documenting the results of the audit, and deliver that report to, at a minimum, the sponsor of the audit. If your project was involved in the audit, a copy of that report should eventually find its way to you.

External software capability audits all share the common characteristic of striving to be as objective as possible. It is generally in the best interests of all involved parties for the results of these audits to be highly accurate. However, it is not uncommon for external auditors to encounter unnecessary obstacles, and for you and your project personnel inadvertently to misrepresent your process capability.

PREPARING FOR AND PARTICIPATING IN AN EXTERNAL AUDIT

To avoid unnecessary problems, use the following guidelines to help you prepare your project, your personnel, and yourself for participating in an ESCA. All project personnel need to be able to help you:

- accurately present process capability,
- clearly show project strengths,
- facilitate the audit team's gathering of evidence, and
- support the audit team's accurate interpretation of evidence.

Although not all these guidelines will be applicable to all ESCAs, some are certain to be of value on any type of process audit that may be conducted on your project. Additionally, as a universal guideline, remember that the audit team members are looking for insights and, as a result, they tend to notice just about everything. Although only a subset of what they observe is directly applicable to the quality framework they are using, virtually everything they see and hear has potential implications concerning their audit. Hence, during the entire audit period, never relax your efforts.

Stay Organized

It is easy for projects to fall gradually into a state of general disarray. This does not mean that you have lost control of the project. It merely means that the organizational documentation, plans, and evidence are more or less scattered around in a variety of places. The lead time provided by the auditors may not be enough to allow you to organize your project plans, documentation, and evidence in a manner that permits easy review and examination. Should this happen, one of several undesirable developments may occur:

- Auditors may miss important information because they cannot find it.
- Auditors may overlook important information that is in front of them as a result of a confusing or misleading organization and presentation of the information.
- Auditors may spend excessive time reorganizing your information, and correspondingly less time analyzing that information for compliance.

Generally, external audits are carefully planned, and then conducted in accordance with the plan. A finite amount of time and resources is allocated for the various activities. The amount of information you put in front of the audit team normally does not have an impact on the plan. If the team has, for example, allocated two days for examining the plans, documents, defined procedures, and other evidence available on your project, then two days is how long it will take. Regardless of whether you give the audit team three or thirty notebooks of information, the auditors will attempt to perform the best examination they can within the time they've allocated.

You are nearly always better off when the auditors have more time to find evidence of compliance. When the auditors are looking for information, they will, at a certain point, conclude that since they are unable to find the evidence they are seeking, then that evidence must not exist. By keeping your project data organized, you substantially increase the likelihood that the audit team can find what they are looking for easily and efficiently.

Truly Be a Capable Project

Forget trying to fake your way through an audit. It almost never works, and it is quite painful for everyone involved. Indeed, if your primary objective is to manage a successful software project effectively, and if you are following the essential elements of good software project management, then your project may already be substantially in compliance with a software process quality framework. From that position, striving for complete compliance may be a relatively minor effort. By working to be a truly capable project, you stay focused on the primary objective of ensuring project success. However, in this instance, you are also using a quality framework to help you identify those areas on your project that may need special attention.

No single quality framework will be perfect for your project. Any framework is bound to impose requirements that seem excessive, unnecessary, or even inappropriate for your project. Most frameworks are sufficiently flexible that the audit team has some liberty to interpret the requirements of the framework as they apply to the circumstances and characteristics of a particular project. This is the traditional dichotomy between the "spirit" of compliance and the "letter" of compliance. Most teams expect to find at least an effort, on your part, to comply with the spirit or intent of any particular quality requirement.

Faking compliance with a requirement often involves making a very literal, simplistic interpretation; for example, making some trivial effort to produce something that is supposed to represent evidence, and then smugly producing that pseudo-evidence during the course of an audit. Keep in mind that most audit teams have participated in numerous audits. They've seen quite a variety of ways in which projects have legitimately achieved compliance. This experience serves as background for auditing your project.

Three things commonly happen when you put artificial evidence in front of an audit team:

- They almost instantly recognize it as artificial or at least highly suspect.
- They become more suspect of any future evidence you may offer.
- They become less confident about evidence that they previously considered acceptable.
- Your credibility, as well as the credibility of the project team, is potentially weakened.

In an effort to avoid these problems, some organizations or projects try, incredibly enough, to put together much more robust—and, they hope—more convincing, artificial evidence. This requires considerable time, effort, and money. However, most audit teams will recognize this data for what it is: very costly artificial evidence. Even worse, they now will believe virtually nothing that you say and very little of what they see, and they will feel compelled to dig very deeply to find the truth.

Know the Applicable Quality Framework

It is quite difficult to become, and to remain, in compliance with a quality framework purely by accident. Although nearly all successful projects, and numerous software process quality frameworks, share a considerable number of common characteristics, there are also key differences. Moreover, when the details of a quality framework are investigated and understood, you may find a large number of requirements embodied in that framework. For example, the Software CMM®, which is a five-level model, has more than a hundred requirements just within Level 2. The likelihood of accidentally being in compliance with such a large number of requirements is remote.

At a minimum, you as the software project manager should have a reasonably comprehensive understanding of any quality framework that applies to your project. There is no need to understand it as thoroughly as an auditor typically would, but you should be able to carry on a conversation about the quality framework and how the details of that framework apply to your project.

Most quality frameworks were developed over many years and involved large numbers of people who wrote, reviewed, argued about, negotiated, and wordsmithed every sentence within the framework. Simply reading the requirements of a framework, or attending a one-day orientation, will not be sufficient for you to acquire an adequate understanding of the framework. On the contrary, doing so will take a substantial amount of study.

As with software requirements, throughout the life of your project, you should periodically revisit and study the requirements of any applicable quality framework. Ask yourself the following questions:

- Does this requirement potentially apply to my project?
- Have I properly interpreted this requirement?
- Is the project currently in compliance with this requirement or, if not, has action been taken to bring the project into compliance?
- Is there an alternative approach available that allows me to achieve compliance more easily and effectively?

Occasionally you will look at the efforts you are making either to implement or to sustain compliance with a particular requirement and you will find yourself thinking, "This makes no sense." Learn to trust such thoughts. When something doesn't make sense it is usually a result of excessively concentrating on compliance, and not concentrating primarily on the success of your project. Remember: The primary objective is a successful project. Compliance with a quality framework is only a method for helping to ensure success. When you stay focused on project success, efforts to comply with quality frameworks become much more sensible.

Understand the Initial Questionnaire

Some ESCAs use an initial questionnaire as an early means for gathering information about the activities performed on one or more projects within the organization. Indeed, in some quality frameworks, the majority of the investigation is conducted by means of a questionnaire. Usually, the questions asked on these questionnaires are either publicly available or can be provided to you ahead of time.

Take the time to read, study, and understand the subtleties of the questions being asked. Be certain that you understand how each question applies to your project. Compare the questionnaire to the details of the quality framework that it supports. Understand the range of responses that you might have for a question, and how those responses might be interpreted in the context of compliance with the requirements of the framework.

Look for relationships between questions and your possible responses to those questions. For example, there will likely be questions where, if one is answered "no," then one or more other questions would also clearly have to be answered "no." For example, if you respond to the following statement with a "no":

> "A plan exists that details the schedule, milestones, and required resources for. . . ."

then it would be illogical to respond to the following statement with a "yes":

> "The plan was developed based on historical data and input from. . . ."

In some cases, such inconsistencies in your answers will be a result of interpreting one question using one context, and interpreting another question using a substantially different context or a different set of assumptions. By studying and attempting to answer the questionnaire, you will be able to identify those areas where the questionnaire is confusing, or even where the quality framework is hard to understand. This gives you the opportunity to explore these issues, discuss them with others, and take steps to increase your understanding of all three of the following elements:

- the quality framework,
- the questionnaire, and
- how best to apply the framework to your project.

It is certainly helpful for the project team to deal with these issues before the auditors arrive. Note that ultimately it is the last element—your understanding of how to apply the framework to your project—that is the most important. Understanding the questionnaire is a direct and highly effective method for helping you achieve this goal.

Additionally, consider using the questionnaire on a monthly or quarterly basis to help you monitor the overall health of your project.

Develop Your Own Investigative Questions and Answers

A critical part of some ESCAs is the interviewing of management and technical personnel. The questions asked during these interviews are often prepared prior to the conduct of the interview. The questions usually are designed to elicit the greatest amount of usable information in the least possible time. Unlike the questions on the questionnaires, these are not "yes/no" or multiple choice questions, but are instead more like essay questions.

As part of preparing for an ESCA (and, more importantly, as part of monitoring the status of your project), you should periodically assume the role of an external auditor and develop a set of questions that relates to the requirements of the quality framework. These questions should help you investigate whether or not:

- activities are occurring according to plans,
- plans are being maintained in accordance with applicable processes, and
- everything is in compliance with the quality framework and any other applicable standards.

These are issues you want to monitor on an ongoing basis regardless of whether or not your project has been selected for an ESCA.

It is relatively easy to develop questions that facilitate gaining insights into process capability and framework compliance if you remember a few principles:

- Ask general, sweeping questions that are conducive to long answers.
- Ask questions that, without rewording, are understandable by both senior and junior project personnel.
- Ask questions that allow functional specialists and experts to provide long, detailed answers, but that do not prevent responses from nonspecialists.
- Ask questions that are not targeted to a specific level of management.

Examples of questions that do not meet these criteria include:

- Do you manage the requirements on your project?
- Are you using a configuration management tool?
- Please explain how you analyze the design of low-level modules and estimate the number of user inputs, user outputs, internal files, external interfaces, and reports that are required, and how you use that information to develop software size estimates.
- Please describe how you developed the quality assurance plan.

- How often do you have meetings to track the progress of the subcontractor's work?

Instead of using questions like these, consider using questions similar to the following:

- Please describe how requirements are managed by the project.
- Please describe any automated support you use that assists with performing configuration management.
- Please explain how you estimate the time and effort required to implement a designated part of the system, or how you verify that someone else's estimates are reasonable.
- Please explain any responsibilities you had, or activities you performed, that were related to the development of the quality assurance plan.
- Please describe any involvement you have in monitoring and managing the work being performed by the subcontractor.

Remember that your objective is to gain detailed insights into the current activities and relevant history of your project. To ensure that you gain comprehensive and complete insights, develop a sufficient number of questions to cover all major areas of requirements within the quality framework that you are using.

Avoid asking one question for each quality requirement. Instead, each question should allow someone potentially to speak for two to five minutes. A good set of approximately ten to twenty questions will normally be sufficient for an interview of about thirty to forty-five minutes' duration. Typically, this is enough time to develop a good understanding of the interviewee's day-to-day activities and his or her perception of the major activities occurring within the project.

Conduct Dry Runs of Interviews

Now that you have a set of questions that is likely similar to the questions that an audit team will ask, you can conduct a dry run of the ESCA interviews. Ideally, have several project personnel perform the role of the interview team. Designate one person to ask the questions, and have the others take notes.

Interview the project personnel one at a time. Each interview should simulate, as closely as possible, the actual interview experience. For example, the following steps should occur for each interview:

- Confirm that the interviewee is the person you were expecting.
- Welcome the interviewee and thank him or her for taking the time to support the process audit.
- Introduce the interview team members.
- Tell the interviewee that he or she will be asked a series of questions and that:
  - One person (that is, the lead interviewer) will be asking the majority of the questions, but that other team members may occasionally ask a question.
  - The questions are intended to elicit long answers, so please speak freely.
  - Some of the questions will overlap with other questions, so it is fine to repeat something previously said and add more details.

  - If you do not understand a question, please ask for a clarification.

  - There are no wrong answers.

  - Ultimately, the interview team is simply trying to understand what you do, and how the project looks from your perspective.

- Ask the interviewee if he or she has any questions at this time.

- Ask the interviewee the prepared questions; allow ESCA team members the opportunity to asked additional clarifying or follow-up questions.

- When you have asked all the prepared questions, or when you have used the time allotted, conclude the interview.

- Ask the interviewee if there are any last comments he or she would like to make.

- Inform the interviewee that the questions asked and the answers provided are all confidential, and ask the interviewee to refrain from discussing the interview with anyone.

- Thank the interviewee again for his or her support.

As indicated, although during the interview you are asking a prepared set of questions, it is sometimes necessary to ask additional questions. These are questions that either help elicit additional details from the interviewee or help clarify something already said.

When conducting these dry-run interviews, rotate project members through the interview team. It is very hard to observe how an interview is going when you are the one being interviewed. On the other hand, it is relatively easy to observe when you are watching someone else being interviewed.

The overall objective of conducting the dry-run interviews is not to have people practice their answers until they have them memorized. Indeed, that would actually be detrimental (more on this later). Instead, the objectives are (1) to gain real insights into your project, and (2) to allow project personnel to become more comfortable with the entire interview process and more comfortable with their ability to articulate clearly and easily what they know.

Cross-Reference Your Evidence to the Quality Framework

Another important step you can take when preparing for an ESCA is to develop a cross-reference or mapping between your project evidence and the quality framework you are using. To make life easier for the auditors, organize this mapping according to the requirements of the framework. That is, list the requirements in the order they are found in the framework and, for each, show where there is evidence of compliance. As noted, this evidence may be in the form of policies, activity descriptions, standards, meeting minutes, project notebooks, various logs, reports, and even e-mail archives.

Clearly, one objective is to ensure that you have all the evidence required for the quality framework you are using. Two important types of evidence are:

- evidence that required items exist, and
- evidence that required processes are occurring.

Although no two quality frameworks are identical, they usually share common characteristics. For example, most frameworks require that plans are developed and used, and that activities occur in accordance with the plans. Indeed, a single quality framework may require different plans for a large variety of activities. These need not be physically separate plans, but the identified activities must occur according to some type of documented plan. Examples of different types of plans that may be required include:

- project plan,
- risk management plan,
- staffing plan,
- training plan,
- requirements management plan,
- configuration management plan,
- quality assurance plan, and
- test plan.

All these plans constitute one type of evidence (evidence that required items exist). Of course, it is not sufficient merely to have plans. The plans must be kept current, and the activities must occur more or less in accordance with the plans. This results in the second type of evidence: evidence that required activities are occurring. Ideally, your cross-reference matrix can point to several different types of evidence that all provide support for the fact that a particular activity is being done.

For example, suppose that your quality framework requires you to perform comprehensive risk management. The fact that you have a policy for performing risk management, an activity description that explains how to perform risk management, and a detailed risk management plan, still does not prove that risks are actually being managed on your project. As evidence of active risk management, you should be able to show additional evidence such as:

- meeting memoranda that announce the occurrence of risk management meetings,
- risk management meeting minutes,
- action items (from an action item log) that clearly resulted from efforts to manage risks,
- regularly updated risk-tracking artifacts (such as a "top ten risks" spreadsheet),
- regular updates to your risk management plan, and
- entries in the project decision log that are clearly related to risk management.

Generally, the lower the mapping between the requirements of your quality framework and the evidence you have to prove satisfaction of those requirements, the more believable your assertion that the requirements are being met.

Ensure Excellent On-Site Logistics

Most ESCAs are characterized by at least part of the audit being conducted on-site at a location where actual project work is occurring. This is especially true when interviewing project personnel. However, the audit team may also elect to audit documents and evidence at the on-site location. In light of the large number of people typically interviewed, and the considerable number of activities occurring during the on-site period of an ESCA, the on-site visit is usually quite carefully planned and conducted in accordance with a detailed (sometimes down to the minute) schedule.

It is to your advantage to make every reasonable effort to ensure that the entire on-site visit occurs as smoothly as possible. A well-orchestrated, efficient on-site visit implies a well-orchestrated, efficient organization. In theory, if the on-site visit degenerates into confusion because your project personnel are late for interviews, the wrong people are showing up for interviews, the ESCA team is accidentally held by Security for half a day, etc., none of this is supposed to influence the ESCA team in the slightest. After all, they are there simply to evaluate project evidence and processes with regard to the requirements of the quality framework. However, the typical ESCA team will find it very difficult to believe that you have well-planned and well-run projects when the on-site visit logistics are completely chaotic.

Additionally, poor on-site logistics may force the ESCA team to start making changes to the on-site plan and schedule. These changes may include selecting new or different project personnel for project interviews. In some cases, these new interviewees may be given only an hour or so of advance notice. If these personnel were not included in your efforts to prepare for the ESCA, they may perform weakly when being interviewed.

Respect Confidentiality Requests

Generally, ESCA teams establish a variety of policies or rules with regard to nondisclosure, confidentiality, and the handling of sensitive or proprietary information. Be sure that you:

- understand all such restrictions,
- communicate these restrictions to your project personnel, and
- ensure compliance with the restrictions.

Definitely avoid using recording devices. Most people, including those on ESCA teams, become uncomfortable when they realize they are being recorded. You want the ESCA team members to feel like they can continue asking questions if they feel the need. Remember, if they are continuing to ask questions, it likely means that they have not yet heard what they need to hear. If recording devices are inadvertently causing the ESCA team to ask fewer questions, they simply may not hear enough information to ascertain that your project is meeting the requirements of the quality framework.

Even worse, recording devices may inhibit your own project personnel from speaking freely. This too can lead to inadequate information being communicated. Even if the ESCA team is relatively persistent in asking additional questions while striving to find additional information, if your project personnel are giving very brief answers with little or no content, the ESCA team members may not hear what they need to hear.

Additionally, don't grill the interviewees for the exact questions asked by the ESCA team. First, ESCA teams tend to change at least some of the questions between interviews. They are especially likely to shift questions toward the end of the on-site period. By attempting to capture and document actual questions, you may cause people to fail to listen carefully to the question actually being asked. An ESCA team may revise a question slightly in an effort to elicit a more accurate response. If project personnel have been rehearsing their answers, they may unintentionally answer the original question, miss the changes, and not provide the information the ESCA team is seeking.

Although the ESCA team members don't need to hear everything from everyone, they do need to hear important information from at least a few people. Hence, it's usually to your disadvantage if everyone has been studying actual questions and thereby gravitating toward saying the same thing.

Avoid Short Answers

ESCAs are an exercise in positive proof. The team has to find the evidence it needs. Otherwise, one or more requirements will be deemed unsatisfied. Again, the general rule used by most ESCA teams is: If they can't find it, or if they don't hear about it, then it doesn't exist or it's not happening. Therefore, short answers reveal very little positive proof of compliance.

Presuming that your answers contain usable information, the more you say, the more evidence you are providing. And virtually all ESCAs base their results entirely on the actual evidence found—not evidence that is believed to exist, or that might exist, or that used to exist but is no longer available.

Moreover, consistently short responses tend to indicate:

- a comprehensive lack of understanding of the requirements of the quality framework,
- someone who truly does not know what is happening around them, or
- someone who does not know how they are supposed to be performing their responsibilities.

Of course, some people are simply shy and they tend naturally to provide short answers. Encourage these people to be as forthcoming as possible.

Avoid Quoting the Quality Framework

As discussed, you should strive to understand the requirements of your quality framework. However, do not study it so thoroughly that you end up quoting expressions or statements directly from the framework. Quoting may give the impression that the statements being expressed are a "studied" or memorized response, rather than an actual response. If so, such statements are generally taken to be unreliable.

For example, suppose your quality framework contains the phrase: "A mechanism exists to ensure. . . ." During an interview, you do not want project personnel to say something like, "We use a mechanism to ensure. . . ." It sounds completely artificial.

If you do find it necessary or convenient to use terms or phrases directly from the quality framework, be sure to augment those statements with organizational or project-specific terms and expressions.

Resist Trying to Look Perfect

As with a job interview, it is reasonable to strive to look as good as possible during an ESCA. However, realistically, there is no such thing as a project where everything is going perfectly. This is especially true on software projects. We always have problems. Unsuccessful projects keep having the same problems. Successful projects have constantly changing problems. But all software projects have problems.

No single quality framework (or, for that matter, no combination of quality frameworks) will guarantee that all potential problems will be prevented. Instead, the proponents of a quality framework typically assert that if you meet the requirements of the framework, then you:

- are more likely to have a successful project, and
- are less likely to fall victim to the common problems that occur on most projects (that are not using the framework).

So, by using the framework, you should have fewer problems and a more successful project. However, you can be completely in compliance with the framework and still have all types of major problems occurring. This is not necessarily a reflection that you are doing anything wrong, nor that there is something wrong with the framework. It may just be that you are developing a very complex system under extremely challenging circumstances.

The ESCA team knows this. They know that real projects have real problems, even when they are completely in compliance with a quality framework. In theory, they are likely having fewer problems than they otherwise would have had, but there is no expectation from an ESCA team that compliance equates to a problem-free project. Hence, when a project looks or sounds "too perfect," almost any ESCA team will immediately become suspicious.

For example, it would be highly unusual to hear the following assertions when interviewing project personnel from a more or less normal software project:

- "We regularly hold software inspections, but we don't have any defect logs because our software doesn't have defects in it."

- "We appreciate it when quality assurance prevents us from putting changed software into production. Around here, quality always come ahead of schedules or deadlines."

- "There hasn't been any need for us to update the requirements specification because the requirements have been completely stable for the last two years."

- "Oh, I have no problem at all filling out four different timesheets; after all, we certainly don't want to inconvenience the accounting clerks."

- "We constantly seek daily oversight by senior management because it is always so helpful."

Clearly, there are things you might say in the interests of trying to look as good as possible that actually come across as, if not outright false, then at least exaggerated. And if the ESCA team begins to suspect your credibility, then everything you state during the interview becomes questionable.

Slow Down the Interviews

There can be a tendency during the interview process for the interviewee to try and speak quickly, answer briefly, and get the interview over as soon as possible. You should strive to do just the opposite.

You need to ensure that what you say actually gets into the notes being taken by the ESCA team. They are not professional stenographers. Their note-taking skills are probably just about as good (or as bad) as any average person's. If your information does not get into their notes, they may not remember it later. To help ensure that all important information is captured in the ESCA team's notes, take the following steps:

- Speak slowly.

- Repeat anything important.

- If they don't ask, tell them anyway.

These steps will have the effect of slowing down the interview and improving the transfer of information from the interviewee to the ESCA team. Speaking slowly will help ensure that the information you provide is captured by multiple note-takers. Repeating important information will help ensure that this information is documented in multiple places within their notes. If you know that there are important requirements in the quality framework that seem indirectly related to the question they just asked, then include that additional information in your response. If the auditors do not need the information, they will just ignore it. But, it could be that they were striving to ask "nonleading" questions (a very common practice) and that the additional information you are providing is actually highly relevant to what they are looking for.

Conduct End-of-Day Debriefings Carefully

It is natural during an ESCA to try to do whatever is reasonable to achieve a successful outcome. Therefore, you may want to consider having an end-of-day debriefing during the on-site period. These debriefings should involve only you and the project personnel who were interviewed during that particular day.

During these debriefings, ask that day's interviewees about any general impressions they have regarding areas of emphasis or importance. Stress that you do not want details of questions asked nor their responses to those questions. Instead, ask them how they think their interviews went, and ask them to discuss any high-level observations they made during the interviewing process. In particular, you should ask if there is any general advice they could offer to those who have yet to be interviewed.

Some advice may be trivial, but useful to know. This might include suggestions like:

- "Don't bring a notebook because they don't want you taking notes."
- "They'll be asking you to sign a confidentiality agreement, and they've left a copy out in the room in case you want to read it ahead of time."

- "Arrive out at the building early; it'll take at least twenty minutes to get processed through security and escorted to the interview location."

Other advice will be more substantial, and may be similar to the following:

- "They seem to be concentrating entirely in the area of requirements management; they didn't ask me a single question from the other nine areas of the quality framework."

- "They really want dates and durations for any training courses you attended that were provided by the company. Be sure to bring that information with you."

Of course, some of the advice may be wrong or misleading, so consider any advice carefully and use it cautiously. For example, the fact that the ESCA team concentrated only on requirements management for a single day may indicate that they are completely done with that area and they will be investigating a different area the next day.

Nevertheless, use the end-of-day debriefings to help you gain insight into the objectives and methods of the ESCA team, and to help you prepare the people who have not yet been interviewed.

Conduct Start-of-Day Debriefings Carefully

Consider starting each day of the on-site period by having a brief meeting with the group of people scheduled to be interviewed that day. During this meeting, review the basics for having a successful interview. For example, you may want to stress one or more of the following principles:

- Talk only about what you know for a fact—avoid speculation.

- Do not exaggerate, and do not minimize or trivialize.
- If you don't understand a question, ask for clarification.
- After being asked a question, take a brief moment to compose your thoughts.
- Speak slowly and clearly; give the team time to take notes.
- Feel free to repeat anything you've already told them if you consider that information important.
- If, later in the interview, you realize that you answered a previous question impartially or incorrectly, verbally express this, and then provide the additional or correct information.
- Do not complain about those parts of the quality framework that you think are really stupid. The ESCA team is not responsible for determining the appropriateness of the quality framework; they are only authorized to investigate degrees of compliance.

In addition, you should also provide any additional suggestions or advice that you think will help the interviewees understand and respond to the types of questions being asked by the ESCA team. At a minimum, relate:

- anything that you've learned (during the end-of-day debriefings) about what seems to be particularly important to this ESCA team; and
- an edited summary of the advice offered by those already interviewed.

Start-of-day briefings are a very careful balancing act. You want to help the interviewees be sufficiently informed that their contributions are highly valuable. However, you want to avoid interviewees accidentally becoming misdirected or unduly nervous and thereby inadvertently interfering with the accurate, concise, clear, and effective communication of information to the ESCA team.

Of course, for the start-of-day briefings (as well as the end-of-day debriefings), do nothing that violates any confidentiality or nondisclosure agreements that the ESCA team has invoked.

In Your Weakest Areas, Try for Partial or Alternative Compliance

This particular point of guidance is likely to be something you learned back in junior high school. The primary issue here is that a "questionably compliant answer" is infinitely better than a nonanswer. Hence, you and your project personnel should strive to avoid blatant, obvious, and incontestable noncompliances. For example:

- Suppose your quality framework contains a requirement that "A defined procedure exists that explains how to. . . ." A five-page documented procedure might get the ESCA team members arguing among themselves about whether or not your defined procedure has sufficient detail to result in consistent performance, but at least a defined procedure exists. No procedure at all guarantees instant, complete consensus that your project is clearly noncompliant.

- Suppose your quality framework contains a requirement that "Executive management regularly monitors the status and progress of the project." Executive status meetings held about every three to six months may seem infrequent, and don't seem particularly regular, but they demonstrate that at least some level of executive oversight is occurring.

Most quality frameworks define only what needs to be occurring, and what products or artifacts need to be produced or used. How you perform those activities and construct those artifacts is left to the organization or project. There are a virtually unlimited variety of ways that you can implement compliant processes and products. Hence, ESCA teams are quite used to looking at a process that is unique to an organization or project, and evaluating that process relative to the framework. The fact that they have never seen exactly that process before is not uncommon. Indeed, it's the norm.

Since the ESCA team will be interpreting the quality framework with regard to your project, give the team as much opportunity as possible to interpret compliance with the quality framework creatively. Always have something that you can show to the ESCA team, and always have some type of story to tell regarding how your activities and products satisfy the requirements of the quality framework. Avoid obvious noncompliances that prevent any type of partial credit.

Strive to Exceed Minimum Quality Requirements

Some quality frameworks are based on "levels," where you become progressively more compliant by moving to progressively higher levels in the framework. The Software CMM®, for example, is a five-level model where Level 1 is the lowest and is characterized by the least mature processes, and Level 5 is the highest and is characterized by the most mature processes.

Suppose that you have a contractual requirement to maintain an operational capability on your project of at least Level 2. Also suppose that a government agency is sending an audit team to investigate your level of compliance. One approach is to focus on ensuring that your project satisfies all the Level 2 requirements. However, a better approach will be to show that you are solidly on your way to complying with Level 3.

For example, Level 3 has a set of requirements related to the performance of peer reviews. Hence, if your project is performing code reviews, walkthroughs, or inspections, you might be able to demonstrate compliance with requirements above the minimum required level.

Being only minimally compliant is generally high risk. If you falter anywhere, then you fall below minimums. By striving to achieve a level of compliance above the minimum required, you introduce somewhat of a reserve capability that can more easily accommodate minor fluctuations in performance without necessarily causing you to fall below minimum requirements.

Don't Torture the Audit Team

This is a minor point, but something that you may want to pay attention to. Whenever an audit team arrives, you will find yourself having to maintain a careful balance between being a hospitable host, and yet avoiding even the appearance of attempting to influence the ESCA team inappropriately. For example, there is certainly no problem with providing free coffee to the team. However, a catered lobster lunch will invariably look like you are trying to buy (versus legitimately achieve) a favorable report from the ESCA team.

Auditors are often treated like they are some type of enemy. Needless to say, most auditors don't think of themselves this way. Many sincerely try to help you come through the audit as successfully as possible. They will—within the limits of professional integrity and the outright constraints imposed by the quality framework—make every effort to help you come through the audit successfully. Typically, they will do this in spite of everything you might be doing to irritate and annoy them. Nevertheless, the best approach is to seek a balance where you are hospitable to the audit team, but not excessively so.

Read Between the Lines of the Audit Report

No one ever complains about positive results documented in an audit report. Hence, the ESCA team really hopes that you are in compliance. If you are, it is much easier for them to write the final report because the report will generally receive much less scrutiny. However, in any areas where your project has noncompliances, weaknesses, violations, or anything else that reflects an unmet requirement, then the audit team has to document the issues very carefully and phrase every statement as precisely, accurately, and unambiguously as possible.

In virtually any audit, there are areas where a project is clearly in compliance. There is also the possibility that there are other areas where the project is clearly not in compliance. None of these presents a problem. However, there are almost always a few areas where compliance is really difficult to confirm or reject. In these areas, the ESCA team will reevaluate evidence, reinterpret the quality framework, gather additional information, and otherwise do whatever is possible to make an objective determination regarding compliance or noncompliance. Even if the audit team finally takes the position that you are in compliance, they are likely to send a message to you via the audit report.

Accordingly, be sure to read the audit report carefully. Look for any statements that contain qualifiers, conditional expressions, or subtle (and maybe not so subtle) warnings.

Consider the following examples:

- *What the report states*: "Nearly all requirements were managed in accordance with the project's defined procedures, even though a recent project reorganization has caused some minor inconsistencies in the way requirements are handled."

  What the ESCA team might have meant: Although the project used to manage requirements in a compliant manner, due to the reorganization, the project looks to be on the verge of losing control over its requirements management processes.

- *What the report states*: "Plans were developed prior to activities occurring, and were updated whenever there was slack time available for administrative work."

  What the ESCA team might have meant: Keeping plans current seemed to be a low priority. Unless slack time becomes available, plans will become outdated.

- *What the report states*: "It appeared that the project was beginning to use a configuration management tool to ensure consistency in configuration control activities."

  What the ESCA team might have meant: Configuration control is weak and will apparently depend upon the successful deployment and use of a new automated tool.

As shown in these examples, any given assertion can be interpreted in a variety of ways. Unless a statement is outright absolute, there may be more to the message than what is written. Most of the time you know the relative strengths and weaknesses of your project and you will have no trouble getting the real messages from the report. Just make sure that you look for them.

In the same vein, virtually all ESCA teams are required to make one or more judgment calls during the performance of an audit. In some cases, the audit team will give you the benefit of the doubt, note that you are in compliance, and then send some type of message via the ESCA report that the area was hard to investigate, or that compliance was achieved but seemed fragile or otherwise at risk. Be sure that you take steps to address these issues.

It is very common, and sometimes required, for an ESCA team to perform a follow-up audit by using the report resulting from a previous ESCA. After carefully studying the report, they usually conduct another round of evidence reviews and interviews. Using the above examples, if an ESCA team returns a year later and finds persistent inconsistencies in requirements management, plans that have not been updated, and a failure to implement the configuration management tool successfully, the audit will likely have a very different outcome.

Start Preparing Now

Although this entire chapter seems dedicated to helping you prepare for an ESCA, there really is a more important motivation. Nearly all the activities presented as part of preparing for an ESCA are excellent ways for you to gain insight into the overall health of your project. Even if you are not yet aware of your project being selected for an audit, to be a successful manager, you still must know your project's areas of strength and weakness.

The next several chapters examine how to detect and recover from a variety of control problems. However, keep in mind that you should periodically ask yourself about the state of your project with regard to compliance with an overall quality framework. If necessary, you can always conduct your own audit of the activities occurring on your task. This is not an external audit, of course, but as long as you strive for objectivity, you can still derive all the benefits of adherence to a quality framework.

You should start preparing now for an audit of your project against a quality framework. If your company or organization does not use such frameworks, then consider obtaining a copy of the Software CMM® from the Software Engineering Institute.

Study the quality framework and compare it to the activities being performed and evidence being generated by your project. Wherever you identify weaknesses, take steps to implement corrective action in a manner that makes business sense for your project. In other words, do not allow this effort to degenerate into an exercise of merely achieving compliance. Instead, strive for the far more important objective of improving your project's overall likelihood of success via use of the quality framework.

Make such actions a regular and periodic part of monitoring and controlling your project, and you will typically reduce overall project risk, increase the likelihood of project success, and improve the quality of the products you are producing. As a side benefit, you'll also have far fewer concerns in the event you are told that an external team will be arriving on Monday to audit your project's activities and records. Additionally, the insights you gain as a result of using quality frameworks and performing quality audits are an excellent foundation for you to perform any necessary project recovery efforts.

8 Recovering Projects from Insufficient Control

"When implementing additional controls, always strive to implement the least amount of control necessary to achieve the intended results."

When you are in control of a project, your expectations of future events are sufficiently accurate that your plans are relatively stable and you are taking actions in advance of events. These actions improve your ability to take advantage of positive developments and to mitigate or prevent negative developments.

Insufficient control of a project is characterized by just the opposite: Events keep occurring that are not expected, and you spend the majority of your time reacting to developments instead of controlling those developments.

IDENTIFYING THE SYMPTOMS OF INSUFFICIENT CONTROL

A simple measure of the degree to which you are in control of a project is the ratio of time spent responding to expected events versus time spent responding to unexpected events. The most significant symptom of insufficient project control is when you find yourself spending more time responding to unexpected events than you spend responding to expected and planned events. At this point, you are no longer controlling the project. The project is, literally, controlling you.

Other major symptoms of insufficient project control include:

- accelerating loss of project personnel,
- loss of configuration control,
- disproportionate effort on nonengineering activities,
- inability to finish planning,
- excessive time spent doing rework,
- frequent renegotiation of commitments, and
- persistent need to work required overtime.

Each of these areas is somewhat subjective. For example, what is an "excessive" amount of time when it comes to rework: 20 percent of the original development time? 200 percent? However, in the absence of discrete formulas quantifying project control effectiveness, an accumulation of subjective evidence can be highly convincing. If you recognize any one of these symptoms on your project, be suspect. If you see two or more, take action.

Accelerating Loss of Project Personnel

One of the greatest determinants of project success is the team that you put together. Studies have reported productivity differences of 10 to 1, and even as high as 27 to 1. Building and protecting an effective team is one of the most important actions you take. You don't go through the time and effort of staffing and building a team with the intent that key people will start leaving during the middle of the project. Certainly, some attrition is to be expected—indeed, planned for—but an accelerating loss of project personnel means that something has gone drastically wrong.

Issues relating to team building and staff retention were discussed in the "fundamentals" chapters. However, one of the main reasons people leave a project is the belief that the project is failing and recovery is either impossible or simply not worth the effort. Projects fail as a result of a variety of factors, and insufficient project control is certainly one of the most significant.

Loss of Configuration Control

Loss of configuration control is a very common, incredibly wasteful problem on software projects. When a customer calls and tells you that a problem fixed in an earlier release has reappeared in the most recent release, you've lost control of the configuration.

You may recall from the earlier chapters that configuration control consists of ensuring the integrity of software through access control, version control, baselining, and periodic baseline audits. A primary objective of configuration control is to ensure that developed software components are not lost, and fixed components remain fixed. When older versions of software components are accidentally mixed in with new releases, then enhancements, new developments, and defect corrections can all be lost. When loss of configuration control is sufficiently severe, project managers—and sometimes entire companies—have been forced to order a product recall.

Control of the products and software components you are developing is central to overall project control. Insufficient control of configurations is essentially synonymous with insufficient project control.

Disproportionate Effort on Nonengineering Activities

On all projects, it is necessary to spend time on activities other than the central engineering activities of requirements specification, design, software development, documentation development, testing, etc. Quality assurance and configuration management, for example, are two activities that are necessary but are not generally considered engineering. Additionally, there is the need to hire staff, provide training, conduct status and review meetings, develop reports, deliver briefings, etc.

However, the purpose of the project is to deliver the expected product, ideally, within time and budget targets. When projects are falling out of control, it is very common (and not necessarily wrong) to try to regain control by having additional meetings. However, when developers are sitting in meetings, they are not doing development. If the project continues to slip further out of control, there is commonly an increase in the frequency and type of executive management oversight reviews, and a corresponding increase in the number of project and team status meetings. On some projects, this has deteriorated to the point of having daily meetings.

You can monitor the ratio of time your project personnel spend doing work versus the time they spend having to talk about their work. If progressively more time is going to nonengineering activities, it is almost always a sign of slipping project control.

Inability to Finish Planning

Plans take time to develop. Often, the project is already underway. As initial versions of the plans become available, they are sent out to senior management for review. If the plans keep being returned, with indications to make changes and to resubmit for another review, it indicates a potential problem.

When project management and senior management cannot reach agreement on the project plan, it is usually because of significant differences in expectations regarding the amount of time, effort, or money needed to deliver the final product. Such differences are often based on fundamentally different assumptions regarding project requirements. When the various layers of management cannot come to agreement on a project plan, the planning process, of course, drags on.

In parallel, there may be ongoing and rapid changes within the project itself. In light of these changes, the project manager may find it necessary to make major changes to the next version of the plan. Upon receiving the updated plan, senior management may be surprised by the magnitude of the changes, feel compelled to make its own markups (again), and still not approve the plan.

It is not uncommon for projects to be well into the design effort, and sometimes into development, without an approved plan. Since the project plan is the primary expression of the project control activities, an inability to get an approved plan in place may indicate that controlling actions are being hampered or delayed.

Excessive Time Spent Doing Rework

The purpose of all the activities occurring on a project (management, technical, and support) is to build a working product. There is a discrete point in time when a given team member asserts that his or her software is complete—and working. This may be the time that the developer submits the software for a formal software inspection, or submits the software for integration testing. Any additional time spent to correct deficiencies found during inspection, testing, or beta or field usage should be tracked as rework time.

It is virtually impossible to develop a complex system that is defect-free on the first try. However, the minimum objective is to make it as good as possible. Some amount of rework is normal and expected. But how much?

You need to set a target for what you consider to be an acceptable amount of rework. Use any available historical data or, in the absence of data, your best estimate based on current, recent, or similar project activities. If rework ratios start exceeding your thresholds, consider the possibility that controls are insufficient.

Frequent Renegotiation of Commitments

Project plans are characterized in part by a set of negotiated commitments between you and other managers or groups. As circumstances change, it is usually necessary to reexamine commitments and determine if (1) they still make sense, and (2) you can still honor your part of the commitment.

In the case of commitments that no longer make sense, you will need to meet with affected individuals and groups, present your rationale, and request renegotiations. Since these are commonly caused by changes in events or circumstances beyond your control, such renegotiations are not usually symptomatic of insufficient controls.

However, if the need to renegotiate a commitment is not caused by external factors, but is instead a result of internal factors such as falling behind schedule, excessive defects, or understaffing, then it might indicate the need for additional project controls.

Persistent Need to Work Required Overtime

Most software projects are planned on the assumption that a full-time professional will work a 40-hour week. Most software professionals routinely work more than that. However, their motivation for overtime is typically their own professional standards and their motivation to deliver high-quality code on time.

When projects start having problems, it is not uncommon to see overtime switch from discretionary to mandatory. The latter typically happens by decree. The project manager calls a meeting and announces that henceforth, everyone will work 10-hour days, 6-day weeks. Of course, all vacation is cancelled. When such extreme measures seem necessary, it is a clear indication that the project is out of control and has been for a substantial amount of time.

DETERMINING TYPES OF ADDITIONAL CONTROL

Almost universally, the best way to respond to insufficient control is to implement additional control. Determining the appropriate types of additional control is a three-step process:

1. Identify symptoms of insufficient control.
2. Perform root cause analysis (i.e., what is behind the symptom?).
3. Outline a new control process.

When you see any of the symptoms discussed, or other symptoms that you consider indicative of insufficient project control, you need to determine what is actually behind those symptoms. In the absence of hard metrics and historical data, you can attempt root cause analysis based on your own experience. However, to the greatest degree possible, strive to find causes by studying actual data.

Typically, an area of insufficient control may manifest itself in several symptoms. For example, the mere absence of a project plan can lead to every one of the symptoms described. Additionally, the lack of several control mechanisms may all be combining their impact within one symptom. In any event, you need to analyze the symptoms carefully and ask repeatedly, "What is causing this to happen?" If need be, bring in some of your senior technical personnel for a brainstorming or Delphi session.

When you think you've found a cause for a symptom, ask again, "What is causing this to happen?" Keep going backward through the causal chain until you think you have found the root cause. You should regard as root causes those areas that you can potentially affect by implementing additional controls.

While performing root cause analysis, you need to examine how root causes can be reduced or eliminated by developing and implementing additional controls in any or all of the following four categories of control processes:

- management processes,
- engineering processes,
- support processes, and
- project interface with other groups.

Increasing Control of Management Processes

One of the first areas to investigate is whether you can eliminate one or more of your root causes by increasing your control over the key management processes on your project. These processes include:

- your own processes for project planning,
- your own processes for project tracking and oversight,

- the requirements management process,
- the configuration management process, and
- the defect management process.

Some of these processes may not seem to be internal to your project. For example, the configuration management group may be external to your project.

However, you may be having configuration problems precisely because you need some configuration management activities to be internal to your project, but they are not being performed. Hence, just because some of the management activity is the responsibility of a group external to your project, you may still have to implement some controls to ensure that everything that needs to occur within your project, does occur.

Increasing Control of Engineering Processes

When examining the possibility of reducing or eliminating root causes through increased control of engineering processes, examine your engineering processes in reverse lifecycle order. For example, you may examine the impact of implementing increased control over:

- software system test,
- software integration test,
- software unit test,
- software inspection and review,
- software development,
- software detail design,

- software preliminary design, and
- software requirements specification.

The reason for examining engineering disciplines in reverse lifecycle order is to further your insights into potential root causes (see Figure 18). For example, by examining root causes relating to software integration testing, you may discover issues that are actually caused by lack of controls relating to software unit testing. Similarly, problems in software unit testing may be related to a lack of controls in the area of software development.

By working in reverse lifecycle order, it is often easier to see cause and effect relationships between earlier lifecycle control inadequacies and later lifecycle problems.

Increasing Control of Support Processes

A variety of support processes may be affecting your project. Generally, if you are using support processes, they can have a substantial impact on the overall success of your project. These processes include:

- administrative support,
- documentation support,
- human resources support,
- shipping and receiving support, and
- training support.

Unless the support processes are internal to your project, there is relatively little you can do to control these processes

Figure 18
Control of Engineering Process in Reverse Lifecycle Order

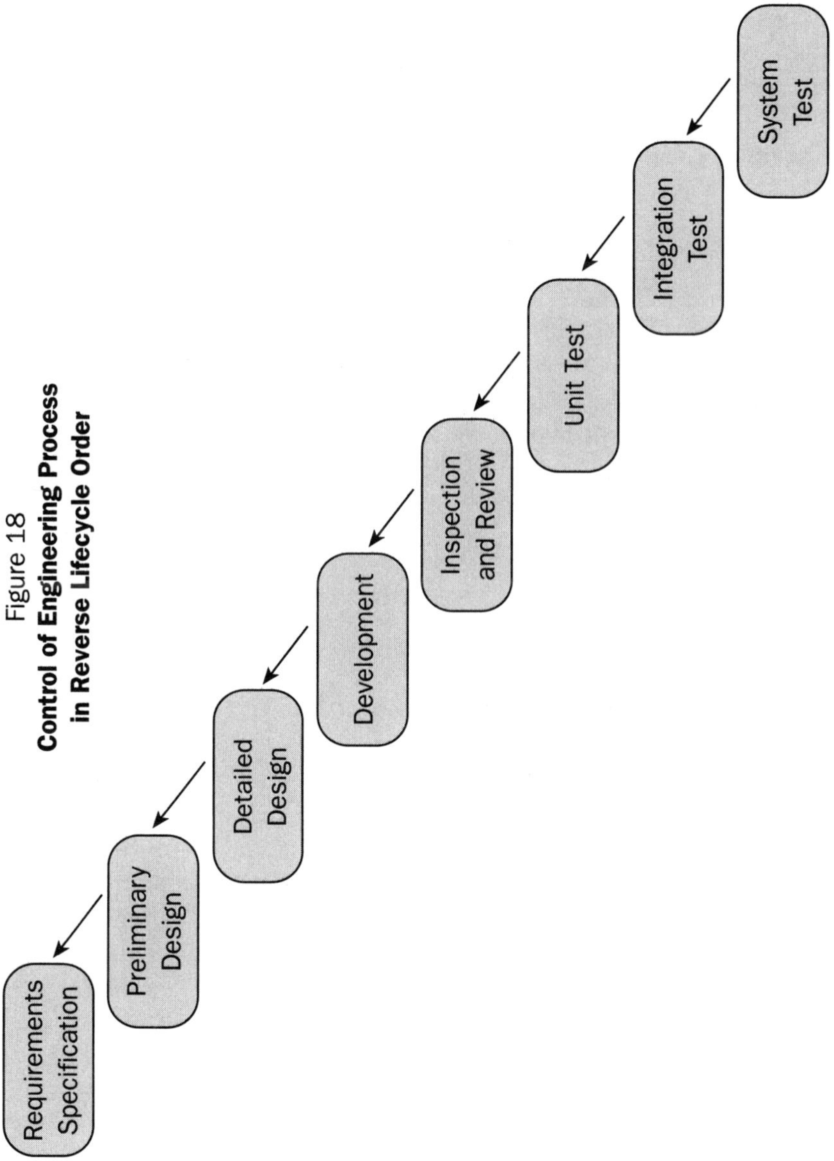

directly. However, you typically will have some influence over your interaction with these groups. You may be able to increase your control indirectly by, for example, becoming more specific about what you will provide to them and what you need them to provide to you.

Increasing Control of Project Interface with Other Groups

Other groups that you may need to interact with that are not explicitly considered support groups include:

- beta-test groups,
- customer groups,
- marketing,
- proposal teams,
- research labs, and
- systems engineering.

These groups often can influence the long-term success of your project significantly, but may also make considerable demands in the near term. Some project symptoms may be directly traceable to insufficient project controls relating to how you interact with these groups.

As with support groups, your primary option for increasing control over the impact that these groups has on your project is to increase the amount of control you have over how your project interfaces with them. You can potentially diagnose interface problems as a function of any of the following symptoms:

- feature creep,
- resource distractions (to work on proposals, committees, etc.),
- inadequate quality in items provided by external groups,
- repeated rejection by external groups of provided information or products,
- poor quality of information or products received from external groups, and
- ongoing changes in the stated needs of external groups.

Generally, as organizations become progressively larger, the opportunity for specialization increases and the need to interact and coordinate with other projects or groups becomes more apparent. Sometimes the need to interact with an external group results in a net loss of value to the project. That is, the project may need to expend a significant amount of time working with the external group, and the project receives, in return, little or nothing of obvious benefit. However, such interactions are typically intended to benefit the overall organization. For example, providing technical resources to help write a proposal is almost entirely an expense to the project (in time, though typically not in dollars), with no obvious benefit to the project. However, a year later, when the project is wrapping up, and there are new projects to transfer personnel to, the organizational and personal benefits become obvious.

DEFINING ADDITIONAL CONTROLS

As a result of the prior activity, you will have a list of potential additional controls. However, you need to select the efforts that will provide the maximum benefit.

To do this, take the following steps:

1. Identify additional controls.
2. Describe the controls.
3. Prioritize the controls.
4. Verify impact.
5. Develop a timetable.
6. Define new responsibilities.
7. Document new process rules.

When you have completed these steps, you will be ready to test the benefits of the new controls. Each of these steps is discussed below, and the next section addresses how to verify that benefits are being realized.

Identify Additional Controls

Pick five to seven areas where you intend to increase control. Generally, use greatest impact as the criterion for determining how to prioritize the initiatives. However, also factor in the amount of effort required to make the change and the probability of achieving the expected benefit. For example, a high impact change should be skipped if it will be very difficult to implement and the success of the effort is highly uncertain.

In this step, however, don't spend too much time on whether or not a change should be made now—prioritization comes later. Instead, just select the best seven (or fewer) candidates from the opportunities that you've previously identified.

Describe the Controls

For each of the opportunities you've selected, develop a brief description of what the new change is, and what you think the expected benefit will be. Generally, a one-paragraph description will be sufficient. The purpose of these descriptions is to ensure that you have a clear understanding of what you are planning to do, and what you expect the consequence to be.

As you develop the descriptions, you may find that two of them are rather similar. If so, they are likely to be describing the same effort under two different titles. If they are, combine them under one title. Conversely, you may find that describing one of the initiatives is quite complex and hard to complete in a single paragraph (or page). When this occurs, you may actually have two or more efforts needed, but grouped under a single title. In this case, try to identify the specific efforts and separate them under unique titles.

Prioritize the Controls

At this point, you have maybe five to seven initiatives that seem to offer potential for improving control over your project. The obvious question is: which ones to concentrate on and which ones to defer until later?

As a general rule, pick three or four initiatives to implement. This will allow you to concentrate your efforts on a set of changes intended to minimize disruption but maximize benefit. Moreover, by not focusing on just a single initiative, you are more likely to have at least some success resulting from your efforts. That is, if one or even two of the new control initiatives are of questionable success, you can shut them down and still realize benefit from the other one or two initiatives that are demonstrating positive results.

Verify Impact

Perceptions of success can range from highly subjective to rather objective. Generally, the more you rely on measures and metrics, the more objective you can be regarding whether or not an initiative is having positive benefit.

For each of the three or four improved control initiatives you have selected, identify the measures or metrics you will use so that you know whether or not control is improving. Commonly, these measures or metrics may be closely related to the symptoms that originally warned you of insufficient project control. For example, as a consequence of implementing improved controls, you may expect to see some or several of the following:

- increased software detection ratio (found by the project versus found by the customer),
- reduced software defect density,
- increased features per product size,
- reduced customer problem reports, and
- increased inspection defect counts (that is, the inspection process is becoming better).

It is very, if not extremely, important that you identify two or more measures that you will use to verify positive benefits from implementing increased controls. Your subjective feeling that "things are getting better" or "things are getting worse" is, virtually by definition, lacking in objectivity.

Develop a Timetable

Once you have identified the actions you intend to take, it is necessary to develop a timetable or schedule that documents when, where, and how you will take specific actions to implement the new control processes. This timetable needs to document the estimated resources required, effort required, budget required, and any internal relationships between the initiatives. That is, if a particular initiative must be completed before another initiative can commence, the dependencies need to be documented and communicated.

Define New Responsibilities

Generally, most control changes will affect the work you need to perform more than they will affect the work performed by others. However, in some cases, you may need project personnel to perform differently. These changes may be as simple as completing a timesheet on a daily basis, or as complex as regular participation in formal software inspections.

If you need people on the project to change, you will need to define and document the changes in their responsibilities. If you have documented roles and responsibility descriptions, you will need to update them. Otherwise, consider distributing a simple responsibility description memorandum that provides an overview of your new expectations regarding how project personnel will perform their work.

Document New Process Rules

Unless you are under severe schedule pressure, take the time to develop a high-level description of the overall process. If you don't have the time or inclination to document how things should be done, at least document any rules that should not be broken.

Process descriptions are helpful for communicating an overall approach for how work is performed and coordinated between groups. While role descriptions make it easy for an individual to understand his or her own work, process and activity descriptions make it easy for project personnel to understand everything that is happening around them.

Remember, you have prioritized your new controls. If you find that time is short, undertake the implementation and documentation of new controls in priority order.

TESTING ADDITIONAL CONTROLS

Before deploying the increased controls across the project, you should test them and verify that they will have a positive impact. To test the additional controls, identify the specific individuals who will be affected by changes in their responsibilities. On larger projects, pick just one team or a portion of the project.

To those individuals who will need to change their actions, send e-mails or hold an orientation meeting, and explain that a forty-five-day beta test period will commence on a certain date (at least two weeks away). Provide these people with the documented changes to the responsibility descriptions and with any updated process descriptions. Ask that they provide feedback to you at least one week prior to beta rollout.

Incorporate the feedback from project personnel into updated role descriptions and process descriptions. Redistribute the updated information.

Commence the beta test period with a one to four week baselining effort. During this period, the only changes that occur are those related to collecting process- and product-related measurements and metrics. Use this data to develop a baseline of your project performance capability.

After the baselining phase, commence with any other planned changes in implementing the additional controls. Ensure that you and others continue collecting metric and measurement data.

At the end of the beta phase, continue operating using the new processes. In parallel, conduct a detailed examination of the metrics. Compare the latest metrics with all prior metrics, especially those collected during the initial baselining effort. Are the values of the metrics moving in intended directions? Although changes in the metrics may not be as significant as you had estimated, they should at least be moving in the correct direction. For example, you might have been hoping for a productivity increase of 20 percent, but the metrics indicate an increase of only 5 percent. This still indicates that the improved controls are having a positive effect.

Regardless of what the metrics indicate, collect another round of feedback from practitioners. Ask them what their perceptions are regarding the new processes now that they've had a chance to practice them for a month or two. Document their feedback and consider another set of revisions to the responsibility and activity descriptions.

If none of the metrics is changing, consider a thirty-day extension to the beta phase. Alternatively, consider changing the metrics. In particular, can you find metrics that are more sensitive than the existing ones? Similarly, can you make the existing metrics more sensitive?

If, at the end of the beta test period, the metrics appear to be changing for the worse, it is likely to be a temporary downturn. The introduction of virtually any new process or tool usually results in a temporary reduction in productivity. When project personnel become familiar and comfortable with the new process or tool, productivity increases again. However, in such circumstances, you may want to continue the beta test evaluation period and verify that the metrics eventually reverse and start showing the intended trends.

DEPLOYING ADDITIONAL CONTROLS

When you are satisfied that the increased controls are having a positive effect, take some time to add more content to the responsibility descriptions and the activity descriptions. Provide at least an orientation describing the changes to the rest of the project personnel. Where necessary, provide training. For all project members, provide any supplemental information, documentation, templates, etc., that you've developed.

Announce a ninety-day trial period. The notion of a trial period is less intimidating for project personnel. The fact that you are having a trial period clearly communicates that your intention is to improve the project, and that steps to increase control over the project will be reconsidered the moment it becomes clear that they are not having a positive impact. Stress to the project personnel that increased control does not mean that you will have more control over them. Instead, it means that all project members will have more control over project activities and events.

As during the beta test phase, solicit feedback. Tell project personnel that there is no need to wait until the end of the ninety-day trial period; they can send feedback to you at any time. During this period, continue to watch the metrics carefully. As you receive feedback, update any of the material you've developed to help document and deploy the increased controls.

At the end of the trial period, if the metrics are showing the intended change, then announce that the new processes are now a part of the project's standard processes. Update your software development plan to document this fact. If the metrics are not confirming positive change, and feedback from the team members indicates that they do not think the increased controls are having the intended effect, go back to step 1 and begin analyzing symptoms and root causes again. Since you've already been through the entire exercise once, the likelihood of success is substantially greater on subsequent efforts.

MONITORING ADDITIONAL CONTROLS

As part of your regular project monitoring activities, continue to watch for symptoms of insufficient control, excessive control, and inappropriate control. In an environment where you are progressively increasing project controls, be especially sensitive to any symptoms of excessive control.

Your earliest warnings will typically show up either in your metrics or in the form of complaints from project personnel. If you start getting warnings from either, attempt to find the source of the problem. First, determine whether any of the project circumstances are changing. For example, relocating the project from one building to another, significant changes in organizational policies, or having your company be acquired by another company, can all have significant impacts on your project metrics. It is very hard to isolate the impact of increased control if the project environment or circumstances are changing significantly. However, it is typically true that during such times, it is especially important to have adequate controls in place, and thereby minimize the disruptive aspects of the other changes.

When implementing additional controls, always strive to implement the least amount of control necessary to achieve the intended results. As a general rule, software development continues to be a highly creative activity. For people to manifest creative talent, they need a certain degree of freedom.

It is definitely not true that more control is always better. Although most software projects fail because of insufficient control, some fail because of excessive control. This possibility is examined in the next chapter.

9 Recovering Projects from Excessive Control

"In the process of relaxing controls, you face the risk of relaxing too far and starting to lose control of the project."

Most organizations tend to increase the number and variety of control mechanisms they require slowly and progressively. Therefore, on longer duration projects, and in older organizations, it is not uncommon to find relatively large numbers of controls being used. If the addition of new controls continues unchecked, project personnel may begin to find themselves overconstrained. When this happens, the excessive controls actually impede the project and reduce the likelihood of overall project success.

IDENTIFYING THE SYMPTOMS OF EXCESSIVE CONTROL

As with insufficient control, your first indications of excessive control are usually revealed by one or more symptoms or problems resulting from excessive control. Major symptoms of excessive control include:

- work queued up at multiple locations,
- groups or individuals waiting to get started,
- regular interruptions for decisions,
- high rejection rate of process artifacts,

- numerous meetings requiring your attendance,
- regular reversal of technical decisions,
- skip-level management direction , and
- tasking conflicts.

While not exhaustive, this list illustrates the types of inefficiencies that can result from excessive control. Each symptom is discussed below.

Work Queued Up at Multiple Locations

When work is queued up at one or more locations, you should investigate the consequences, and potentially the cause. If the backlog of work is not holding up anyone else, then the consequences are likely to be relatively benign, and the backlog acceptable. However, if the backlog delays other people's work, or delays the release of project deliverables or process artifacts, then the backlog is detrimental and potentially indicates either understaffing or excessive controls.

If there are backlogs of work at a variety of locations, then your project is either chronically understaffed or may be subject to multiple instances of excessive control.

Backlogs are often caused by excessive procedural requirements. These requirements might include the need to have artifacts reviewed, the need to collect a variety of signatures, or the need to wait for a variety of permissions or approvals. While oversight, signatures, and approvals are an essential part of any project, an excessive amount of such requirements can start to impede work.

Groups or Individuals Waiting to Get Started

Similarly, when people are ready to work, but either don't have the necessary authorizations to commence work, or are waiting on needed tools or documents, it can be indicative of excessive procedural requirements.

This problem can be hard to detect. People typically don't sit around doing nothing. In software development, there is almost always something useful that can be done if the time is available. There are design documents to study, requirements to analyze, tool capabilities to explore, etc. While all of these are beneficial, when they happen in lieu of primary assigned work, the affected developers become less productive.

Regular Interruptions for Decisions

As project manager, you will regularly be making decisions that affect the overall project. Significant decisions should be documented in a simple decision log. Really significant decisions should also be documented in your software development plan.

Most decisions will usually be made during regularly scheduled review meetings (such as weekly meetings with senior technical personnel) and during regularly scheduled executive oversight meetings (where you are briefing management regarding your project's status). However, if you are frequently interrupted by phone, e-mail, or in person by project or other personnel who need you to make a decision, it may be a warning of excessive control over details that really could be handled by senior technical staff.

Generally, when someone else needs a decision made, they often have to stop whatever they were working on until the decision is made. The need for a project manager to make numerous decisions outside of regular meetings is usually warranted only when working with very junior teams.

High Rejection Rate of Process Artifacts

Process artifacts include everything produced as a consequence of developing the software product. Examples of artifacts include:

- project plans,
- software change requests,
- problem reports,
- action item log,
- status meeting minutes,
- inspection logs, and
- test descriptions.

Some of these artifacts stay internal to the project, and others are sent to groups outside the project. A high or increasing rejection rate of any project artifacts may indicate excessively strict acceptance standards.

Acceptance standards are either documented or undocumented. If artifacts are being rejected based on documented standards, examine the standards for reasonableness relative to the needs of your specific project. In the event of rejections based on undocumented acceptance criteria, ask the individual or group rejecting the artifacts to document the minimum criteria for acceptance.

As with other controls, acceptance criteria generally become increasingly restrictive. This progression toward increasingly severe constraints usually continues until it becomes obvious—often as a result of high rejection rates—that acceptance criteria or other controls have become excessive.

Numerous Meetings Requiring Your Attendance

As with other overhead activities, meetings should be kept to the minimum necessary to ensure effective progress, communications, tracking, controlling, and decision-making. But even with a minimum number of meetings, it is highly unlikely that the project manager needs to attend all of them.

If you find yourself going to a significant majority of the meetings being held on your project, investigate the role you play at those meetings. If you typically attend just to listen, facilitate, and answer questions, then your attendance is not indicative of excessive control. However, if you do most of the talking, and make all the decisions, including low-level technical decisions, this is likely to indicate excessive control for all but the most junior of teams.

Regular Reversal of Technical Decisions

This is similar to the symptoms of frequent interruptions to make decisions, and attendance at numerous meetings. As with these other two symptoms, this one is traceable to a reluctance to allow others to make decisions. In this case, the processes are in place to allow others to make decisions, but for whatever reason, you or others find it necessary to reverse those decisions regularly.

On any project where you have delegated authority to others to make decisions, there will be times when someone else makes a decision that you feel compelled to overrule. This might occur, for example, when you are aware of some significant factor that the decision-maker was not aware of. However, delegated authority means that other people do have the authority to make certain decisions. Generally, those decisions need to be respected if you want those individuals to be effective in their roles. If you find yourself having to reverse a large number of decisions, you have put the wrong people in those roles, delegated too much authority, or implemented excessive controls on the project.

Skip-Level Management Direction

Fortunately, most symptoms of excessive control are attributable to factors that you can influence. Skip-level management direction is one that you usually cannot influence unless (1) you are a second-line or higher manager, and (2) you are the source of the problem. Skip-level management direction is characterized by a level of management bypassing one or more lower levels of management and giving direction or control to personnel two or more levels away.

In virtually all companies, this is quite permissible, but rarely exercised. For example, the president of a company might bypass four levels of management and tell a mailroom employee to make a special delivery to the post office; however, the president usually doesn't do that. Bypassing or skipping the management chain is, at a minimum, disruptive. It is also conducive to potentially conflicting directions. When practitioners are subject to controls coming from multiple levels of management, the consequence can easily be excessive control.

Tasking Conflicts

In addition to skip-level management direction, there are many other potential sources of tasking conflicts. For example, if your technical personnel tell you that your requests are in conflict with requests from other managers, this could be indicative of excessive (or at least confusing) management controls.

Tasking conflicts may occur more frequently in matrix management environments. This is especially true in any environment where the matrix has three or more dimensions. For example, if a company has designated you to be the project manager (responsible for budget and schedule), someone else to be the product line manager (responsible for ensuring that your products adhere to the strategic direction of the company), and someone else to be program manager (responsible for customer satisfaction), and if all three managers feel that they can microtask and redirect technical personnel, it is virtually certain that tasking conflicts will occur.

DETERMINING TYPES OF CONTROL REDUCTION

Generally, excessive control is characterized by less productivity. People are waiting for decisions or approvals. Forms are being rejected for format problems. The configuration management group says they won't have time to release that software until next week at the earliest.

For this discussion, assume that you have identified the following symptoms on your project:

- work queued up at multiple locations,
- groups or individuals waiting to get started,
- numerous meetings requiring your attendance, and
- regular reversal of technical decisions.

The impact of excessive controls on efficiency provides an excellent means for determining where and how to take corrective actions. To identify where to apply control reduction techniques, take the following steps:

1. Identify inefficiencies.
2. Estimate maximum throughput.
3. Determine restriction factor.
4. Estimate implementation difficulty.
5. Rank control reduction opportunities.
6. Adjust rank ordering.

Identifying Inefficiencies

An inefficiency is anything where productivity, or throughput, is less than it otherwise could be. With software development, the notion of throughput is more difficult to quantify than it is in manufacturing, but it is still possible to develop "guesstimates" that help provide insight into where the greatest inefficiencies are occurring. To identify potential inefficiencies, list the primary symptoms you see on the project, and for each symptom, list one or more specific project events that are related to that symptom. Some project events will likely seem related to two or more symptoms.

When you have finished the list, isolate the specific processes that you think are candidates for improved efficiency. Briefly document general characteristics or factors that may be contributing to inefficiency.

Continuing with the previous example, the project manager looks at each of the symptoms, and relates them to specific project events. The project manager develops the following symptom/event list:

1. Work queued up at multiple locations

   – Software is ready for inspections, but inspections are not occurring.

2. Groups or individuals waiting to get started

   – Testers are ready to start testing product, but very little product is available.

   – The configuration management team says there are too few components for them to form a baseline.

3. Numerous meetings requiring your attendance

   – The detail design review team insists that you attend their meetings to arbitrate disagreements between designers and developers.

4. Regular reversal of technical decisions

   – The design group is asking frequently for restructuring of code.

Analyzing this list, the project manager determines that there are apparent inefficiencies in each of the following processes:

- inspection,
- testing,
- configuration management, and
- detail design review.

The project manager performs additional investigation and determines that the inspection process was recently changed and now requires twenty-four hours of preparation time and eight hours of inspection meeting time per inspection artifact. The developers do not feel that they have that amount of time available.

Additionally, the configuration management group has been rejecting four out of five components due to improper completion of configuration management submittal forms. Developers have finished product, but they are not submitting it to configuration management because it will likely be rejected.

The project manager also finds that the documented process for performing software integration testing requires that artifacts be part of a baseline released from configuration management before they can become part of the integration test.

The project manager sees a variety of potential improvements, and attempts to estimate what might happen as a result of relaxing some potentially excessive constraints.

Estimating Maximum Throughput

Estimating maximum throughput is a simple exercise of determining how to quantify the work being done in one or more areas of a project, and then estimating the increased work that might occur if the controls were relaxed (but not entirely removed). On software development projects, there are so many interrelationships between factors, processes, and people that it is nearly impossible to predict exactly the throughput of a changed process. Indeed, since software development is an intellectually intensive activity, in some cases, it is nearly impossible to quantify the units of work being performed within a given activity. Therefore, all that is needed at this step is a very general notion of what the consequences might be of relaxing the controls.

To continue with the prior example, the inspection process could be relaxed from the current four-day process to a four-hour process: two hours to prepare, and two hours for the inspection meeting.

Regarding the configuration management process, it could be changed so that the configuration management group is required to accept any software where the only reason for rejection is related to improperly completed forms. The configuration management group can then take steps to get the forms completed properly. Additionally, there may be an opportunity to have fewer required fields on configuration management forms.

Examining the integration test process, it could be redefined so that once a product has been inspected, it can go directly to integration test. This removes the requirement that it must go to configuration management first.

As shown in these examples, during this step, you hypothesize ways that you might be able to change the process to improve the likelihood that project personnel can work easier, faster, and more effectively.

Determining Restriction Factor

This is an optional step and makes sense only on those activities where you can clearly quantify the work being done. For example, consider a design group that is using a word processing package to develop graphics of the detailed design. The project tracking data indicates that for each software module, it takes three days to develop the detailed design. Another project is using a graphics design software package, and they take an average of one and a half days to develop the detailed design for a module.

Restriction factors can be calculated by simply taking the potential throughput (always a larger number) and dividing it by the current throughput. The larger the resulting number, the more severely the throughput is restricted.

In this step, for any processes where you can quantify the work being performed, calculate a factor to represent the potential consequences of relaxing the controls.

Estimating Implementation Difficulty

At this point, you have an idea about where the problems are, some briefly documented actions you can take to relax potentially excessive controls, and some notion of what might happen, in terms of improved productivity, as a result of relaxing the controls.

This step involves developing a rough estimate of the difficulty associated with implementing the relaxed controls. Generally, difficulty is reduced as a function of the degree to which you "own" the control. For example, if you are responsible for the configuration management process on your project, it is relatively easy for you to change that process and the associated rules and forms. However, if configuration management is performed by an external group, any changes to that group's processes and forms will have to be negotiated carefully.

For this step, estimating implementation difficulty can be as simple as assigning a difficulty rating of low, medium, or high to each action you might undertake.

Ranking Control Reduction Opportunities

Since you will likely have multiple actions you can take to reduce excessive control, you should rank the opportunities in order from highest to lowest priority. To determine the priority of a particular action, consider the three important factors developed in prior steps:

- restriction factor,
- estimated impact, and
- estimated difficulty.

Higher priority opportunities are those that have the largest restriction factors, the greatest estimated impact, and the least amount of difficulty associated with implementation. Lower priority opportunities are just the opposite and are characterized by small restriction factors, low impact, and high difficulty.

Adjusting Rank Ordering

Before starting to relax controls incrementally, take one last look at the ranked list of opportunities and evaluate it based on your experience and common sense. Consider whether there are any unusual factors beyond those discussed here that might cause you to raise or lower the priority of a particular initiative.

For example, if you are nearing the end of a lifecycle phase, such as software design, there is likely little reason to attempt to make changes in how the design process is controlled when, for example, that process will be completed in the next week or two. It might make more sense to concentrate instead on the processes and controls associated with the next lifecycle phase. Figure 19 is an example of shifting control attention to an imminent phase.

When you are satisfied with the ranking of your initiatives, you can begin to relax excessive control incrementally.

Figure 19
Adjusting Rank Ordering

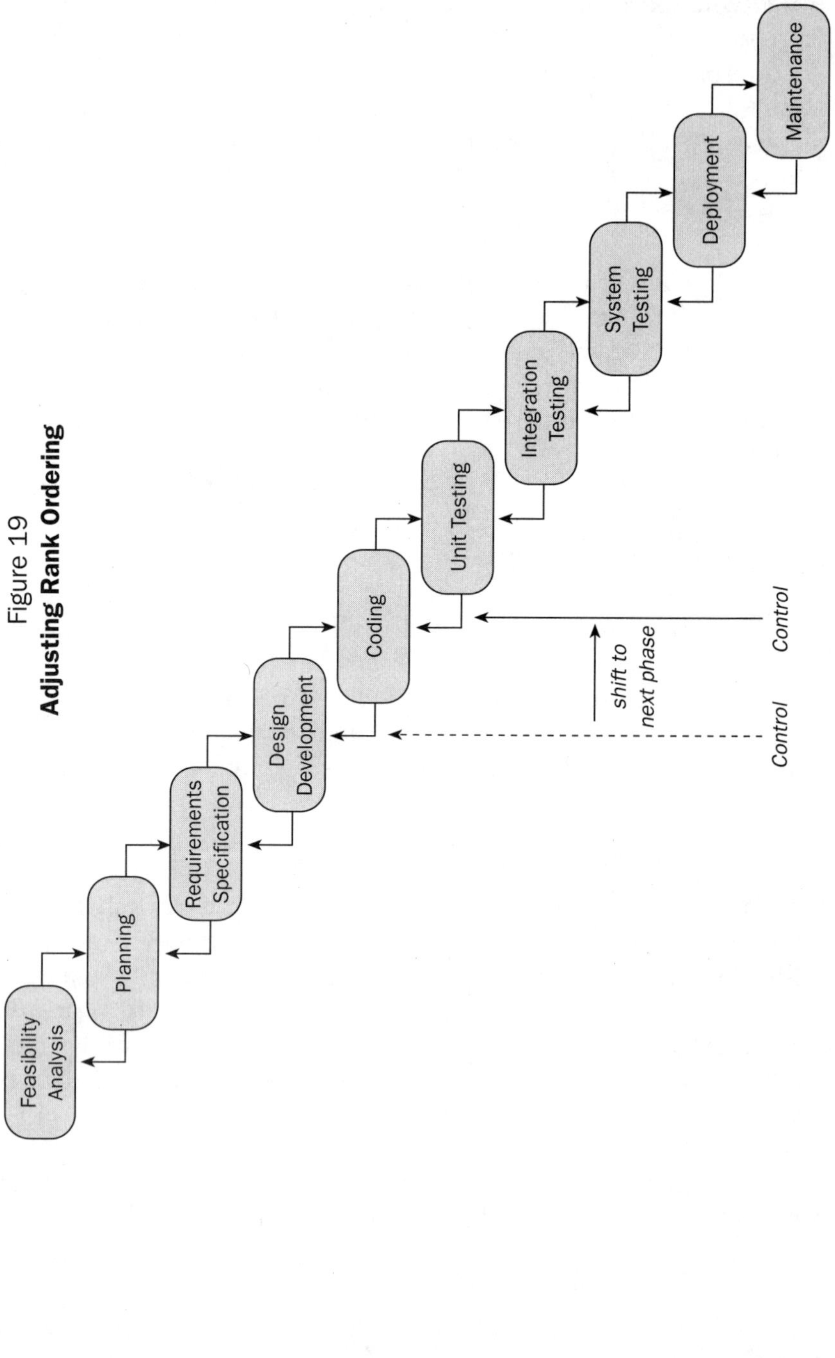

INCREMENTALLY RELAXING EXCESSIVE CONTROLS

Relaxing excessive control is typically a higher risk activity than implementing additional controls. In the latter case, things are generally out of control anyway, so there is little downside risk. In the former case, the project is likely in control, but in a way that creates inefficiencies, waste, and unnecessary delays. Hence, in the process of relaxing controls, you face the risk of relaxing too far and starting to lose control of the project. Given this higher level of risk, relaxing control should be approached as a series of incremental efforts.

Many activities are common to each increment. Thus, within each increment of relaxing control, you should follow a series of steps similar to that described in Chapter 8:

- Identify measures so you know whether or not control is improving (measures may be tied to symptoms).
- List the specific actions you will take, and develop a timetable for implementing them.
- If you need people on the project to change, define the changes to their responsibilities.
- Time permitting, develop high-level descriptions of the overall process.
- At a minimum, if you don't have the time or inclination to document how things should be done, at least document any rules that should not be broken.

When relaxing controls, it is especially important to rely on metrics and measurements to confirm that the actions you are taking are having a positive impact on the project. You want objective confirmation that things are getting better, not just a subjective feeling that things are probably getting better.

Each increment of relaxing controls potentially involves accepting a certain degree of risk. However, with each increment, you are also becoming more familiar with control relaxation activities, and tracking their impact on project metrics. From that perspective, as you become more experienced at relaxing controls, risk exposure diminishes.

You can systematically relax controls by using as many as five increments:

- Increment 1: Relax clearly unnecessary controls
- Increment 2: Relax low-downside controls
- Increment 3: Relax isolated controls
- Increment 4: Relax rapid feedback controls
- Increment 5: Relax remaining excessive controls

Relaxing Clearly Unnecessary Controls

In the first increment, you should strive to relax clearly unnecessary controls. For example, if a particular form has to be routed to five people for successive signatures, and everyone agrees that only two signatures are really necessary, this is likely something that should be implemented immediately.

Another example might be the four-day inspection process described earlier. If inspections are not occurring at all, reducing the required minimum inspection preparation and meeting times to something more compatible with developers' actual schedules likely makes sense. You can keep a close watch on defect counts coming from integration tests to help decide whether more or less time should be spent conducting inspections.

If you are not sure if a control is clearly unnecessary then, by definition, it's not clear. Defer relaxation of that control to a later increment.

Relaxing Low-Downside Controls

A low-downside control is any control for which you perceive little or no risk associated with inadvertently relaxing the control too much. Examples include the completion of forms that may make sense for other projects but that do not seem to have any purpose on your project. In this example, if you use a simpler form, or even resort to unstructured communication such as e-mail, you will not inadvertently lose control of the project. If it becomes apparent that the form actually was useful in, for example, facilitating communications, then you can always reinstate it.

Relaxing Isolated Controls

An isolated control is similar to a low-downside control. With isolated controls, the consequences of excessive relaxation may be more significant; however, those consequences are contained on an isolated part of the project.

Typically, isolated controls are those associated with just a very few people on the project team. Relaxing these controls will affect those few people, but the benefits may extend considerably beyond them. For example, if change requests tend to queue up because of an inefficient change control process within the configuration management team, you can look for ways to improve the change control evaluation and approval process. Although the actual process changes will be isolated to just those people involved in evaluating and approving change requests, everyone else on the project will see the benefit of having their change requests turned around more quickly.

Relaxing Rapid Feedback Controls

The next lowest risk controls to relax are those that will rapidly provide feedback, via metrics, regarding whether or not the relaxation is having the intended effect. This is useful because it allows you to take corrective action, such as reinstituting a greater degree of control. Additionally, you can take this action rapidly and before too much control is lost.

For example, suppose you decide not to relax the inspection process as part of your initiatives in Increment 1. You could relax it as part of Increment 4 on the premise that excessive relaxation of minimum inspection times would quickly show up in the results of integration test runs.

Relaxing Remaining Excessive Controls

In Increment 5, you relax any remaining excessive controls. These controls are characterized by not exhibiting any of the attributes that would allow them to be included in an earlier increment. Hence, these controls are not clearly excessive, have a fair degree of risk associated with their relaxation, affect a significant number of people, and their consequences will take some time to be reflected in the metrics.

In an extreme case, all your control relaxation initiatives may end up assigned to Increment 5. If that is the case, and if you have three or more change initiatives, you should still use multiple increments of releasing the change. Release each initiative singularly in reverse priority order. This allows you time to become proficient at implementing control relaxation before you attempt any high priority initiatives. In this context, high priority means that the requirement for success exceeds the need for speed.

In most cases, however, you will be able to allocate your control relaxation initiatives across at least two or three of the increments, and can therefore follow this low-risk approach to relaxing excessive control.

DETECTING EXCESSIVE RELAXATION OF CONTROL

It is effectively impossible to determine the perfect amount of control appropriate for a given project. However, there are times when control is clearly insufficient and needs to be increased, and other times when control is clearly excessive and needs to be reduced. Increased by how much, or reduced by how much, is a much more difficult question to answer, but at least we sometimes can know which direction to take the controls on a project.

To detect excessive relaxation of control, you once again must rely on project metrics. You have already identified metrics that you will use to verify that things have started improving as a result of relaxing controls.

However, there is another important set of steps you should take. For each control you are relaxing:

- Think of what undesirable consequences might occur if the control is relaxed excessively.
- Identify metrics you can collect that will rapidly signal the occurrence of those undesirable consequences.
- Track these metrics regularly in conjunction with the technique being used to verify success.

By taking this approach, you have two types of metrics. One type is intended to confirm success or warn you of a lack of success, and the other is intended to confirm that a change is not having undesirable consequences or to warn you if undesirable consequences develop.

Consider the following example. A project is using a configuration management (CM) process where one person keeps all the source code on a secure machine. When a developer wants source, he or she must submit a written request to the CM person. That person sends an e-mail to verify that there is an authorized change request indicating that a specific change needs to be made. Upon receiving confirmation, the CM person sends an e-mail to another person who maintains a list regarding who has authority to change which modules. If the developer has the authority, the second person sends an e-mail to the first and authorizes release of the source. The CM person then copies the source across the network to the developer's machine.

The project manager decides that this process is far too labor-intensive, and potentially a reflection of excessive controls accumulating over time. She decides to replace this entire process with a low-cost, easy-to-use configuration management tool.

After making this decision, the project manager examines a variety of undesirable outcomes and documents them as follows:

- Developers might be able to change source code without an approved change request.
- Changes might be made by unauthorized developers.
- Developers might become confused by the new CM procedures, and copy old defective code into the repository.

The project manager calls customer support at the company that sells the CM tool. Naturally, they assure her that none of these undesirable events can possibly happen. She decides to be cautious anyway. Therefore, as part of monitoring the process for potential excessive relaxation of control, she implements and tracks the following metrics:

- number of times source modules were changed without an approved change request,
- number of times source modules were changed by an unauthorized person,
- number of times a previously corrected defect reappears in a new baseline,
- number of times the CM tool correctly refuses to release source in the absence of an approved change request,
- number of times the CM tool correctly refuses to release source to someone not authorized for that source, and
- number of times the CM tool correctly detects that the source being sent back for check-in is an older version than the source that was checked out.

By monitoring these metrics, the project manager doesn't gain much insight into whether or not the overall CM process is more efficient than it was before. However, she does gain comprehensive insight into whether the new CM process and tool are providing adequate control over the configuration management activities.

By using metrics both to verify positive impacts and to warn of negative impacts, you provide yourself and your project with comprehensive protection against excessive relaxation of controls.

10 Recovering Projects from Inappropriate Control

"Typically, you will have no problem staffing a project that is so outrageous that it seems doomed to failure."

Recovering from insufficient control generally involves focusing on basic project management and product engineering issues (requirements, design, configuration management, etc.). Recovering from excessive control typically involves concentrating on process and organizational issues. Think of the former as bottom up, the latter as top down. Recovering from inappropriate control usually involves working orthogonally, or from the inside out.

IDENTIFYING THE SYMPTOMS OF INAPPROPRIATE CONTROL

Inappropriate control can be viewed as a mix of being too relaxed where tighter controls are needed, and being too tight where greater freedom is needed. Symptoms of inappropriate control include:

- Product ships quickly but field defect reports are high.
- Everyone seems busy but nothing is getting finished.
- Quality product is shipping, but costs are way above planned (or are way behind schedule, or both).
- Training is available, but attendance is poor.

- Inspections are being set up, but keep being postponed.
- Quality product is shipping as planned, but the project team is working seven-day weeks.
- The customer is very happy, but we're really delivering junk.
- There's a lot of talk about improving the process, but things actually seem to be getting worse.

Inappropriate control is considered to be, simply enough, any control failure that is not clearly attributable to either insufficient control or excessive control. In this sense, it is a loose collection of a highly diverse set of control failures. The symptoms show that when many aspects of a project appear successful, but there is something that does not seem right with the overall picture, there may be a control problem. If you can't trace it to either insufficient or excessive control, treat it as an inappropriate control problem.

To address inappropriate control, you need to examine each major project attribute and evaluate the controls most appropriate for that attribute (see Figure 20). Major project attributes to examine include:

- lifecycle,
- team,
- product, and
- culture.

For each of these project attributes, you need to examine the types of control that seem most appropriate, and least appropriate, given the needs and circumstances of your specific project.

Figure 20
Project Attributes

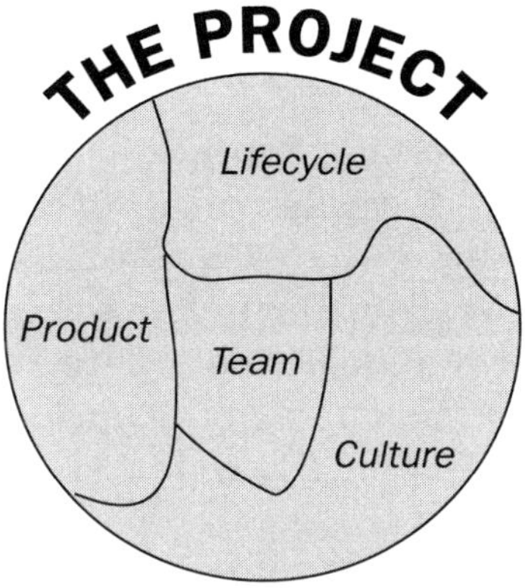

What Types of Control Fit This Lifecycle?

The project lifecycle is the overall organizing influence on the project's numerous activities. Lifecycles differ considerably in terms of the types of control with which they are compatible. The lifecycles discussed in Chapter 2 were:

1. Waterfall
2. Throw-away prototype
3. Incremental build
4. Multiple build
5. Spiral
6. Legacy maintenance
7. Hybrid

Each lifecycle is discussed below in terms of the types of control that are commonly appropriate for projects following that lifecycle.

Controlling the Waterfall Lifecycle

For the waterfall lifecycle, it is very important to have strong product quality controls. The premise of the waterfall lifecycle is that you will be moving on to later phases of development. Once a given phase is complete, a waterfall lifecycle does not readily accommodate going backward and reactivating a previously completed lifecycle phase.

For example, after completing the design phase of a project, you move on to the development phase. You may release the vast majority—if not all—of your designers so that they may work on other projects. Four months into the software coding phase, it starts to become apparent that there are problems with the design. Six months into software coding, it is obvious that there are major problems with the design. You have a big problem and no obvious way to address it. No designers are available for your project (after all, your plan indicates that design has been completed) and the developers do not have the necessary skills.

To help avoid this type of situation, verify that you have:

- strong engineering process controls,
- strong inspection processes, and
- strong milestone reviews.

When using the waterfall lifecycle, ensure that you have tight controls on product quality as you move between the major phases. This will help ensure that the outputs of earlier phases meet the needs of later phases.

Controlling the Throw-Away Prototype Lifecycle

Remember, when developing throw-away prototypes, you are not building the actual system—you are just clarifying the system requirements. However, prototyping projects can be significant efforts in their own right, and any significant effort can founder from a loss of control.

Controls that are compatible with a throw-away prototyping lifecycle include:

- strong feature controls,
- strong customer feedback and capture controls, and
- strong requirements capture controls.

One objective of the throw-away prototype lifecycle is to have sufficient flexibility and freedom to allow the prototype to evolve into something that clearly and accurately captures the customer's needs. Hence, many prototyping projects are characterized by very little control.

As a result, some prototyping projects consume so much time and money that management finally decides there is no time to build another system. Instead, the prototype must be "fixed" until it can be used as the operational system. This typically leads to a high-visibility disaster.

Prototyping projects need to have sufficient flexibility to explore solutions, but also have sufficient control to achieve their objectives in a timely, cost-effective manner.

Controlling the Incremental Build Lifecycle

When using the increment build lifecycle, it is imperative that you have strong controls over the configuration management process. Incremental build is characterized by building the system in pieces and bringing those pieces together effectively. In the absence of adequate controls over your successive system configurations, you will likely experience repeated problems with new features being lost and old defects resurfacing.

Additionally, incremental build is characterized by the successive builds going into system test, but not being released to the customer. Therefore, comprehensive controls over processes relating to system test can help ensure comprehensive testing and accurate and thorough feedback to the development team.

Controlling the Multiple Build Lifecycle

The multiple build lifecycle is very similar to the incremental build lifecycle. The major distinguishing characteristic of this lifecycle is that, typically, each build is released for installation at the customer site and intended for actual customer use.

As important as configuration controls are for the incremental build lifecycle, they are even more important for the multiple build lifecycle. If there are any problems with disappearing features, or with recurring defects, your customer will see these problems too.

When using the multiple build lifecycle, it is also important to have adequate controls over requirements management processes. Since customers are receiving and using incremental deliveries of the system, they will invariably develop opinions regarding what they like, and what they would like to have changed. Unless requirements are carefully documented, managed, and negotiated, the multiple build approach can be conducive to ongoing project redirection and an eventual perception of project failure.

Controlling the Spiral Lifecycle

Spiral lifecycles are characterized, in part, by deferring detailed planning of project activities when those activities are in the distant future. At each successive cycle in the spiral lifecycle, the current risks are analyzed and a plan is developed to implement the functionality allocated to this particular cycle.

When using the spiral lifecycle, it is very important to ensure adequate control over project requirements and, in particular, the criteria for testing the achievement of requirements. One of the major ways in which control is lost of projects following a spiral lifecycle is that the system never seems to come to completion. There is a cycle, then another, and another, and it can become very difficult to stop. Hence, throughout the performance of a spiral lifecycle, both you and the customer must understand clearly the criteria that will be used to signal project completion.

If these criteria cannot be defined clearly at the outset of the project—not an uncommon occurrence—you need to make documentation of completion criteria one of your top priorities.

Controlling the Legacy Maintenance Lifecycle

Legacy maintenance is typically characterized by a variety of microprojects that each follows a regularly repeating pattern of estimating effort, performing effort, brief testing, submission into configuration management, integration testing, and submission into production. Given the comparatively short duration needed to implement a single correction or enhancement, detailed insight into the progress of a single change is often ignored.

With legacy maintenance, one of the most important processes that needs control is the size estimation process and the corresponding derivative estimates of effort and cost. Although the difference between estimating two weeks and spending four weeks on a particular effort may seem trivial, if there is an endemic inability to perform in accordance with estimates and for work to take twice as long as expected or necessary, a two-year project can easily become a four-year project.

Controlling the Hybrid Lifecycle

The hybrid lifecycle is one of the most challenging to implement successfully on a project. Virtually by definition, just as you are figuring out what works and does not work in the context of one lifecycle, it is time to change over to a new lifecycle and attempt to determine which controls work best with that lifecycle. It can become especially dangerous when habits become entrenched in the context of one lifecycle and those same habits extend into the performance of the new lifecycle. There is also considerable risk that the controls developed and exercised during one lifecycle may be highly inappropriate for the next lifecycle.

With the hybrid lifecycle, your primary control problem is essentially one of meta-control. That is, you will need to have considerable control over how you manage and transition the types of control processes needed to ensure project success. You will need to identify and correct problems associated with insufficient, excessive, and inappropriate control rapidly and regularly.

What Types of Control Fit This Team?

Another primary consideration when evaluating appropriate or inappropriate controls is the type of team that you have on the project. Controls appropriate for different types of teams can be evaluated using the following distinguishing characteristics:

1. Senior team versus junior team
2. Small team versus large team
3. Localized team versus distributed team
4. Functionally focused team versus integrated, multidisciplined team
5. Well-established team versus new team

Senior Team Versus Junior Team

Virtually without exception, senior teams need less control than junior teams. The rare exception to this generalization is a junior team that is staffed by aggressively finding some of the most creative young talent available. When these teams are staffed successfully, they can be monitored safely by using postactivity metrics. Typically, these metrics will confirm that processes are being performed efficiently and effectively.

Junior teams need more controls to prevent inefficiencies and defects related to lack of experience. The controls need to emphasize engineering (versus management) discipline. Often, junior engineers are quite capable at working on small, one-person efforts. However, they may be substantially less capable when trying to coordinate their activities with others and participating as a part of a much larger team. Consequently, when using junior teams, it is important to ensure proper control over:

- low-level engineering processes,
- communication processes,
- mentoring or training processes, and
- problem reporting and management processes.

Many of the risks associated with using junior teams can be mitigated by adding a few senior people in lead positions, and delegating authority accordingly.

Small Team Versus Large Team

Team size also has a substantial impact on which control mechanisms will be more or less successful. Small teams typically need less control, and large teams need progressively more control. This is especially true with regard to controls designed to ensure effective and efficient communication and coordination. For example, a team of five can communicate status and coordinate work quite easily just by sitting in close proximity and talking with each other. This is essentially impossible for a team of 200.

Localized Team Versus Distributed Team

With the advent of the worldwide web and associated extremely low-cost technology to support teamwork, collaboration, communication, and coordination, the negative aspects of distributed teams are diminishing. However, there is a lingering and legitimate perception that it is more difficult to control a distributed team than a localized team.

With distributed teams, ensure that you have adequate controls covering:

- communication,
- assignments (including objectives and responsibilities),
- software component interfaces, and
- expectations.

Paradoxically, the larger the pieces of the distributed team, the easier it may be to control those pieces. For example, if a team of ten developers is working in ten different countries, ensuring efficient and effective teamwork will clearly be a challenge. Conversely, three teams at three different locations, each team consisting of ten or so developers, may be easier to control. The latter example presumes reasonably effective management controls within each team. Hence, all that remains is ensuring that the three teams coordinate their actions and work together effectively.

Functionally Focused Team Versus Integrated, Multi-Disciplined Team

During recent years, there seems to have been a migration from functionally focused teams toward integrated, multi-disciplined teams. The perception that integrated, multidisciplined teams are better is based on the premise that one large group of people working toward a single definition of success will be more successful than numerous smaller groups working toward their own individual definitions of success.

In theory, this makes sense. In practice, numerous problems develop. For example, you need each discipline in a multidiscipline team to be, practically speaking, at least a full-time position. If you have someone spending one-tenth of their time on your project, will they really act like a team member? A team member can easily become overworked because, for example, four projects each try to use 50 percent of that person's time. Additionally, on integrated teams, it is preferable to keep the team together throughout the life of the development effort. However, you will need some skills during earlier parts of the project, and other skills later. Finding work to keep people gainfully productive when their expertise is currently not needed can be difficult.

Considering these and related problems, functionally focused teams seem to need less management control than multidisciplined teams. When using a multidisciplined team, controls you need to have effectively in place include:

- decision-making,
- assignment and monitoring of responsibilities and authority,
- negotiation, and
- completion criteria.

Well-Established Team Versus New Team

Finally, control requirements will certainly differ as a function of whether the team is newly formed or has an established history of working together. Typically, the longer a team works together, the less its members depend on external controls. A well-established team, with a history of success, may be more than capable of self-management.

This assumption, however, is based on the premise that team members are free to join or leave at their discretion. A team that has been ordered or otherwise forced to work together may require more controls than a new team composed of relatively compatible team members.

What Types of Control Fit This Product?

The type of product you are building will also influence the types of control you need and the degree to which you need them.

For example, highly user-interface intensive products will need considerable control over the requirements management process. These systems typically involve large numbers of people, especially customers, who will be testing, evaluating, or using the system. Invariably, these people will form opinions about the system; most of those opinions will potentially affect system requirements.

Conversely, you may be developing a highly machine-interface intensive product. In that case, hardware configuration management may be critical to your success. Changes to hardware almost inevitably have significant impacts on the software designed to run on that hardware.

If the software you are developing seems to be highly complex, then you will need strong quality assurance processes coupled with strong configuration management processes.

Keep in mind that the perception of complexity is often a function of experience, talent, and education. The question is *not*, "Is this complicated for someone else?" The question *is*, "Does this feel complicated to me?" If the answer is yes, you need to ensure that strong quality assurance and configuration control processes are in place on your project.

Finally, it is relatively common within the high-technology community that some projects are, frankly, highly speculative. Phrased differently, these are the projects that are expected to fail. Or to succeed wildly.

Typically, you will have no problem staffing a project that is so outrageous that it seems doomed to failure. For whatever reason, software developers seem to line up for such projects. Maybe maximum challenge is what highly talented developers seek.

Regardless, your highest risk projects, especially those building unprecedented products, may be precisely the projects that succeed beyond all documented expectations. For these projects, controls will need to be monitored carefully for any indication of unnecessary interference with talent and creativity.

What Types of Control Fit This Culture?

A company's culture is the composite influence of all the undocumented rules associated with that company. Culture is, without question, the most influential element of an organization or company. Simply stated, nothing contradicts culture and survives. If the cultural tendency is to go east, and the new trend is to go west, over time, everything of consequence will go east. Practically speaking, an interesting, but isolated, new initiative will have no impact on a massive and pervasive culture.

One major characteristic of a culture is its overall acceptance of, or resistance to, anything perceived as high risk. A culture that willingly accepts a higher level of risk will need more control over its projects than is needed in a conservative culture. Risk-tolerant cultures are often exploring new technologies and seeking new opportunities. Hence, new projects can be significantly different from projects historically performed in that organization.

A lack of historical data makes it difficult to estimate the project's cost and schedule accurately. Controls are needed that facilitate close tracking of project performance. Additional controls are needed to ensure that actual performance data is used to recalculate predictions of cost and schedule regularly, and that the project plan is updated systematically to reflect revised estimates.

Another major distinguishing characteristic of organizational culture is the sense of urgency within that culture. Some cultures prefer to be very systematic: arrive at 8:00, leave at 5:00, and don't rush because that just leads to mistakes and rework. Other cultures have a sense of urgency that in extreme cases seems to border on panic. In the latter case, more controls relating to process compliance will be needed to ensure that the perception of the need to hurry does not cause people to start breaking rules and skipping important parts of the process.

When evaluating whether or not a control is appropriate for a given project within a culture, look to see if a similar control is in place on any other projects. If the control is being used successfully on one or more projects in that culture, it will likely work on the given project. If the control is not in place anywhere else in the organization, it could be because it has been tried before and proved to be fundamentally incompatible with the culture. In this case, you should either identify a different control that will achieve the same results, or be sure to have a contingency plan in place regarding the actions you will take in the event that the new control fails.

PLANNING THE CONTROL SHIFT

Planning a control shift in the context of possible inappropriate control differs from recovering control. This difference in planing for and carrying out the recovery techniques is characterized by the need to address having too little control in some areas, too much control in others, and the wrong type of control in still others.

To plan a control shift, list the control change opportunities that you are considering and categorize each opportunity using the following discriminators:

- easy to difficult,
- short term to long term,
- highly certain success to highly uncertain success, and
- high impact to low impact.

Since the risk associated with recovering from inappropriate control is comparatively high, an incremental recovery approach makes the most sense. Within each increment of relaxing controls, you should follow the steps described in Chapter 9:

- Identify measures so you know whether or not control is improving (measures may be tied to symptoms).
- List the specific actions you will take, and develop a timetable for implementing them.

- If you need people on the project to change, define the changes to their responsibilities.

- Time permitting, develop high-level descriptions of the overall process.

- At a minimum, if you don't have the time or inclination to document how things should be done, at least document any rules that should not be broken.

To recover incrementally, try to identify two recovery initiatives that were rated at the positive end of each of the categories. That is, try to pick two that are easy, two that are short term, two that are highly certain of success, and two that are high impact. By selecting a mix of controls to implement, you will have a balance between high likelihood of success and high impact.

To implement the new controls, examine their prevailing characteristics (from the previous categorization) and assign each initiative to one of the following increments:

- Increment 1: Short term

- Increment 2: Highly certain of success

- Increment 3: Easy

- Increment 4: High impact

- Increment 5: Lowest composite score

This will give you an overall approach to implementing the recovery from inappropriate controls. If you feel highly confident in your proposed solutions, consider overlapping two or more increments (especially 1 through 3).

For example, since short-term effort is the distinguishing characteristic for the first increment, it is reasonable to expect that results will show quickly. If these results are positive, you can overlap and commence the second increment without waiting for the first increment to complete the entire beta-test period.

Time permitting, finish your planning by thinking of anything that might go wrong, determining how you can detect the beginnings of things going wrong, and deciding what steps you will take if or when these undesirable events occur. Similar to the discussion in Chapter 9, have one set of metrics dedicated to confirming positive impact, and another set of metrics for confirming the absence of negative impacts. This approach will give you comprehensive insight into the consequences of your changed controls.

IMPLEMENTING AND TRACKING THE CONTROL SHIFT

Chapters 8 and 9 have detailed a variety of issues and considerations with regard to implementing changes specifically intended to affect how you are controlling your project. Those principles are equally applicable when implementing changes intended to recover from inappropriate control. These principles included:

- identifying the controls to change,
- describing the control changes,
- prioritizing the control changes,
- verifying the impact,
- developing a timetable to implement the changes,

- defining any new or changed responsibilities, and
- documenting any new or changed process rules.

However, when recovering from inappropriate control, you need to consider a few additional steps that augment or enhance the preceding steps:

- varying beta periods,
- using multiple overlap,
- minimizing contradictory impacts,
- detecting new symptoms,
- identifying short-term inefficiencies, and
- performing split analysis.

Varying Beta Periods

When implementing a set of new or revised controls, it is always a good idea to beta-test them before actually institutionalizing them. A beta period may range from a couple of weeks to a few months.

When recovering from inappropriate control, there is a high likelihood of significant differences between the specific actions being taken, the risks associated with those actions, the time required before improvement can be confirmed, etc. These differences are in part related to the fact that in some cases you are relaxing existing controls, in other cases you are increasing existing controls, and in still other cases you are introducing new controls. In light of these differences, the duration of the beta periods should be matched with the type of control change being deployed. In particular, the beta periods can be relatively shorter for high-confidence implementations.

Using Multiple Overlap

You can potentially accelerate your incremental deployment of improved controls by overlapping two of the increments. In some circumstances, especially as you become more experienced at improving project control, you may find it useful to overlap three or more increments.

The advantage of overlapping increments is accelerating the rate at which the new controls are implemented and thereby shortening the delay in benefits derived from the new controls. The disadvantages of too much overlap are (1) the increased effort required to monitor the impacts resulting from the changed controls, and (2) an increased possibility that developing problems might not be detected as early.

When using an implementation method involving multiple overlapping increments, consider adding some extra time to the beta period for each increment. This typically does not reduce the benefits received from the improved controls, but does help maintain awareness of any positive or negative impacts associated with the new controls.

Minimizing Contradictory Impacts

Since recovering from inappropriate control often consists of a mix of relaxing some controls while increasing other controls, there is an increased possibility that some of the actions being taken will have contradictory impacts. Hence, it is especially important that you watch the metrics carefully and regularly. You should strive always to have hard evidence available that control effectiveness is moving in the right direction.

If some of the metrics are not moving in the direction you originally anticipated, examine the associated controls and see if they may be having greater impact than you originally intended. In particular, see if the scope of their impact is beyond what you originally expected. Relaxed controls that are having greater influence than you had planned could easily cause some planned increases in control to be less effective. Similarly, increased controls having greater influence than planned could offset the expected benefits of having relaxed controls elsewhere on the project.

Detecting New Symptoms

As you monitor the metrics associated with the new controls, periodically look beyond the metrics and examine the project for any symptoms of insufficient, excessive, or inappropriate control. If your new controls are having the intended effects, then symptoms of control problems should slowly start to diminish.

However, new symptoms will appear periodically. These new symptoms may be attributable to actions you are taking or to ongoing changes in circumstances, technologies, personnel, and priorities. As these all change, the types of control you are using will likewise need to change.

Regular (such as monthly) monitoring of the symptoms of control problems will help you quickly detect the need to revisit your approach to project control.

Identifying Short-Term Inefficiencies

As with implementing any change, be sure to anticipate short-term inefficiencies that typically result from people attempting to do things differently. Whenever possible, make allowances for these inefficiencies by scheduling extra time. Additionally, inefficiencies associated with process or control changes can be reduced through employee orientations and additional training.

Generally, the incremental release approach will help minimize the amount of change occurring during any given increment and thereby help reduce the inefficiencies occurring during that specific increment. To help ensure that inefficiencies are truly short term, for any given control (or for the set of controls being released during an increment), attempt to predict the extent of inefficiencies that might result, and how long those inefficiencies will likely persist. Then monitor the metrics, track the inefficiencies, and compare these with your predictions. If the inefficiencies persist well beyond your predictions, consider the possibility of conflicting impacts, or new symptoms of control problems.

Performing Split Analysis

When implementing recovery from inappropriate control, you may find it easier to track and evaluate the impact of the control changes by splitting your analysis of the three separate types of changes you are implementing:

- increasing existing controls,
- relaxing existing controls, and
- implementing new controls.

By splitting your analysis, you can avoid the problems associated with trying to examine and understand everything simultaneously. For example, if you concentrate first on the new controls being implemented, you can evaluate them in isolation from any other changes and concentrate on the impact they seem to be having. Then you can examine any actions you are taking based on increasing existing controls. Again, look only at the impacts traceable to those controls. Finally, analyze the impacts resulting from relaxing existing controls.

Once you have conducted these three separate investigations, you should find it relatively easy to combine the results of your analysis and identify areas where the impact of control changes are overlapping, reinforcing, or possibly even negating each other.

ADDRESSING HUMAN FACTORS

With regard to the successful implementation of project controls and the successful management of software development projects, the most difficult problems are almost never technical. Human factors tend to be far more influential on project success than technical factors. Generally speaking, most people are resistant to change and, even when you do get them to change, they fall back into old habits easily. Therefore, to sustain your recovery from insufficient control, excessive control, or inappropriate control, you will need to direct special attention to the human factors associated with change and process improvement. This is the focus of the next chapter.

11 Sustaining the Recovery

"Sometimes just a little bit of help at just the right moment has far-reaching positive consequences."

At this stage in the project, you have developed plans, conducted reviews, performed process and product audits, identified ways to improve project management and engineering processes, and implemented those improvements. Though it has likely taken considerable time and effort to reach this point, it is still too early to relax. To ensure that the efforts you've made produce the intended results, you need to concentrate on a variety of human factors that, when handled properly, help project personnel adjust to the changes you've deployed.

Areas related to human factors that you will need to address (see Figure 21) include:

- amortizing the recovery effort,
- overcoming backlash,
- overcoming passive resistance,
- preventing exhaustion,
- gently tempering zealots,
- avoiding artificial victory,
- avoiding polarizing management peers,

- sharing success, and
- identifying and focusing on project management essentials.

Figure 21
Human Factors Areas to Address

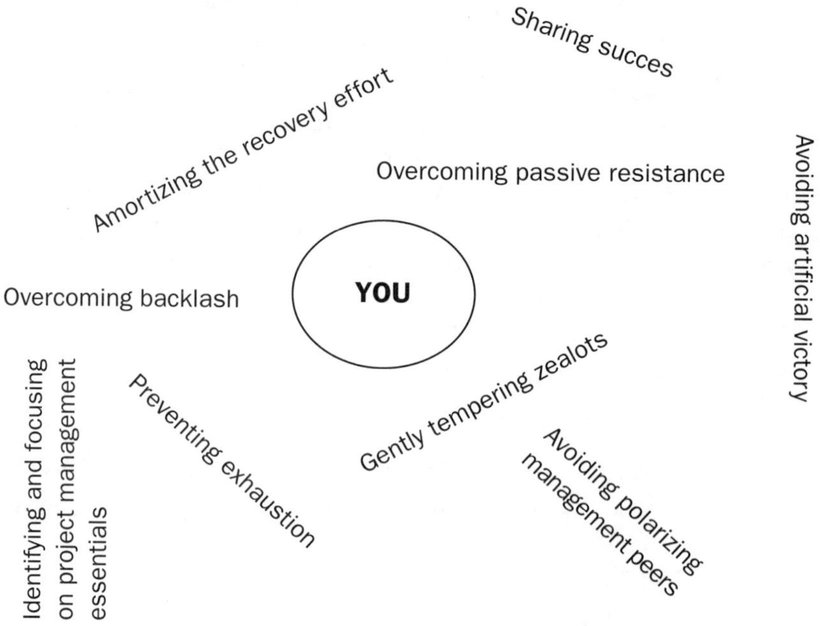

AMORTIZING THE RECOVERY EFFORT

Recovering a failing project typically requires considerable time, effort, and skill. It always involves at least some change, and may require considerable change. Once the changes are in place, it is critical to return to the business of managing and controlling the project as efficiently and effectively as possible.

To leverage the positive benefits of successful change techniques, you must shift the emphasis from introducing change to minimizing change. This shift allows the project personnel, including you, to derive the maximum benefit possible from relatively stable processes. In this way, you amortize across a longer span of time the extra effort you and others have made to recover the project. As discussed, it is very important that your perception of successful project control is confirmed by (relatively) objective evidence of success.

However, while returning your primary focus to day-to-day project management, if you are to sustain the recovery, you will need to monitor the environment for indications that the success of the recovery is under greater risk. Actions that may be required are discussed throughout the remainder of this chapter.

OVERCOMING BACKLASH

Backlash is characterized as clear and obvious resistance to change. When project personnel manifest backlash, they tell you, emphatically, why they think that your actions, initiatives, or objectives are in conflict with their perception of what is necessary. Backlash is, ironically, a low-risk manifestation of resistance and is fairly easy to work with.

With backlash, people are being honest with you. True, they disagree with your actions or plans, but at least they are honest. Such people are not adversaries—they are allies. Their feedback is highly valuable for a variety of reasons. First, they are clearly interested in success; otherwise, they would not care and would not be complaining. Second, they are sufficiently confident in their position that they have no trouble broadcasting it to you. Typically, such confidence comes from experience—they really may have issues that you need to hear about and possibly reconsider. Third, they let you know exactly what they don't like, or are not comfort able with. Hence, evaluating, designing, and implementing steps to address their concerns is relatively easy in the sense that you have the significant advantage of knowing exactly the problem or complaint you are trying to address.

OVERCOMING PASSIVE RESISTANCE

Passive resistance is much worse than backlash. Key people agree with or approve your efforts, others repeatedly confirm that yes, all these actions are important and must be performed, but in spite of all this apparent support, progress remains stalled.

With passive resistance, you have to find the real source of the resistance. This is typically a very difficult and time-consuming task. Judging by appearances, active resistance has been identified and actions are being taken, and all other indications are that progress can be expected. But your metrics (or your experience) indicate that progress either is not happening or is severely impeded.

Passive resistance is characterized by last-minute failures to meet prior commitments. For example, you tell someone that you will be providing an orientation on the new control processes at a meeting. They tell you that the changes are long overdue and they will support you 100 percent. Then, on the morning of the meeting, they call to apologize and explain that a totally unexpected emergency occurred. They ask if you could at least e-mail them the briefing material. You agree. Later, you set up a second orientation. This person again agrees, but again cancels at the last moment for what seems like legitimate reasons.

Passive resistance is one of the most difficult human factors issues you will need to deal with. It requires that you be patient. It also requires that you strive to be as objective as possible.

When trying to determine the source and magnitude of passive resistance, you need to follow two rules:

- Ignore what people say.
- Study and remember what people do.

PREVENTING EXHAUSTION

Whenever someone is asked to change the way he or she works, doing so typically requires additional attention and energy. When someone continually has to apply additional attention and energy, the risk of exhaustion increases proportionately.

The overall objective of change is to implement behavior that is conducive to achieving your goals. Generally, once the goals are achieved, it makes sense to stabilize the processes and let everyone acclimatize to a better life. Only after a protracted period of monitoring metrics and verifying successful application of essential project controls, should you consider introducing another round of control change.

In any event, it is wise to avoid continuous, pervasive, and incessant change. Continuous change leads to exhaustion. Change is usually perceived as something temporary. When change becomes a constant, those who are changing begin to suspect that management does not truly understand the purpose of making the changes.

As a general rule, the people you hire to staff a particular software development project are reasonably intelligent. Hence, they pay attention to their responsibilities and to your expectations. Usually, occasional change for strategic advantage is acknowledged and understood.

But most of them will interpret constant change as a sign of insufficient control or a confused interpretation of required controls. In any event, as manager, you have a bit of latitude regarding the willingness of your project personnel to follow your recommended changes to project control. Practically speaking, they will be thinking, "Do these new changes really help?"

Hence, as stated, it is imperative that you accumulate objective proof of the positive impact that your changes are having. It is likewise imperative that you share this proof with project personnel.

GENTLY TEMPERING ZEALOTS

As someone who is introducing change, you likely expect to encounter considerable resistance to your proposed changes. Resistance will be active, or maybe passive. No matter, the presence of resistance is virtually a given. Regardless of the type of resistance, it certainly makes sense to make contingencies when original plans prove inadequate. Sometimes these contingencies will rely in part on one or more project personnel who actively and vocally support the new changes.

As you struggle to implement change, you will usually find that some project personnel agree with your actions. Indeed, they think that your actions are long overdue. Actually, they think that your actions (which, by coincidence, are similar to what they've been attempting for years) are brilliant and all but ensure success. Such excessive support needs to be leveraged cautiously.

Zealots are wonderful as a source of energy. The risk you must manage is the risk that they are actually representing an approach that is fundamentally and intrinsically excessive to the approach you are taking. When project personnel essentially echo your position with comparatively little "value added," they usually help. When they exaggerate potential benefits, or otherwise distort your position, actions, or objectives, you should carefully reevaluate the advantages and disadvantages of encouraging or discouraging your zealots.

AVOIDING ARTIFICIAL VICTORY

As you pursue improved control of your project, and as you expend additional thought and effort in achieving this goal, you will naturally find yourself periodically asking, "Have I done it? Is my project under adequate control?"

During this time, it is especially important that you remember the original objectives of the project control changes, and compare original change targets, goals, or objectives with those that have been achieved to date.

Predictably, over time you will start to lose energy and then start to lose motivation regarding the implementation of control changes. During this time, you may look around and decide that, all in all, things look rather good. Indeed, as you reconsider the actions you've taken and the results of those actions, it may occur to you that, somewhat suddenly, it seems that you are done—you've succeeded in implementing the essential control changes needed on your project.

Be cautious of early declarations of victory. Strive to adhere to any beta-test intervals you previously identified.

The most reliable defense against premature declarations of victory is objective evidence. To avoid an artificial victory, ensure that you are tracking actual events and actual numbers, and that you have predefined thresholds regarding excesses and insufficiencies.

AVOIDING POLARIZING MANAGEMENT PEERS

Avoiding polarizing management peers is not much of a risk in top-down control improvement initiatives. However, if you are mostly self-motivated to implement the new controls, your project will start to stand out from similar projects. Virtually by definition, if your project starts looking better, other projects may start looking worse.

Generally, you are best served by striving not only to improve your ability to control your project, but also by striving to share openly with other project managers the steps you are taking, the results you are seeing, and even the problems you are encountering. Ask them for advice. Listen sincerely to their recommendations and implement those that seem reasonable.

If you isolate yourself, the more you succeed, the more you increase the risk that other project managers perceive your success as a threat. When you work openly with other managers as peers, seeking advice when needed and offering advice when asked, you reduce substantially the risk of polarizing or alienating them.

SHARING SUCCESS

There is absolutely no way you can be successful without the help of others. At a minimum, your team has to support your efforts. With luck, support groups will also help you. You may even receive cooperation from other project managers. Occasionally, executive management will take an enlightened approach, and visibly support and actively fund your efforts at control improvement.

In any event, achieving successful project controls is not about how you force or coerce others into doing what you think is best. Instead, it is about communicating key issues to others so that, as a team, you share a common understanding of what is required for success.

As you secure major, or even minor, victories related to initiatives you've introduced, you need to share those victories with those who helped you along the path to success. Sometimes, it may feel like everyone was an opponent and you had to do it all yourself. Such feelings are more likely when sustained introduction of changes has led to exhaustion. Almost without exception, when you succeed, it is precisely because one or more key people understood what you were trying to do and decided they would help. It may not have been major, or prolonged, but sometimes just a little bit of help at just the right moment has far-reaching positive consequences.

When you achieve objective confirmation of success, realistically it is impossible to determine accurately who contributed what to that success. Try anyway. Then let them know.

IDENTIFYING AND FOCUSING ON PROJECT MANAGEMENT ESSENTIALS

As discussed, recovering a failing project requires systematic change, but not continuous change. Nor radical change. Systematic process adaptation of essential project control consists of identifying an opportunity, making a change, having everyone verify the benefit, and enjoying the results. Then, everyone concentrates on production, quality, and other development and engineering issues. Periodically, you take the long view and look for new symptoms or opportunities. This approach helps ensure that if something essential needs to happen, it happens on your project. Moreover, nonessential actions are kept to a minimum.

Software project management is very unforgiving. It seems that every mistake has significant costs, and those costs accrue rapidly. If your project falls three months behind and you are a really good manager, then a year later your project will finish three months behind schedule. No additional slippage will be a major success. If you fall three months behind, and you want to recover that time and finish on schedule, it will require virtually a miracle.

The key is to stay ahead of the project, stay in control, and stay focused on essentials. Although the later chapters in this book have concentrated on techniques for recovering control of your project, you can substantially reduce the need to use these techniques by concentrating on understanding and applying the essential project management techniques discussed in the earlier chapters. Successful projects typically can trace their success to the strength of the project team, and the strength and *appropriateness* of the control techniques used to facilitate, coordinate, and protect that team.

As a software development project manager, you are attempting to manage the construction of some of the most complex systems ever developed by humankind. You are attempting to be a successful manager in spite of the extreme rate of change occurring in the tools and components used to construct these systems—and in spite of the considerable uncertainty surrounding the ultimate needs of those who will eventually use the systems. Nevertheless, many complex systems have been developed on time and within budget—unimaginably complex systems that work. It has been done. It will continue to be done. It just requires a very careful mix of freedom and discipline to make it happen.

And a well-managed team.

APPENDICES

APPENDIX A

Managing Defects Using Diagnostic Software Architectures

In addition to managing project personnel, one of your most important management responsibilities is managing (and reducing) defects in your software and software-related products. Generally, your greatest risk exposure is from defects in the software itself (versus, for example, defects in documentation or training material). An important technique you can use when designing the software system is to incorporate a diagnostic software architecture.

THE NEED FOR DIAGNOSTICS

A common challenge in all software systems is determining the ideal amount of internal error checking and management. The objective is to have a sufficient, but not excessive, amount of error management. Excessive error management typically causes unnecessary complexity, increased software size, and decreased software performance.

Software systems are usually designed with error detection and management as an integral part of overall system functionality. To support insight into alternative error management approaches, analysts and designers might employ model-integrated environments, patterns, and formal techniques. Even with such techniques, very few systems can be asserted to be defect-free.

Therefore, as the architecture forms, most analysts and designers strive to ensure sufficient error management routines to accomplish two objectives: (1) to prevent errors from happening; and (2) if prevention fails, to manage the impact of errors as an expected part of overall system processing.

Outside of mission-critical, life-rated systems (flight control being an excellent example), designers often fail to consider an equally important third objective: to design the software architecture to support aggressively after-the-fact identification and diagnosis of system errors and anomalous behavior. This diagnostic approach to software architecture provides the same type of recovery and corrective options to software development and maintenance personnel that diagnostic systems provide in mission-critical software systems and systems resulting from other engineering disciplines.

To summarize, in principle, all systems should be designed to achieve perfect error detection and management. However, given the chance that the actual system might be less than perfect, systems should also be based on architectures that help diagnose problems that were not detected or managed successfully. In the event of anomalous system behavior, a diagnostic architecture helps you rapidly focus the search for defects to the fewest modules, fewest objects, fewest lines of code, and fewest data elements possible.

CONSTRUCTING DIAGNOSTIC SOFTWARE ARCHITECTURES

When you, as a software project manager or engineer, are first informed of a problem in the performance of a software-intensive system, you usually are given three types of information: (1) context—the system's general environment while executing, (2) sequence—the series of actions immediately prior to problem detection, and (3) consequence—the known and probable results of the problem. A diagnostic architecture must augment this information to provide the most comprehensive insight possible into the probable source of the problem.

Generally, insight regarding how best to augment problem information can be achieved after preliminary system design, or after development of the system invention and design rules. At this point, the software architecture is beginning to take shape, and is driven primarily by key elements within both the problem domain and the solution domain. This is an ideal time to adjust the architecture so that it also supports diagnosis of system anomalies.

To identify where in the architecture you should consider making changes to accommodate diagnostic support, you need to ask the following four questions:

1. Where can the most comprehensive insights be gained? (breadth of insight)

2. Where can the most important insights be gained? (depth of insight)

3. Which modules will dominate the behavior of the system? (type of insight)

4. Which interfaces will reveal behavior? (frequency of insight)

A key principle in developing a diagnostic software architecture is that the diagnostics are intrinsic to the architecture, not to the code. That is, at certain locations within the overall system, a call is made or a message passed that results in the storage of diagnostic data. Keeping the diagnostic algorithms out of the application code helps preserve maximum flexibility for modifying and updating the code without negatively affecting your ability to perform software diagnostics.

Numerous locations within the architecture are good candidates for answering the four questions. Consider, for example, using diagnostic routines:

- immediately upon receiving data from external systems,
- immediately before passing data to external systems,
- upon exchange of data with persistent data stores,
- between major system states,
- before/after complex data manipulations,
- before/after high-visibility behavior, and
- before/after critical no-visibility behavior.

Some of these areas are usually well-protected by error detection and management routines. For example, checking data from external systems, and rejecting bad data, is a fairly common practice. However, if some of these areas are not well-protected, then diagnostics could be critical when trying to isolate the source of system problems. As another example, any type of persistent data store is a candidate for diagnostics since sometimes these data stores are not nearly as persistent as originally designed.

In addition to determining how to adjust the architecture to support diagnostics, it is necessary to determine the most appropriate types of diagnostic techniques.

DETERMINING APPROPRIATE DIAGNOSTIC TECHNIQUES

Diagnostic techniques can be classified using two characteristics: (1) what is being diagnosed, and (2) what the limitations are on the diagnosis.

With regard to the first, the two primary options are to diagnose the process or to diagnose the product. Process diagnosis generally consists of tracking the activation or invocation history of various objects, modules, subroutines, etc. Product diagnosis typically consists of tracking the creation, manipulation, storage, and destruction of data.

With regard to the second characteristic, limitations are usually a reflection of acceptable negative impact on available resources. Common limitation categories include:

- Frequency limitations (e.g., log no more than the last one hundred change instances)
- Time limitations (e.g., log nothing older than the last ten seconds)
- Activation limitations (e.g., log data only from the last three times the system was activated)
- Negative feedback loop limitations (e.g., limit when data recording threatens to result in excessive computational demand)
- No limitations (e.g., always record everything) Note: this is generally unrealistic.

After identifying areas in the software architecture that

are candidates for diagnostic insight, it is necessary to answer two fundamental questions:

1. What do I need to diagnose (process, product)?

2. What limitations exist regarding my ability to implement diagnostic intelligence (time, space, frequency, other)?

By carefully considering the insights to be derived from using different diagnostic techniques at various places within the system, you can strive to have the most revealing and informative set of data while simultaneously minimizing negative performance impacts and the use of critical system resources. Properly designed diagnostic architectures may also yield highly reusable architectural components.

SUMMARY

As a result of market competition, innovation, technology advances, and other factors, embedded systems are often subject to considerable updating and evolutionary change. Ideally, the architecture for these systems is designed to anticipate, accommodate, and even facilitate rapid change. However, the insertion of new or upgraded features always introduces the possibility of inserting defects that result in system performance anomalies or outright failures.

Error capture and management routines are an essential part of even simple software systems. However, with increasing complexity, it becomes progressively more difficult to determine if you have successfully implemented an appropriate amount of error management.

Although the ideal is for systems always to work perfectly, if your system ever starts exhibiting anomalous behavior, you must have the means to conduct a successful investigation into the source of the anomalies. As discussed, one means to improve your ability to conduct such investigations efficiently and successfully is to design the software architecture with the express purpose of supporting the diagnosis of behavioral anomalies within the family of systems derived from the architecture.

APPENDIX B

Sample Approach for a One-Semester Course in Software Project Management

The following material is intended to help you develop a syllabus for a one-semester undergraduate or graduate course in software project management, using this text as the primary reference book. For an undergraduate-level course, this text contains more than enough content to fill the entire semester. As reflected in the following material, emphasis should be placed on core project management objectives, such as planning, tracking, and controlling. Topics such as risk management, process improvement, and even metrics can be deferred until later in the semester and introduced only if time permits.

If you are teaching a graduate-level course, consider either adding a text containing a set of recent papers on software project management, or augmenting this book with recent papers in all areas you consider especially important. In light of the complexity of the subject matter, it can be useful to find seemingly contradictory papers on various topics. This discourages students from simply looking for the right answer, and encourages them to pursue right thinking.

The following material is designed to assist you in building a syllabus for a sixteen-week semester. It presumes some type of mid-semester break of one week. The following layout does not allocate time for a mid-term exam, and presumes that the final exam will require an entire class period.

You will find that the scope of the material from the text allows you considerable flexibility in focusing on topics you consider most important and augmenting this material with information from other sources.

Included as part of the suggested assignments are three major items: a term paper, a term project, and weekly reading summaries. The weekly summaries are intended to encourage students to keep up with the reading by providing a summary of what they consider to be the top ten major points that were made within the assigned reading. The term project and term paper are whatever you think will help students understand and retain the key principles of successful software project management.

Week 1: Semester Overview

Agenda:
- Course introduction
- Instructor introduction
- Student introductions
- Review of the syllabus
- Review of term paper assignment
- Review of term project assignment
- Review of student reading and other assignments
- Review of grading criteria

Due at Start of Class: —

Comments to Instructor:

The primary objective of the first class is to ensure that all students understand what they are expected to learn during the semester, what they are expected to do, what they are expected to produce, and how their activities and products (assignments) will be graded. With this type of class, it is often quite useful to spend a fair amount of time on student introductions. In particular, allow the students to provide a brief overview of both their project management experience and their software development experience. You may find it useful to establish the following rules:

1. Whenever a student is discussing a bad project experience, it is always to be discussed in the context of a job they previously had, not their current job.
2. No company names are to be used in a negative context.
3. Company names, or references to a current project, are allowed only when relating positive experiences and insights.

Reading assignment for next week:

Chapter 1 (all):
Project Management in the Software Development Environment
- Why Do Project Management?
- Different Approaches to Project Management
- The Challenging Environment of Software Development
- What is Project Management?
- The Role of the Project Manager in Today's Software-Intensive Environments
- Where to Start?

Week 2: Project Management in the Software Context

Agenda:
- Brief review of syllabus and student assignments
- Project goals
- Project obstacles
- Project resources
- Alternative approaches to project management
- In-class exercise: major software challenges
- Overview of project planning

Overview of project tracking
Overview of project control
Principles of leadership
Reminder: Resumes and project proposals are due next week.

Due at Start of Class:
Summary of ten key points from reading assignment (Chapter 1)

Comments to Instructor:
The primary objective of this class is to provide a reasonably comprehensive overview of the major responsibilities of a software project manager. Emphasis should be placed on the wide variety of software projects and the corresponding wide variety of approaches to software project management. Time permitting, conduct an in-class exercise to develop a list of the primary causes of software project failure. For each cause, discuss the degree to which a project manager may be able to detect the cause and reduce its impact.

Reading assignment for next week:
Chapter 2 (all):
Selecting the Best Processes
Identifying Your Project's Key Strengths
Selecting the Best Lifecycle
Selecting the Best Engineering Method

Week 3: Selecting the Best Processes

Agenda:
Project strengths
Typical software project activities
Common lifecycle models
Common engineering methodologies
Reminder: Preliminary term paper abstract and outline are due next week.

Due at Start of Class:
Summary of ten key points from reading assignment (Chapter 2)
Student resume or short biography
Proposal for term project

Comments to Instructor:
During this lecture, ask students to augment the set of lifecycle models with other lifecycles that they are familiar with or have studied. Similarly, discuss engineering methodologies not presented in this book. Stress the importance of understanding the impact that various lifecycles have on project risk management. Since this is the only time that lifecycle models are discussed as a major, stand-alone topic, plan on spending a majority of the class time explaining various lifecycles and the impact they have on management techniques. Generally, most students are quite familiar with common software engineering methodologies, such as object-oriented techniques, but not lifecycle methodologies (with the exception of the waterfall lifecycle).

Reading assignment for next week:
Chapter 3 (part):
Developing Plans
Developing Preliminary Plans
Developing Intermediate Plans

Week 4: Developing Preliminary Plans

Agenda:
Iterative development of project plans
Feasibility analysis
Project initiation
Contents of a project plan
Project organizational structures
Staffing the project
Planning the project environment and tools

Preliminary work breakdown structure
Preliminary resource breakdown structure
Detailed requirements analysis
In-class exercise: Develop a WBS for any one of the following:

- summer vacation
- moving from one residence to another
- finding and purchasing a new car
- getting an "A" in a difficult class

Due at Start of Class:

Summary of ten key points from reading assignment (Chapter 3, part)
Preliminary term paper abstract and outline

Comments to Instructor:

Consider placing the major emphasis during this lecture on human factors. That is, emphasize the topics of project staffing and finding software talent. Try to leave sufficient time for the suggested in-class exercise, and have the students develop some preliminary work breakdown structures. A useful approach is to first allow students about 15 minutes to work individually. Then pair up students who are working on the same type of WBS and allow them to work as teams of two. After another 15 or 20 minutes, see if you can form some teams of four (again, all four will need to be working on the same type of WBS). Conclude this exercise with voluntary presentations of one or more work breakdown structures, a discussion of any problems encountered while creating the WBS, and a discussion of techniques used to overcome those problems.

Reading assignment for next week:

Chapter 3 (part):
Developing Plans
  Developing Detailed Plans
  Developing a Risk Management Plan

Organizing the Project Plan
Maintaining the Project Plan
Developing a Staffing Plan

Week 5: Developing Detailed Plans

Agenda:

Estimating product size
Estimating project effort
Milestone scheduling
Precedence networks
Resource scheduling
Planning, mitigating, and managing risks
Completing the project plan
Maintaining plans as "living documents"
Project roles
Finding software talent
In-class exercise: Creative methods for finding software talent
Reminder: Detailed term project outline and detailed term paper outline are due next week.

Due at Start of Class:

Summary of ten key points from reading assignment (Chapter 3, remainder)

Comments to Instructor:

This is a very full class so you'll want to be deliberate about time management. It is quite useful to walk students through the process of manually constructing a simple precedence network and analyzing it for dependencies, critical path, and slack time. Although many students are familiar with mainstream project management tools, they are often unfamiliar with the principles behind those tools.

Risk management is also a major topic, and you may want to devote an entire class to it (and combine two other classes into one). Stress that risk management can be done simply and implemented easily.

Reading assignment for next week:
Chapter 4 (part):
Product Management
Managing Software in a Systems Context
Managing Requirements
Managing Product Complexity
Managing Configurations

Week 6: Managing Product Quality

Agenda:
Overview of systems engineering
Software in a systems context
Managing requirements
Reducing software complexity
Principles of software configuration management

Due at Start of Class:
Summary of ten key points from reading assignment (Chapter 4, part)
Detailed term project outline
Detailed term paper outline

Comments to Instructor:
The two primary topics for this class are requirements management and configuration management. Each topic is easily worthy of an entire semester, and you may want to adjust the syllabus to split these topics into different classes so that you can devote more time to each. In any event, stress to the students that, as project manager, they will either need to accept these responsibilities and perform these activities themselves, or delegate these responsibilities to someone else on the project. Also stress that

these are essential management responsibilities that are applicable to and critical for the success of even the smallest projects.

Reading assignment for next week:

Chapter 4 (remaining):
Product Management
- Managing Defects
- Ensuring Quality
- Tracking Your Project Using Earned Value Management
- (Skip: Using Product Measurements and Metrics)
- Maintaining Product Focus

Week 7: Defect Management and Earned Value

Agenda:
- Management software reviews
- Senior software reviews
- Software walkthroughs
- Software inspections
- Planning and tracking defect management
- Software quality assurance
- Calculating and tracking earned value
- Importance of maintaining a focus on product delivery

Due at Start of Class:
- Summary of ten key points from reading assignment (Chapter 4, remainder, except metrics)

Comments to Instructor:

The primary topics for this class are software reviews and software quality assurance. Stress the importance of having a choice of review processes on the project so that the type of review used is appropriate for the amount of risk associated with the software being reviewed. Although it is not practical, or necessary, to teach the students how to perform these types of reviews, it is important that they understand that even a brief review process is capable of detecting significant software defects. As the lecture transitions into the larger topic of software quality assurance, be sure to stress that software quality assurance is not limited just to product quality, but is also very concerned with ensuring adequate process quality. Note that the topic of metrics (from Chapter 4) is deferred until the next class session.

Reading assignment for next two weeks:
- Chapter 5 (all), Chapter 4 (part):
- Process Management
  - Managing Software Processes in a Systems Context
  - Managing Your Project Staff
  - Managing Negotiations with Affected Groups
  - Managing Process Support Technology
  - Managing Process Complexity
  - Managing Interactions with Customers
  - (Skip: Using Process Measurements and Metrics)
  - (Optional: Managing the Acquisition of Software Subcomponents)
  - Controlling Your Project Control Activities
- Product Management
  - Using Product Measurements and Metrics
- Process Management
  - Using Process Measurements and Metrics

Week 8: Semester Break

Week 9: Managing Process Quality

Agenda:
- Impact of system-level processes on the software project
- Managing a team of software professionals
- Motivating and retaining software professionals

Negotiating with affected groups
Leveraging tools and technology
Techniques for reducing software complexity
Interacting with customers
Interacting with executive management
Fundamentals of measurements and metrics
Dangerous metrics
(Optional: Managing the acquisition of software subcomponents)

Due at Start of Class:
Summary of ten key points from reading assignment (Chapter 5, and the metrics section from Chapter 4)

Comments to Instructor:
The topic of metrics can easily fill this entire class, so you will want to ensure that you budget a considerable amount of time for it. However, metrics can be a comparatively dry topic, so encourage class participation. Ask students about the various ways that they, or their work, have been measured in the past. Ask what their reaction was to such measurement. Ask the students about any failed software measurement initiatives they've witnessed, and what they think caused the failure of those initiatives.

Reading assignment for next week:

Chapter 6 (all):
Diagnosing Project Control Effectiveness
Detecting Control Problems
Performing Routine Project Tracking
Leveraging Safety-Net Functions

Week 10: Diagnosing Project Control Effectiveness

Agenda:
Common project control problems
Tracking the progress of work packages

Analyzing and projecting milestone achievement
Plotting and comparing project trendlines
Overview of software quality frameworks
The Software Capability Maturity Model®
IEEE standards
Formal project capability audits

Due at Start of Class:
Summary of ten key points from reading assignment (Chapter 6, all)

Comments to Instructor:
This class is an excellent opportunity to review everything that has been discussed previously during the semester. In effect, the primary diagnostic technique the manager has is the routine use of project plans and the routine tracking of project activities, products, and related metrics. This class is also a good time to discuss more specialized diagnostic approaches such as software project capability appraisals and assessments. Depending on your familiarity with the topic, describing a comprehensive approach to examining the capability or risk exposure of a given project may take a majority of the class time. Such techniques appear to be becoming more widespread, and students should understand the value of these techniques to a software project manager.

Reading assignment for next week:
Chapter 7 (all):
External Software Capability Audits
The Purpose of External Audits
External Audit Approach
Standard Rules for External Auditors
Preparing for and Participating in an External Audit

Week 11: External Software Capability Audits

Agenda:

Purpose of external audits
Types of external audits
Preparing your project for an external audit
Participating in an external audit
Leveraging the audit results
Reminder: Term papers are due next week.

Due at Start of Class:

Summary of ten key points from reading assignment (Chapter 7, all)

Comments to Instructor:

Depending on the particular students in your class, and the types of organizations they work for, this topic will be of greater or lesser value. Although the use of external software capability audits by commercial organizations is becoming more common, government agencies and contractor organizations performing work for government agencies currently show the most interest in this technique. Depending on the mix of students in your class, consider using some of this class time for any earlier topic that you want to give additional emphasis (such as software size estimation, risk management, requirements management, configuration management, quality assurance, or metrics). Generally, you should still have the students read Chapter 7, and hand in their summaries of what they consider to be the ten key points.

Reading assignment for next week: Chapter 8 (all):

Recovering Projects from Insufficient Control
Identifying the Symptoms of Insufficient Control

Determining Types of Additional Control
Defining Additional Controls
Testing Additional Controls
Deploying Additional Controls
Monitoring Additional Controls

Week 12: Recovering from Insufficient Control

Agenda:

Major symptoms of insufficient control
Root cause analysis
Increasing control of management processes
Increasing control of engineering processes
Increasing control of support processes
Increasing control of project interface
Identifying and describing additional controls
Prioritizing additional controls
Planning control rollout
Documenting new responsibilities and roles
Testing additional controls
Deploying additional controls
Monitoring additional controls

Due at Start of Class:

Summary of ten key points from reading assignment (Chapter 8, all)
Term papers

Comments to Instructor:

This class covers a lot of fundamental material that will all be applicable to the next two classes. Hence, if you cannot get through all the material in the available class time, it is better to allow this material to continue into the next class than to rush or to cut short the discussion. With this and the next two chapters, be sure to stress the importance of identifying symptoms. Typically, no corrective actions are taken if the project manager does not realize that a problem is beginning to develop. Stress the importance of early diagnosis and early treatment.

Reading assignment for next week:
  Chapter 9 (all):
  Recovering Projects from Excessive Control
    Identifying the Symptoms of Excessive Control
    Determining Types of Control Reduction
    Incrementally Relaxing Excessive Controls
    Detecting Excessive Relaxation of Control

Week 13: Recovering from Excessive Control

Agenda:
  Major symptoms of excessive control
  Identifying project inefficiencies
  Estimating impact of improvements
  Estimating implementation difficulty
  Prioritizing control reduction opportunities
  Relaxing clearly unnecessary controls
  Relaxing low-downside controls
  Relaxing isolated controls
  Relaxing rapid feedback controls
  Relaxing remaining excessive controls
  Monitoring for and detecting excessive relaxation
  Reminder: Term projects are due next week.

Due at Start of Class:
  Summary of ten key points from reading assignment (Chapter 9, all)
  Late term papers

Comments to Instructor:
  If you are having students volunteer to present their semester projects or term papers, this class and the next class are

the best times for these presentations. If you provided a thorough explanation of the principles presented in Chapter 8, Recovering from Insufficient Control, then you can focus on the unique aspects of this (and the next) chapter. Be sure to stress that excessive controls can become a major problem on any long-term project and on virtually all legacy system maintenance projects.

Reading assignment for next week:
  Chapter 10 (all):
  Recovering Projects from Inappropriate Control
    Identifying the Symptoms of Inappropriate Control
    Planning the Control Shift
    Implementing and Tracking the Control Shift
    Addressing Human Factors

Week 14: Recovering from Inappropriate Control

Agenda:
  Major symptoms of inappropriate control
  Matching controls to the project lifecycle
  Matching controls to the project team
  Matching controls to the products being developed
  Matching controls to the project and organizational culture
  Planning a shift in project controls
  Incrementally shifting project controls
  Implementing and tracking incremental shifts
  Monitoring and detecting new symptoms
  Overview of human factors
  In-class exercise: case study analysis and recovery

Due at Start of Class:
  Summary of ten key points from reading assignment (Chapter 10, all)
  Term projects

Comments to Instructor:
  The topics covered in this class can leverage off the topics discussed during the prior two classes. Try to set aside ap-

proximately half the class time for an in-class exercise that allows students to apply the principles from the three chapters on project recovery (Chapters 8, 9, and 10). Consider having the students form into teams of four to six students each. Provide each team with an example case study (either fictional or real) that describes a particular software project and the problems being experienced on that project. Have each team document what they consider to be the major symptoms being manifested on the project, the possible root causes of those symptoms, the corrective actions that should be taken, and a draft sequence of steps for implementing those corrective actions. Save time near the end of class for open discussion of the scenarios, symptoms, and techniques the teams would use to recover the project in their scenario.

Reading assignment for next week:
- Chapter 11 (all):
- Sustaining the Recovery
  - Amortizing the Recovery Effort
  - Overcoming Backlash
  - Overcoming Passive Resistance
  - Preventing Exhaustion
  - Gently Tempering Zealots
  - Avoiding Artificial Victory
  - Avoiding Polarizing Management Peers
  - Sharing Success
  - Identifying and Focusing on Project Management Essentials

Week 15: Sustaining the Recovery

Agenda:
- Amortizing the recovery effort
- Overcoming backlash
- Overcoming passive resistance
- Preventing exhaustion
- Gently tempering zealots
- Avoiding artificial victory

Avoiding polarizing management peers
Sharing success
Identifying and focusing on project management essentials
Reminder: Final exam is next week (not that anyone needs reminding)!

Due at Start of Class:
Summary of ten key points from reading assignment (Chapter 11, all).
Late term projects

Comments to Instructor:
This is, of course, the last lecture night of the semester. You may want to deemphasize somewhat the topics in Chapter 11 to leave more time for a review of important highlights from throughout the semester. Although not a topic within the book, if you have the time, this is a good class for discussing the future of software project management. Students find the topic very interesting and enjoyable. Additionally, it allows students to gain better insight into the fact that the vast majority of project management techniques discussed during the semester are fundamental and persistent techniques, independent of the changes in technologies and tools used in software project management.

Reading assignment for next week: Review chapters 1 through 11.

Week 16: Final Exam

Agenda:
Take attendance
Review ground rules for taking the exam
Distribute exam
Preread of exam, student questions, and instructor clarification
Exam
Optional: Postexam review of major points

Due at Start of Class:
All past-due material

Due at End of Class:
Final exam
Three pages, double-sided, reference notes for final exam

Comments to Instructor:

Some instructors prefer to allow students to bring a few pages of notes to the final exam (which is otherwise closed-book, closed-notes). These notes can be on anything the student thinks is important and that might be helpful during the final exam. Given such an opportunity, most students will spend considerable time studying their lecture notes and the course material, analyzing that information for the most important concepts, principles, and techniques, and then transferring that information onto their few pages of "essential" notes. This translates into an extremely valuable period of learning and assimilation.

Consider asking students to turn in their notes with their exam (or to turn in a duplicate copy of their notes). This will allow you to investigate what the students consider to be the most important topics and lessons from your semester course. If necessary, the next time you teach the class you can adjust the amount of time devoted to different topics to stress those areas that you think are most important for the students to learn.

APPENDIX C

Sample Schedule for a 40-Hour Certificate Course in Software Project Management

The following sample schedule and agenda illustrate one approach to developing a 40-hour certificate course using this text as the primary reference book. The material is structured into a morning session from 8:00 to 12:00 (with a 15 minute break) and an afternoon session from 1:00 to 5:00 (also with a 15 minute break). Generally, fewer topics are covered in the morning than in the afternoon. This allows time in the morning to review prior material and to answer questions related to prior material. In view of the large amount of material to cover, you will likely need to manage your time quite carefully during the afternoon sessions.

The overall schedule and agenda follow the organization of the book rather closely. Therefore, you may want to encourage students to follow along in the book and add comments, highlights, or notations directly to the book whenever they wish.

If you are teaching a less experienced group, consider placing the emphasis on the fundamentals of software project management. Indeed, you may want to adjust the following material so that you take four days to teach the fundamentals (instead of three) and take only one day to teach recovery techniques (instead of two). Conversely, with a more experienced set of students, you can likely accelerate the discussion of project management fundamentals, and place more em phasis on specialty topics such as project recovery, risk management, metrics, and software process improvement.

Day #1

Agenda, 8:00 to 10:00, 10:15 to 12:00
Course introduction
Instructor introduction
Student introductions
Comprehensive review of the course agenda
Project goals
Project obstacles
Project resources

Comments to Instructor:
The primary objective of the first segment is to ensure that all students understand what they are expected to learn during the course, what they are expected to do, and what they are expected to produce. With this type of class, it is often quite useful to spend a fair amount of time on student introductions. In particular, allow the students to provide a brief overview of both their project management and their software development experience. Establish the following rules:

1. Whenever a student is discussing a bad project experience, it is always to be discussed in the context of a job they previously had, not their current job.
2. No company names are to be used in a negative context.
3. Company names, or references to a current project, are allowed only when relating positive experiences and insights.

Agenda, 1:00 to 2:45
Alternative approaches to project management
In-class exercise: Major software challenges

Overview of project planning
Overview of project tracking
Overview of project control
Principles of leadership

Comments to Instructor:

The primary objective of this segment is to provide a reasonably comprehensive overview of the major responsibilities of a software project manager. Emphasis should be placed on the wide variety of software projects and the corresponding wide variety of approaches to software project management. Time permitting, conduct an in-class exercise to develop a list of the primary causes of software project failure. For each cause, discuss the degree to which a project manager may be able to detect the cause and reduce its impact.

Agenda, 3:00 to 5:00:

Project strengths
Typical software project activities
Common lifecycle models
Common engineering methodologies
Iterative development of project plans
Feasibility analysis
Project initiation
Contents of a project plan
Review of Day #1

Comments to Instructor:

During this segment, ask students to augment the set of lifecycle models with other lifecycles that they are familiar with or have studied. Similarly, discuss engineering methodologies not presented in this book. Stress the importance of understanding the impact that various lifecycles have on project risk management. Since this is the only time that lifecycle models are discussed as a major, stand-alone topic, plan on spending a majority of the class time explaining various lifecycles. Generally, most students are quite familiar with common software engineering methodologies, such as object-oriented techniques, but are much less familiar with lifecycle methodologies. At the end of the day, save time to discuss the material relating to the contents of the project plan.

Day #2

Agenda, 8:00 to 10:00, 10:15 to 12:00:

Review of Day #1
Preview of Day #2
Project organizational structures
Staffing the project
Planning the project environment and tools
Preliminary work breakdown structure
Preliminary resource breakdown structure
Detailed requirements analysis
In-class exercise: Develop a WBS for any one of the following:

- summer vacation
- moving from one residence to another
- finding and purchasing a new car
- getting an "A" in a difficult class

Comments to Instructor:

Consider placing the major emphasis during this segment on human factors. That is, emphasize the topics of project staffing and finding software talent. Try to leave sufficient time for the suggested in-class exercise, and have the students develop some work breakdown structures. A useful approach is to first allow students about 15 minutes to work individually. Then pair up students who are working on the same type of WBS and allow them to work as teams of two. After another 15 or 20 minutes, see if you can form some teams of four (again, all four will need to be working on the same type of WBS). Conclude this exercise with voluntary presentations of one or more work breakdown structures, a discussion of any problems encountered while creating the WBS, and a discussion of techniques used to overcome those problems.

Agenda, 1:00 to 2:45:

Estimating product size
Estimating project effort
Milestone scheduling
Precedence networks
Resource scheduling
Planning, mitigating, and managing risks
Completing the project plan
Maintaining plans as "living documents"
Project roles
Finding software talent
In-class exercise: Creative methods for finding software talent

Comments to Instructor:

This is a very full segment so you'll want to be deliberate about time management. It is quite useful to walk students through the process of manually constructing a simple precedence network and analyzing it for dependencies, critical path, and slack time. Although many students are familiar with mainstream project management tools, they are often unfamiliar with the principles behind those tools.

Risk management is also a major topic and you may want to devote an entire segment to it (and combine two other segments into one). Stress that risk management can be done simply and implemented easily.

Agenda, 3:00 to 5:00:

Overview of systems engineering
Software in a systems context
Managing requirements
Software complexity reduction
Principles of software configuration management
Review of Day #2

Comments to Instructor:

The two primary topics for this segment are requirements management and configuration management. Each topic is easily an entire certificate unto itself, and you may want to adjust the agenda to split these topics into different segments and thereby devote more time to each. In any event, stress to the students that, as project manager, they will either need to accept these responsibilities and perform these activities themselves, or delegate these responsibilities to someone else on the project. Also stress that these are essential management responsibilities that are applicable to and critical for the success of even the smallest projects.

Day #3

Agenda, 8:00 to 10:00, 10:15 to 12:00:

Review of Day #2
Preview of Day #3
Management software reviews
Senior software reviews
Software walkthroughs
Software inspections
Planning and tracking defect management
Software quality assurance
Calculating and tracking earned value
Importance of maintaining a focus on product delivery

Comments to Instructor:

The primary topics for this segment are software reviews and software quality assurance. Stress the importance of having a choice of review processes on the project so that the type of review used is appropriate for the amount of risk associated with the software being reviewed. Although it is not practical, or necessary, to teach the students how to perform these types of reviews, it is important that they understand that even a brief review process is capable of detecting significant software defects. As the lecture transitions into the larger topic of software quality assurance, be sure to stress the fact that software quality assurance is not limited just to product quality, but is also very concerned with ensuring adequate process quality. Note that the topic of metrics (from Chapter 4) is deferred until the next class segment.

Agenda, 1:00 to 2:45:
Impact of system-level processes on the software project
Managing a team of software professionals
Motivating and retaining software professionals
Negotiating with affected groups
Leveraging tools and technology
Techniques for reducing software complexity
Interacting with customers
Interacting with executive management
Fundamentals of measurements and metrics
Dangerous metrics
(Optional: Managing the acquisition of software subcomponents)

Comments to Instructor:
The topic of metrics can easily fill this entire segment, so you will want to ensure that you budget a considerable amount of time for it. However, metrics can be a comparatively dry topic, so encourage class participation. Ask students about the various ways either they, or their work, have been measured in the past. Ask what their reaction was to such measurement. Ask the students about any failed software measurement initiatives they've witnessed, and what they think caused the failure of those initiatives.

Agenda, 3:00 to 5:00:
Common project control problems
Tracking the progress of work packages
Analyzing and projecting milestone achievement
Plotting and comparing project trendlines
Overview of software quality frameworks

The Software Capability Maturity Model®
IEEE standards
Formal project capability audits
Review of Day #3

Comments to Instructor:

This segment is a good time to discuss specialized diagnostic approaches such as software project capability appraisals and assessments. Depending on your familiarity with the topic, describing a comprehensive approach to examining the capability or risk exposure of a given project may take a majority of the class time. Such techniques appear to be becoming more widespread, and students should understand the value of these techniques to a software project manager. Ideally, also plan on spending a fair amount of time discussing the Software Capability Maturity Model®.

Day #4

Topic: External Software Capability Audits

Agenda, 8:00 to 10:00, 10:15 to 12:00:

Review of Day #1, Day #2, and Day #3
Preview of Day #4 and Day #5
Purpose of external audits
Types of external audits
Preparing your project for an external audit
Participating in an external audit
Leveraging the audit results
Major symptoms of insufficient control
Root cause analysis
Increasing control of management processes
Increasing control of engineering processes
Increasing control of support processes
Increasing control of project interface

Comments to Instructor:

Today's material begins the transition from fundamentals of project management and control, to identifying and correcting control problems. Therefore, begin this day with a review of all the material presented, and an overview of all remaining material.

Depending on the particular students in your class, and the types of organizations they work for, the need to understand external software quality audits will vary. Although the use of external software capability audits by commercial organizations is becoming more common, government agencies and contractor organizations performing work for government agencies currently show the most interest in this technique. Depending on the mix of students in your class, consider using some of this time for any earlier topic that you want to give additional emphasis (such as software size estimation, risk management, requirements management, configuration management, quality assurance, or metrics).

Agenda, 1:00 to 2:45:

Identifying and describing additional controls
Prioritizing additional controls
Planning control rollout
Documenting new responsibilities and roles
Testing additional controls
Deploying additional controls
Monitoring additional controls

Comments to Instructor:

This segment covers a lot of fundamental material that will all be applicable to the next two segments. Hence, if you cannot get through all the material in the available time, it is better to allow this material to continue into the next segment than to rush or to cut short the discussion. With this and the next two chapters, be sure to stress the importance of identifying symptoms. Typically, no corrective actions are taken if the project manager does not realize that a problem is beginning to develop. Stress the importance of early diagnosis and early treatment.

Agenda, 3:00 to 5:00:
Major symptoms of excessive control
Identifying project inefficiencies
Estimating impact of improvements
Estimating implementation difficulty
Prioritizing control reduction opportunities
Relaxing clearly unnecessary controls
Relaxing low-downside controls
Relaxing isolated controls
Relaxing rapid feedback controls
Relaxing remaining excessive controls
Monitoring for and detecting excessive relaxation
Review of Day #4

Comments to Instructor:
If you provided a thorough explanation of the principles presented in Chapter 8, Recovering from Insufficient Control, then you can focus on the unique aspects of this (and the next) chapter. Be sure to stress that excessive controls can become a major problem on any long-term project and on virtually all legacy system maintenance projects.

Day #5

Agenda, 8:00 to 10:00, 10:15 to 12:00:
Review of Day #4
Preview of Day #5
Major symptoms of inappropriate control
Matching controls to the project lifecycle
Matching controls to the project team
Matching controls to the products being developed
Matching controls to the project and organizational culture

Planning a shift in project controls
Incrementally shifting project controls
Implementing and tracking incremental shifts
Monitoring and detecting new symptoms
Overview of human factors
In-class exercise: case study analysis and recovery

Comments to Instructor:

The topics covered in this segment can leverage off the topics discussed during the prior two segments. Try to set aside approximately half the class time for an in-class exercise that allows students to apply the principles from the three chapters on project recovery (Chapters 8, 9, and 10). Consider having the students form into teams of four to six students each. Provide each team with an example case study (either fictional or real) that describes a particular software project and the problems being experienced on that project. Have each team document what they consider to be the major symptoms being manifested on the project, the possible root causes of those symptoms, the corrective actions that should be taken, and a draft sequence of steps for implementing those corrective actions. Save time near the end of this segment for open discussion of the scenarios, symptoms, and techniques the teams would use to recover the project in their scenario.

Agenda, 1:00 to 2:45, 3:00 to 5:00:

Amortizing the recovery effort
Overcoming backlash
Overcoming passive resistance
Preventing exhaustion
Gently tempering zealots
Avoiding artificial victory
Avoiding polarizing management peers
Sharing success
Identifying and focusing on project management essentials
Review of all material
Course evaluations

Comments to Instructor:

You may want to deemphasize somewhat the topics in Chapter 11 to leave more time for a review of important highlights from throughout the week. Although not a topic within the book, if you have the time, this is a good class for discussing the future of software project management. Students find the topic very interesting and enjoyable. Additionally, it allows students to gain better insight into the fact that the vast majority of project management techniques discussed during the week are fundamental and persistent techniques, independent of the changes in technologies and tools used in software project management.

Appendix D
References and Additional Readings

Articles

Adolph, W. Stephen. "Cash Cow in the Tar Pit: Reengineering a Legacy System." *IEEE Software*, Vol. 13, No. 3: May 1996.

Bechtold, Richard T. "Maximum-Leverage SCE Techniques." *Crosstalk*, May 1998.

Boehm, Barry, et al. "The COCOMO 2.0 Software Cost Estimation Model: A Status Report." *American Programmer*, July 1996.

Boehm, Barry. "A Spiral Model for Software Development and Enhancement." *IEEE Computer*, May 1988.

Boehm, Barry. "Anchoring the Software Process." *IEEE Software*, Vol. 13, No. 4: July 1996.

Boehm, Barry. "Software Engineering Economics." *IEEE Transactions on Software Engineering*, January 1984.

Boehm, Barry, and Tom DeMarco. "Software Risk Management." *IEEE Software*, Vol. 14, No. 3: May–June 1997.

Brown, Norm. "Industrial Strength Management Strategies." *IEEE Software*, Vol. 13, No. 4: July 1996.

Burrows, Clive. "Configuration Management Coming of Age in the Year 2000." *Crosstalk*, March 1999.

Charette, Robert, Kevin Adams, and Mary White. "Managing Risk in Software Maintenance." *IEEE Software,* Vol. 14, No. 3: May–June 1997.

Crawford-Hines, Stewart. "Software Inspections and Technical Reviews: Transcending the Dogma." University of Colorado, Department of Computer Science, Technical Report, 1995.

Fagan, Michael E. "Advances in Software Inspections." *IEEE Transactions on Software Engineering*, Vol. SE-12, No. 7: July 1986.

Gill, Ted. "Stop-Gap Configuration Management." *Crosstalk*, February 1998.

Glass, Robert L. "Short-Term and Long-Term Remedies for Runaway Projects." *Comm. of the ACM*, Vol. 41, No. 7: July 1998.

Hall, Tracy, and Norman Fenton. "Implementing Effective Software Metrics Programs." *IEEE Software*, Vol. 14, No. 2: March–April 1997.

Hansen, G. A. "Simulating Software Development Processes." *IEEE Computer*, Vol. 29, No. 1: January 1996.

Ishihara, Katsuyosh, Ysoji Akao, and Shigeru Mizuno. "QFD: The Customer-Driven Approach to Quality Planning and Deployment." *Quality Resources*, January 1994.

Jones, Capers. "Project Management Tools and Software Failures and Successes." *Crosstalk*, July 1998.

Lee, Earl. "Software Inspections: How to Diagnose Problems and Improve the Odds of Organizational Acceptance." *Crosstalk*, August 1997.

Lutz, Richard Covington, John Kelly, Yoko Ampo, and David Hamilton. "Lightweight Fromal Methods for Requirements Modeling." *IEEE Transactions on Software Engineering*, Vol. 24, No. 1: January 1998.

Mackey, Karen. "Beyond Dilbert: Creating Cultures that Work." *IEEE Software*, Vol. 15, No. 1: January–February 1998.

Moynihan, Tony. "How Experienced Project Managers Assess Risk." *IEEE Software*, Vol. 14, No. 3: May–June 1997.

Nesi, Paolo. "Managing OO Projects Better." *IEEE Software*, Vol. 15, No. 4: July–August 1998.

Nolan, Andrew J. "Learning from Success." *IEEE Software*, Vol. 16, No. 1: January–February 1999.

Olsen, Neil C. "Survival of the Fastest: Improving Service Velocity." *IEEE Software*, Vol. 12, No. 5: September 1995.

Pressman, Roger. "Fear of Trying: The Plight of Rookie Project Managers." *IEEE Software*, Vol. 15, No. 1: January–February 1998.

Simonson, Norman F. "Engineering Disasters. . . ." *Crosstalk*, April 1998.

Sorensen, Reed. "CCB—An Acronym for Chocolate Chip Brownies? A Tutorial on Control Boards." *Crosstalk*, March 1999.

Books

Demarco, Tom. *The Deadline: A Novel About Project Management.* Dorset House Publishing, Dorset House, July 1997.

El Emam, Khaled, Jean-Normand Drouin, and Walcelio Melo. *SPICE: The Theory and Practice of Software Process Improvement and Capability Determination.* IEEE Computer Society, November 1997.

Humphrey, Watts S. *A Discipline for Software Engineering.* Addison-Wesley, January 1995.

Ishihara, Katsuyoshi, Ysoji Akao, and Shigeru Mizuno. *QFD: The Customer-Driven Approach to Quality Planning and Deployment.* Quality Resources, January 1994.

Jackson, Michael A. *Software Requirements & Specifications: A Lexicon of Practice, Principles and Prejudices.* Addison-Wesley, July 1995.

Joint Logistics Commanders, Joint Group on Systems Engineering. *Practical Software Measurement: A Foundation for Objective Project Management, Version 3.1a,* April 17, 1998.

Karolak, Dale. *Software Engineering Risk Management.* IEEE Computer Society, October 1995.

McCarthy, Jim, and Denis Gilbert. *Dynamics of Software Development.* Microsoft Press, August 1995.

McConnell, Steve. *Rapid Development: Taming Wild Software Schedules.* Microsoft Press, July 1996.

Phillips, Dwayne. *The Software Project Manager's Handbook: Principles that Work at Work.* IEEE Computer Society, June 1998.

Putnam, Lawrence H., and Ware Myers. *Industrial Strength Software: Effective Management Using Measurement.* IEEE, February 1997.

Reifer, Donald (editor). *Software Management, 5th edition.* IEEE Computer Society, 1997.

Software Engineering Laboratory. *Manager's Handbook for Software Development, Revision 1.* SEL-84-101, National Aeronautics and Space Administration, 1990.

Thayer, Richard. *Software Engineering Project Management, 2nd edition.* IEEE Computer Society, October 1997.

Yourdon, Edward. *Death March: The Complete Software Developer's Guide to Surviving "Mission Impossible" Projects.* Prentice Hall Computer Books, April 1997.

INDEX

A

D

F

S

T

V

W

Z